The Creation of Mythology

The Creation of Mythology

Marcel Detienne

Translated from the French
by Margaret Cook

The University of Chicago Press
Chicago *and* London

MARCEL DETIENNE is director of studies at the Ecole
pratique des Hautes Etudes in Paris.

Originally published as *L'invention de la mythologie*,
© Editions Gallimard, 1981

The University of Chicago Press, Chicago 60637
The University of Chicago Press, Ltd., London
© 1986 by The University of Chicago
All rights reserved. Published 1986
Printed in the United States of America

95 94 93 92 91 90 89 88 87 86   5 4 3 2

LIBRARY OF CONGRESS CATALOGING-IN-PUBLICATION DATA

Detienne, Marcel.
  The creation of mythology.

  Translation of: L'invention de la mythologie.
  Bibliography: p.
  Includes index.
  1. Mythology.   I. Title.
BL311.D4713   1986   292'.13   85-24658
ISBN 0-226-14350-3
ISBN 0-226-14348-1 (pbk.)

Contents

Note on the Translation

In translating Detienne I have tried to render his thought accurately while maintaining linguistic felicity. This has been an interesting challenge. For instance, his sentences tend to be long and I was tempted to cut them up into shorter ones. This has not been done because of the risk of ambiguity or, rather, the certainty of ambiguity. If one sentence were made into two, for example, the second would have to repeat the subject of the first with soporific weight at its very beginning, or else substitute a pronoun whose referent would be too difficult to determine.

Since clarity is primary, his parenthetical phrases usually are kept in place.

Again, in the interest of clarity, I have substituted words commonly in use for technical ones in order to reach the largest number of readers the book deserves. This is consonant with Detienne's repeated denunciations of the purely academic mind and with his main thesis: the poetry of mythology must not be crushed by a heavy load of bookishness and pseudointellectualism.

Because French is less rich than English, some French words have to be translated according to context: the word *esprit* comes readily to mind as meaning both mind and spirit or synonyms thereof.

I have not gone in for the writer's elegant variation when it sometimes occurs.

Detienne tends to mix metaphors, but since that idiosyncrasy adds flavor and vividness to his style I have preserved them. I have also kept his abrupt changes in style from the formally elegant and stately to the vivid vernacular. Some tautologies have been deleted, others left in where needed for emphasis.

I have tried not to use the pronoun "one" (the French *on*) and have occasionally changed the syntax to avoid it. Certain arcane words such as *mythologema* have been translated by their rudimentary meaning, this again being consistent with Detienne's expressed desire to avoid technicalities in behalf of preserving the beauty and humanistic wisdom underlying mythology. It is not always possible for the writer to keep his enormous fund of erudition from showing through, but it is my hope that this appears subordinated, in translation as in the original, to Detienne's fervid independence of thought.

MARGARET COOK

Once Upon a Time

When young we become so inured to the conventional concept of myths that on reaching the age of reason we are no longer aware that they are surprising. But if we can rid ourselves of the eye of habit, as Fontenelle wrote in 1724,[1] we cannot help being astonished to observe through what strange works we have attempted to understand the functioning of the human mind. Today as in the past everyone thinks he knows that no people exists whose history does not begin with fables or mythology. Fontenelle, both learned and wise, added: "except for the chosen people whose foresight preserved the truth."[2] And we know to what extent in the heads of some nineteenth-century thinkers the question of mythology is linked with that of polytheism from which Israel liberated us but without thus sparing us the trouble, even so recently, of "demythologizing" the New Testament.

Twenty years after the structuralist movement it is not irrelevant conscientiously to examine mythology in general. First, because we thought—and in good company—that new theoretical consideration of it would enable us to write a real grammar of mythological language after several years of unpublished applications of theory and formative principles. Second, because a Greek scholar naively thinks that mythology, the term and the thing, stems more or less from his curiosity if not from his powers.

For us myth is like a force of nature. In mythology everyone feels more or less at home without being restricted to choosing between fascinating or miraculous stories and ways of thinking that are not necessarily ours. To the reader of myths what difference does it make that, in 1724, Father Lafitau decried their "carnal thoughts"? Why would he care about the opinion of a Jesuit rereading Plutarch among the Hurons unless those sublime and fabulous poetical works offered us so much charm and voluptuous pleasure (as Lévy-Bruhl confessed in 1935) that, despite such brilliant scientific enlightenment, we have let them exert over us all their former sovereign power—over us whose memory goes back four or five centuries and who are acquainted with so many huge imaginary libraries? In effect, the symbolic animal or daydreaming person who seeks and finds himself in myths, local or foreign, always listens to both the intuitive and sophisticated interpretations of myth collectors, whether they be unpretentious or mythologists with a reputation for learning.

Ever since the eighteenth century, everything stemming from the realm of fable, such as the gods and heroes of Ovid, has been dealt with in a hermeneutic way, from ideas concerning the origin of fables to ways of explaining the layout of the Pantheon or why the Greeks of Plutarch and of Homer told each other the same stories. In mythology, which voice shall we hear, which thought discover? Is it a language, the first language, that of the childhood of the race? The naiveté of ignorance or the original Word? Song of the earth or Nature's tragedy? Discussions of primitive or antiquated societies about themselves? Is it a religious phenomenon of a high order which endows others with efficacy and meaning and whose guarantors, in Dumézil's Indo-European domain, are the solemn administrators, memory, and collective thought? Or else, in the nursemaid philosophy of Tylor, is it the founding Father of Anthropology? Is there a concept of myth in which all forms of culture are as though dressed and enveloped by some figure out of a myth? Does this kind of universal thought universally applicable to the human spirit forever engender new legends according to specific and infallible rules of transformation? Is it the native land where philosophic thought becomes self-conscious in proportion as it succeeds in becoming abstract and conceptual? Does it require strong faith? Is it wild or cultivated? Or is it both? Does it describe the supernatural? Does it have legitimate status? Is it unconscious, inevitable, and basic behind the deceptive semblance of the pleasure it dispenses without reckoning? Is it ignorance miming profundity or is it the main point as yet unknown?

In a matter of this kind perhaps there should have been a choice between two methods: dealing with mythology as with a hammer stroke or else working as theoretician of the human spirit outside of history and of genealogies for amateurs of heraldry. The course having been mapped out, it behooves each individual to decide between it and others which are possible or necessary. At the beginning, a slight problem: Claude Lévi-Strauss based the scheme for *Mythologiques*, a genesis of thought, on the evidence that a myth is perceived by every reader in the whole world as being a myth;

and, at the same time, Georges Dumézil, publishing at the outset of his old age *Myth and Epic*, admitted that he had never understood the difference between a story and a myth. Why urge a reader of Greek "myths" to rethink mythology[3] rather than to continue to narrate it while enjoying the complicity, both ancient and always renewed, between the Greeks and ourselves, islanders of the West and of its culture? Whence stems this learning so glib that the same word, mythology, designates simultaneously straight narratives, tales with which we are all familiar, and interpretative dissertations which, ever since the middle of the nineteenth century, speak of it in the manner and tone of a science? Why is to speak of mythology always, more or less explicitly, to speak Greek or to be influenced by Greece?

It has not been a question of rewriting *De l'origine des fables*, two-and-a-half centuries after Fontenelle, but of conducting an inquiry in the form of a family tree going from the Greeks to Lévi-Strauss and, conversely, from Lévi-Strauss to the Greeks. First of all, it has been a question of demolishing the concepts of a scholarship seemingly proximate and well-founded and of rectifying the strange practices brought into play by Xenophanes, philosopher treating of causes, and resumed by Fr.-Max Müller, innovator of comparative mythology, and also by the historian Thucydides which were taken up again by Tylor the anthropologist—all of them so smug in their newly acquired erudition. And then, asking ourselves whether or not Greek mythology is more to be believed than that of our scholars, of discovering that its heterogeneous shape, delineated by exclusionary acts and shocking behavior from the first thinkers of archaic Greece to the heirs of modern mythologists, has been uncovered slowly, diversely, between paths of memory and written outlines. An archaeology of "myth" led to the conclusion that, indubitably, mythology exists, at least since Plato devised it in his own way; but nevertheless without controlling autonomous territory or indicating a form of universal thought whose pure essence should await its philosopher. Other ideas advanced: that "myth" is an untraceable genus, in Greece and elsewhere; that the Science of the myths of Cassirer and Lévi-Strauss is incapable of defining its subject-matter, and for good reason. Have we not, only yesterday, experienced the illusion that structural analysis of myths begins with the Greeks thinking of their own "mythology" as conceptual interpretation or yet that "mythic thought" in its perfection attains, here and there, a formal logic, outstripping itself?

It is not, to be sure, a question of going into mourning for so many unforgettable stories but also of depriving whomever it may be of the right to find his mythology where he sees fit. It is the logical admissibility of a "science of myths" that we question, as well as our imagination and its inventiveness from the Greeks to the present in a mode of progression which promises to become ridiculous. "The more solitary I become," said Aristotle, "the more I like stories, myths."[4] A confession, in old age, for which it would be pedantic to reproach the theoretician of the *Poetics* to whom what we call mythology was so unknown that he applied the word "myth" both to a well-constructed plot and to a well-told tale. But what a lovely subject of conversation between Fontenelle, always the academician in dressing gown, and Aristotle, ultimately an old baby giving way to babble. I prefer to conjure up another Aristotle, the visionary convinced that civilizations have been innumerable, that in the darkness of *Time* some beginnings have eclipsed others, that all discoveries have been made infinite times[5] and that, after so many obliterated progressions, there only remain fossils or traces in the form of proverbs, souvenirs of antique wisdom which have come down to us thanks to their brevity and truth.[6] Subterranean thoughts in which the eye hears ageless tidings; stones of memory, in "mythology" more precious than the fantasies of Hermes, the epic of Asdiwal, or the death of Ryangombe.

No doubt in order to "rescue" a certain idea of mythology I have implied too often that memory and forgetting are equally inventive. The mists of a journey through uncharted lands are no excuse for inaccuracy. Have forgetfulness and memory really lived in perfect harmony as naturally as Philemon and Baucis? Is it only nowadays that "the struggle between memory and forgetting"[7] has become so alive and real, now that there has come about proliferation of learned societies in which historians have ultimately become civil servants and official bureaucrats and in which the fight against power, truth, totalitarianism, has caused to rise up in the night those women and men who repeat against all hope their dying words bereft of documentation, or the fleeting but unforgettable verses of proscribed and assassinated poets?

There is no paradise either for memory or forgetting. Only the workings of both and ways of working that have a history. A history to be made.

Chapter One
Ambiguous Borderlines

Nothing is more familiar to us than mythology, and everyone agrees that "a myth is perceived by every *reader* in the whole world as being a myth."[1] Furthermore, the same figure of speech has been in use from Panckoucke's treatise entitled *Les études convenables aux demoiselles* (Lille, 1749) to the *Mythologiques* of Lévi-Strauss (1964–1971). And the extension into *ique*, introduced by structural analysis to evoke the rise of logic in ancient mythology, only serves to accentuate the semantic double-entry system that we notice right away in speaking of "mythology." On the one hand, it is a combination of discursive statements, of matter-of-fact narratives or even, as the saying goes, of narratives and stories—those stories sufficiently decent for young girls to know, which actually were known to everybody in the eighteenth century. But at the same time mythology is represented as a dissertation *concerning* myths, a scholasticism that understands myths in general, their origin, their nature, their essence; a scholasticism that lays claim to being transformed into science, today as of yore, through customary usage; that lays claim to structuring some of its subjects, systematizing different scholastic pronouncements as it designates, and formalizing concepts and schemes. Intuitively, mythology is for us a semantic crossroads of two discourses, the second of which speaks of the first and springs from the interpretation of it. Why is it that what is called "myth" resides in or is possessed by a need to discuss, a wish to know, to search out the meaning, the reason for its own manner of speaking? From what remote distance arises this figurehead formed by naive introspection? How to set up the scholarly method that wishes to speak of myths and that, ever since the nineteenth century, means to establish a science of myths "at last examined within themselves"? The same questions can be put differently. What prompts mythology-science to speak? And whence does it speak? How, through what applications of theory, has this erudition defined its territory? From what divided opinions has it taken form?

Let us take as point of departure for this procedure a state in which scholarship in mythology tries to be a science of myths and to become institutionalized: when public teachings begin to speak of "the science of myths" or of "comparative mythology."[2] In other words, when scholarship draws up a chair and sits down, when it begins, in Molière's phrase, to preach in a chair or in the pulpit of truth—the piece of furniture designating such scholarship as a science. Between 1850 and 1890 Europe was covered with pulpits: History of Religions, Science of Myths, Comparative Mythology. From Oxford to Berlin and from London to Paris, on the same chairs the same things were said. From Frédéric-Max Müller (1823–1900) to Andrew Lang (1844–1912) and from Edward Burnett Tylor (1832–1917) to Paul Decharme (1839–1905) and Adalbert Kuhn (1812–1882). They all give explicit reasons for holding—over a period of forty years—scientific discourse concerning myths. Their spokesman, Andrew Lang, firmly pronounces the task assigned to the new discipline.

> The difficulty that mythology faces (as "science") lies in explaining the following points among other seemingly irrational elements contained in myths: the *barbaric and absurd* stories concerning the beginnings of things, the origin of mankind, of the sun, of the stars, of animals, of death and of the world in general; the vile and ridiculous behavior of the gods; why divine beings are considered incestuous, adulterous, murderers, thieves, cruel and cannibals; why they take the form of animals; myths of metamorphosis into plants, animals and stars; *repulsive* stories of the kingdom of the dead: descent of the gods to the regions of the dead and their return from those places.[3]

Here is the quarry of the science of myths: barbaric and absurd stories; acts of incest, adultery and cruelty, murders, thefts, cannibalistic practices, repulsive stories. Though he puts it more concisely, Fr.-Max Müller does not say anything else: the task set aside for comparative mythology—a discipline that in his eyes stems from the Science of Language—is to explain the *foolish, barbaric,* and *absurd* element in mythology. In 1884, Paul Decharme confirms that the subject of the science of myths consists of fables which are grisly, offensive, and immoral.[4] What motivates the new mythologists, it seems, is no longer mythology but "fantasies which are foolish or disgustingly immoral." What is this about? Whence come those offensive fables? From which continents, which distant journeys do such horrors arise? For everyone to be so excited and to say that all those tales are so shocking and embarrassing there must be a reason, a motive, or at least a pretext.

Now the reason that is always given is, in our eyes, so strange that a digression in the second half of the nineteenth century via the science of myth seems, today, to arise from an erudite spirit of inquiry except that it gives evidence of a strange attraction to the grotesque and the obscene. Indeed, what prompts the science of myths to speak out is that suddenly it has been observed that Greek mythology is filled with indecent stories, that its subject matter is incongruous and expressed senselessly. It is shameful that in his Oxford lectures Professor Müller attacks as follows:

> The Greek poets have an instinctive aversion to all that is ex-aggerated or grotesque. Now then, the Greeks attribute to their gods things that would make the most savage of redskins shudder. . . . Even in the most backward tribes of Africa and America we are hard put to find anything more hideous or revolting.[5]

What is it that makes Fr.-Max Müller's redskin shudder? The vile adventures of adulterous gods who are incestuous, murderers, cruel, and cannibalistic: Demeter, gluttonously devouring her plate laden with Pelops the day Tantalus invited the gods to dine; Cronus, the rascal, gulping down his crying babies, one after the other; Uranus, father castrated by his sons in a great splashing of blood and sperm. But there are other stories no less hideous and revolting: Dionysus cut up into pieces and roasted on a meat skewer, Zeus taking the form of a bull, etc. A whole lexicon narrates the scandalous. A Victorian lexicon, which begins with the shocking and embarrassing, branches off toward the preposterous and ridiculous, then oscillates from the absurd to the vile, the barbaric, the hideous, the revolting.

The new mythology is revealed straight off as a science of the scandalous. But, for the science of Müller and of Tylor to be entrapped in a state of scandal—both of them having decided to speak of myths in themselves—some far-reaching earthquake must have shaken up the familiar landscape of classical mythology. Could tales of a mythology always well-known thus brutally provoke a scandal?

The obsessional reference to the savage, to the Iroquois hidden behind the external appearance of the Greek, seems to locate the commotion in the confrontation between ancient societies and Nature's Peoples. Especially since the new science calls itself "comparative mythology." And because, in giving itself a history it chooses as precursors of its daring and its own development the two minds which, by separate paths, have simultaneously attempted to show "an astonishing conformity between the fables of the Americans and those of the Greeks."[6] The essay by Joseph-François Lafitau, *Customs of American Savages Compared to the Customs of the Beginnings of Time*, appeared in 1724, the same year as Fontenelle's *De l'origine des fables*. When Lafitau set sail for the Jesuit missions in French Canada, the Americas were already peopled by the Greeks of Homer and by Romans wearing the toga: physically and morally the American savages are contemporaries of Plutarch.[7] They are as handsome as the gods, and the eighteenth-century travelers never tire of admiring their "stature, the proportions of their limbs and majestic and noble physiognomy," and, like Yves d'Evreux the memorialist of Maragnon, invoking Crates, the philosopher, who calls the body a "solitary Kingdom."[8] But to this privilege bestowed by nature the savages add the virtues of Sparta: courage, moderation, generosity, justice. The originality of Lafitau lies in extending the comparison to the "intellectual" plane, in showing the strange "conformity" of manners and customs between the savages of America and the Ancients:[9] in the practice of abstinence, initiation rites, sacrificial rituals, the shape of huts, the institution of the Vestal virgins. So many forms which designate "an aggregation of duties" and "a civil religion" where cult practices are interpreted as a public service and a function useful to Society.[10] Upon this great body of unwritten law extending from the Ancient to the New World are inscribed the stigmata of the Holy Religion in its very beginnings at the time of Adam: hieroglyphics, symbols and emblems, mysterious forms dedicated to dispensing instruction in the secrets of initiations and of mysteries.[11]

In this project of discovering, beyond Christianity and the Bible, a religion of the earliest heathenism[12] which lays the foundations of "conformity" between Greeks and Savages, fables and mythology tell of decadence; they show the havoc wrought by corruption. Mythology proliferates due to ignorance, it swells with the passions, it appears when dogmas disintegrate and Religion is overshadowed. It appears with change. And Lafitau likens the beastly fables of the Greeks to the carnal and no less beastly ideas that canker the religion of the Savages[13] and undo the lofty "aggregation of duties."[14] Furthermore, this Jesuit holds against the Greeks who brought Science and the Arts to their highest perfection so that they spoiled Religion "by an infinite number of very ridiculous and very rapid fables,"[15] despite all their enlightenment and philosophy. Whether they come from the Iroquois or from the Ancient Greeks, the fables are never more than excrescences, a foreign body, an external filth; they evoke the same moral condemnation. But their "conformity" is no cause of shame.[16] Lafitau trots out with equal indifference the Lacedemonians in Iroquois villages and the Hurons in the Athens of Cecrops or of Plutarch without wishing in any way to ensavage the Greeks or to Hellenize the American Savages.[17]

No greater feeling is revealed by Fontenelle though he is sagacious about "Greek and Roman silliness."[18] For if Reason feigns horror when looking back on the earliest men, so gullible since all of ancient history is only a mass of chimaera, of dreams, and of absurdities, it does not doubt for an instant that barbarousness is a state of ignorance and that the barbarian is he who does not yet speak Reason's language.[19] Neither madness nor the uncanny, nothing but the usual: to explain the course of events and thus devote themselves to philosophical work—the only work possible in "these vulgar times"—men have recourse to stories and they invent fables. But the more ignorant one is the more marvels one sees. Besides, philosophy at that time was always propitious to the birth of invented wonders. Whether here or elsewhere—among the Kafirs, the Lapps, the Greeks, and the Iroquois, "in glacial zones as well as torrid ones"[20]—the fable is only the result of ignorance, but of an inquisitive ignorance trying to account for phenomena and for the world itself. Ignorance tidily distributed amongst all peoples, without exception, which makes Fontenelle zealous for conclusions:

> Since the Greeks, with all their intelligence, did not, when they were still a new people think more rationally than the barbarians of America who were also according to all appearances a new people when they were discovered by the Spanish, there is ground for thinking that the Americans would have, at last, come to think as rationally as the Greeks if they had had leisure for it.[21]

There is no more Greek "miracle" than there is real enlightenment in their philosophy whence comes, as Lafitau says, "a kind of ruling Atheism."[22]

Inversely to Lafitau who places Religion at the beginnings, Fontenelle holds that it is the nature of the fabulous "to turn into religion" at least as concerns most peoples. To which is added that, with the Greeks in particular, fables "turn into *pleasurable entertainment*, so to speak."[23] In order to explain the seductiveness wrought by the forms of ancient fable on civilization and the plastic arts throughout his period, Fontenelle invokes pleasure. Pleasure of eye and ear, but above all pleasure of the imagination.[24] For that is what urges us on still to see and to listen to stories "by which reason is not taken in."[25] In proportion as narrative follows its natural trajectory, error is adorned by the miraculous. That is true of the earliest men telling their children—in whom is duplicated the earliest age of the human species—tales often in themselves false and already elaborated by exaggeration[26] as well as stories embellished by fake wonders through efforts of talebearers led astray to say only what is most pleasant to hear.[27]

Those are the most common works of the imagination, to which poetry and painting adapted all the better because in bringing them into play they brought to our imagination the sight of its own activity: the extreme pleasure of deceiving itself while contemplating its own image in the mirror of fine arts.[28] With *pleasurable entertainment* Fontenelle delineates with one sure stroke a trait of the culture of his society in which resided a certain idea of well-being.[29] But which is doubly so when applied to ancient fictions knowledge of which is indispensable "to whomever wishes to understand the subject of many paintings and to read without difficulty the most beautiful works of literature."[30] Dispersed among the settings of civilized life, in salons and pier glasses, in the eighteenth century the fable is a criterion of readability for the whole cultured world.[31] It therefore has neither place nor contour distinctive in itself. No comparative mythology can arise from the project of studying the human spirit "in one of its strangest works."[32] The comparison that affirmed "a surprising conformity between the fables of the Americans and those of the Greeks" goes wrong. Given that "the same ignorance produced almost the same effects concerning all peoples,"[33] there is no need to interpret fable or mythology. That which substitutes for interpretation is its origin which reveals the inaccuracy of the fable and its vanity which is to Fontenelle,[34] infantile, just as it is in Lafitau's opinion, perverse.

Fontenelle and Lafitau, two directions that anthropology originating in the nineteenth century has not maintained by chance, but both of which lead to excluding mythology recognized by Reason as guilty of error and of ignorance. And if it is true that the fable recounts barbarities in tales which are vulgar but ridiculous, absurd but insipid, none of this barbarism affects Reason which feigns fright without allowing itself to worry. That barbarism brings with it silence of interpretation. It does not let others speak to the extent that itself remains dumb. Where the Greeks and the Iroquois, envisaged by Tylor's Anthropology, seemed to hold the same *barbaric* and *absurd* discourse, there is no room for scandal, just as there is no room for scholarship concerning mythology.

For mythology to become spoken word, for that voice to be heard both in itself and its harmonics and no longer through an intellectual classification or in the dungeon of an ethical problem combining conventional civilized attitudes and religion, it was essential that a space reserved for language be opened up and that a new linguistic horizon be discovered. The "comparative mythology" of Fr.-Max Müller is deployed within a *Science of Language*, and when Tylor's Anthropology proposes to show the existence of a *natural* mythology of the inferior races it takes as its point of departure an analysis of the original forms of the language spoken by the most ancient human species. A series of ingenious advances and discoveries change the rules of language in the first half of the nineteenth century.[35] Publication of the books of Veda which lay the foundations of Sanskrit philology; the first works on the Kathas and the Avestan language; in 1816, the comparative grammar of Franz Bopp: so many innovations which make language into an organic thing, stemming from a natural science. Toward the end of the eighteenth century there appears an innovative approach to phonetics which is no longer dedicated to research in the earliest means of expression but rather to analysis of sounds, their interconnections and possible intertransformations.[36] Instead of being discourse, made up of a series of words each containing a meaning whose only possible definition is vertical and refers to what Michel Foucault calls the "pre-Babel," the language becomes a system of sounds, "an aggregate of sounds freed from the letters which can transcribe them."[37] The inflexion thus discovered confers on language its inner architecture: sounds, syllables, and roots are so many formal elements whose modifications are controlled by the rules of a system of phonetics. Natural science thanks to which the naturalist, when his name is A. Schleicher, can, with Darwin, study the struggle for survival of the languages scattered throughout the world,[38] struggle from which emanates, triumphant and as though impatient of other victories, the Judo-European that Klaproth, beginning in 1823, had mobilized in the service of nationalism, rebaptizing it Judo-Germanic.[39] Parallel to the transformations borne along by the new disciplines—philology and comparative grammar—dawns the idea of language as speech emanating from the people, the shifting sonority of which betrays a constant activity which seems inseparable from the movement of a history unceasingly in the making.[40] Speech of the People and of the Nation of which mythology can only be the forgotten or lost voice. Simultaneously word and chant, a primitive language sets about speaking to the origins of humanity or the nation; it knows neither lies nor abstractions; it resides in faithfulness of expression whence it derives the energy and magnificence lacking in civilized languages.[41]

It is in this new sonant space that the mythology of Antiquity suddenly becomes a grotesque and insane language that the ancient people who were supposed to have reached the ultimate in civilization seem to converse with each other in a way more marked by savagery than that of Nature's Peoples. The conjuncture of Greek and Iroquois no longer takes place in the same history now that German romanticism and Hegelian philosophy have conferred on Greece the distinction of being called their native land. The native land of cultured European man, as Hegel says.[42] The first land of our beginnings where is born a new humanity, noted for what Husserl, in the same tradition, will call *theoretical* knowledge, based on ideal truth which becomes the absolute value.[43] At the dawn of the nineteenth century, the Greek no longer has a legal right to error or foolish things: born in the land where arises consciousness of the self, where is formed the spiritual universe which is still ours (and Husserl thus speaks a century after Hegel), the Greek is the bearer of Reason. Thenceforth when one begins to suspect that the guarantor of the new rationalism speaks in his mythology the language of a "mind temporarily demented," scandal erupts. To the strange and hallucinatory voice emerging from mythology, newly written into the language, the reply comes in an interpretation written in the manner of a science.

Between science which speaks and the scandalous which prompts it to speak there is so small a dichotomy and the interpretation follows so closely upon what it censures and tries to catch up with that the scandalous seems inseparable from the terms posited by a science thus motivated. Thus, when Tylor and Lang maintain that the difficulty confronting mythology-science is to explain how so many myths contain elements that are irrational *on the surface*,[44] the workings of science are already in motion; the superficial aspect comes to the rescue of reality, and erudite reasoning is already engaged in talk of public welfare. But science has more than one stratagem. Two large factions rule the discussions of theory prevailing throughout the second half of the nineteenth century: the *School of Comparative Mythology* surrounding Fr.-Max Müller, and the *Anthropological School* founded by Tylor stemming from his *primitive civilization*.[45] Both agree on the urgency of accounting for such crazy

talk: their only difference of opinion concerns justifying the presence of insane subject matter in discussion of myth.

As for Fr.-Max Müller, a contemporary of the discovery of
comparative grammar, the explanation can only be a linguistic one;
it must be sought in the system of language and in its history.[46] That
is what *La science du langage*[47] means to show by drawing up a
stratigraphy of human speech and distinguishing between three
phases of it: thematic, dialectic, mythopoietic. The first period sees
the formation of a primitive grammar; it already contains the germs
of all forms of the Turanian languages as well as the Aryan and
Semitic ones. It was at that time that terms were coined to express
the most essential ideas. During the second period when the two
families of languages—the Semitic and the Aryan—become differentiated, the system of grammar receives, once and for all, its
specific characteristics. The inevitable separation of dialects and
languages opens up a third age in which there are neither laws nor
customs but in which are sketched out the rudiments of religion and
of poetry. This is the *mythopoietic* age. A name that could lead to the
belief that man begins to invent fables and that he makes myths just
as previously he had coined the fundamental expressions of language. Nothing is farther removed from the concept of Fr.-Max
Müller to whom disquisition concerning myths is an unconscious
product of language of which man is always the dupe and never the
originator. Indeed, just as the great structures of grammar are
formed silently in the lowest vegetal depths of language, so also do
the first myths make their appearance as bubbles embedding the
surface of words and phrases which spout from the mouth of
earliest mankind. At the dawn of history the human being had the
faculty of pronouncing words which directly expressed part of the
substance of objects perceived by the senses. Things awakened in
him the sounds which become manifest in *roots* and engender the
phonetic prototypes on which is based the body of the language.
Genesis was right once more: "The entire earth had only one language and one way of speaking."[48] But the human mind did not, for
long, keep the privilege of "giving articulate expression to the
concepts of reason." As soon as mankind ceases to "reverberate" to
the world, the sickness penetrates language. There it is, the victim
of illusions produced by words.

So long as humanity remains sensitive to the primary meaning
of words such as "night, day, morning, evening," these are envisaged as powerful beings endowed with willpower, distinguished by
a sexual type, without, for all that, losing the *physical* character of the

natural phenomena indicated by those words. But once the primary sense of the names given to powerful beings by the language which created them spontaneously has been altered, mythic personages make their appearance: the names of natural forces are transformed into proper names. "Zeus makes the rain fall" arises from the expression "the sky weeps." Language has lost its transparency: the etymological meaning of "Zeus," "luminous sky," has become obscured. Fatal forgetting. Men no longer know anything except language with its "substantive verbs," with its festered swelling of images which speaks more than it says and is pregnant with an "excess of meaning." Ever since the speaker no longer knew that he must strike out a superfluity of meaning, he has become the dupe of the words he pronounces. Mankind has become the prey of the illusions of a language in whose womb the strange and confusing language of myths proliferates.

In its turn, *La science du langage* sets us right: "Mythology, this scourge of Antiquity, is, as a matter of fact, a disease of language."[49] We, deluded just as much as man of the third age when he lost control of language, have let ourselves be taken in. It is through ignorance of linguistic mechanisms that the mythology of the most rational peoples seems to us imbued with "fancies characterized by strange nonsense and shocking immorality."[50] As concerns the linguistics of the Enlightenment, mythology is never spontaneous; it cannot be the naive fabling of the childhood of mankind. On the contrary, it is essential to and inherent in language, this external form of thought. Mythology is, precisely, "the dark shadow that language throws on thought" at a certain time in its genesis.[51] It behooves the science of linguistics to illumine this dark site where our illusions about myth multiply the phantoms and fictions produced by the earliest narrators. Wishing to discover the illusory whence stems mythology, the subject of his erudition, the mythologist Müller makes clear his position: that from which one outlines the world of appearances, a "manner of fiction" contrasting with the reality of things.[52] A believing generation undertook to discover behind the screen of names and mythic personifications the forms of the scene of nature which had impressed earliest mankind.

Mythology, as Stéphane Mallarmé is to say around 1880, tells the "Tragedy of Nature";[53] it is "the anthology of the chitchat in which men in olden times told each other what they had seen or heard";[54] it is an aggregate of tales many of which have been "perverted" and some even became "shocking."[55] Thus—Mallarmé explains in his *New Mythology*, a scholarly treatise intended for young students[56]—"men having said in times of drought that the Sun killed the fruits of Earth who was his fiancée, the Greeks told the story that Tantalus, king of the Orient, killed his own child and had him cooked."[57] Since there seemed to be no doubt that those were figures of speech referring to natural phenomena the good mythologist, according to Paul Decharme, had to evince "a deep feeling for nature."[58] And it is sure that the reaction of the exegetes of the new school has been a function of their temperament. Two families of thought have become differentiated with two different kinds of feeling. With regard to the first of those, led by Fr.-Max Müller, it was the spectacle of the sun and of light that gave birth to language and to myths. "The first subjects of conversation, the first poetic topics of mankind, must have been the birth of the sun, always greeted with new shouts of joy, its fights against darkness, its coming together with clouds, its power mostly beneficial but sometimes crushing and deadly, its disappearance under the horizon which resembled a premature death."[59] With regard to the others, influenced by Ad. Kuhn, it was not the regular phenomena of nature that left their mark on the language of the earliest men but rather its rages, its upheavals, its disturbances. Having soon become indifferent to the daily movements of the heavenly bodies the earliest observers of nature must have felt above all "the divine presence in the unexpected and always marvelous advent of thunderstorms, of lightning and of hurricanes."[60]

To this linguistic interpretation accepted both by the partisans of Sun and the friends of Storm the Anthropological School will raise the relevant objection that an explanatory system formed to account for the whole disquisition about myths is no longer able to justify the *foolish*, *absurd*, and *barbaric* whose scandalous emergence had been universally deprecated.[61] Müller's linguistic prototype sinned through excess. The medicine was certainly too strong. And the operation depended on too cruel a therapy since all of mythology disappeared along with the disappearance of the mists of words and the clouds of sentences. That is why the rival project Lang will undertake in Tylor's footsteps primarily aims at accounting for the only irrational part of mythology. In deciding that myths were only a disease of language the School of Comparative Mythology seems to have forgotten that "the Australians, the Bushmen, the Redskins and the inferior races of South America," as Lang says,[62] in swamps and forests, continued to tell the same barbaric stories no one could dream of explaining as the strange result of a few misunderstood expressions. The present should shed light on the past, not the opposite. And Lafitau was right contrary to his time which was unable to understand him.

Tylor's tactics evoke, in the realm of civilization, the comparison of the primitive to the most advanced without granting to language any other privilege than that of being an original product of mankind. Speech sprang up in the human race when in a state of savagery: actions were named according to sounds; names of animals were given according to their cries; later, the words are modified to adapt sound to meaning. Proceedings, all of which stem from a practical expediency within the scope of a five-year-old child. In the beginning, all languages are subjected to the same intellectual artistry: "a philosophy of nursemaids."[63] And mythology? It is then in flower. "A language of that kind is, in actuality, only the reflection of a mythic world."[64] Mythology is everywhere, it permeates grammar, encroaches upon language through metaphor, and spreads into syntax. Yet its growth is limited; it has one age only, that of childhood. Tylor censures the mistaken notion of an almost unlimited creative power inherent in man's capacity for imagination.[65] The myth, organically and in its earliest developments, belongs to the primordial state of the human spirit which resembles the state of infancy.[66] And in that development, limited to the beginnings of mankind, two phenomena play a determinative part: the attribution of real life to all of nature and the tyranny originally exerted by language on the human spirit. In order to examine the processes employed by earliest man to fabricate myths, Tylor does not need to make the detour either through comparative grammar or through the Indo-Europeans. The childhood of mankind, our own childhood, is right there, before our eyes: in the Americas, on the continent of Africa, everywhere that Savages have cropped up. For the Savages of today are still "in a period of creation of myth."[67]

This discovery should change mythology fundamentally and make it a science, at last. Now, finally, the fictions which seemed to have an entirely spontaneous origin find their *cause*. The interpretation ceases to be a novel odd fancy which has just been added to that plastic and changeable thing called fable or myth. Science can henceforth denote the *real* myths, pick them out of the narrative, recognize them in the fabric of tales and historical erudition. Given that myth is a natural and orderly product of the human mind reacting to certain facts to the extent compatible with the intellectual state of the people who conceived it, true historians must, Tylor proclaims, treat myths "as an excrescence to be sorted out from real history. With precaution, nevertheless: "as soon as they realize that this excrescence does not bear up under proofs furnished by facts and that they can at the same time clearly explain it as myth."[68]

In discovering that the human mind "mythologizes" in certain circumstances, that a certain kind of education leads to a certain kind of ideas and that the savage hordes still speak the primary language of myth, Tylor is sure of having found the method of explaining the shocking and embarrassing Greek tales. Actually, once they have been contraposed to the real mythology of Savages, the absurd data of Greek fable are stripped of their strangeness. Incest, cannibalism, and patricide fill the tales of the Redskins; and theft, adultery, and atrocious cruelty flourish in the mythologies of Africa and Oceania. Those are, of course, unrefined manifestations of the primitive human mind which nowadays can be explained by a state of society and of human intelligence in which acts that now seem to us insane, extraordinary, were then accepted as normal events and obvious facts. In the most advanced civilizations myths finally become fossilized, taking the form of superstition. And it is those *relics* that have sometimes been taken for history and at other times rejected as ridiculous lies.

Doubt is no longer permissible: everywhere, mythology speaks the same language. The savagery which violently erupts under the Tropics amongst Nature's Peoples is in the Greek world the stamp of restraint and discretion, controlled by being possessed of a high order of civilization. Consequently, everything in the mythology of civilized peoples that can shock us is in fact only the remains of a state of mind assumed not long ago by all of mankind and of which the contemporary primitives show us the paramount influence as well as the cohesion.[69]

In those two rival tactics, with respect to Tylor as well as to the School of Solar Mythology, the motivations, often gossipy, are not separate from the proceedings which give form to what Lang calls "the subject of scientific mythology,"[70] that is to say, the insane subject matter, the barbarous utterances, the ridiculous disquisitions. In asserting its authority as science of the scandalous, the new Mythology gives way to a certain number of doings whose dynamics are marked by the idea of scandal. A term of holy Scripture— Voltaire recollects in the *Dictionnaire philosophique*—that denotes momentous indecency, it pertains principally to clergymen. The word is imbued with a strong ecclesiastical odor and evokes various images. First of all, the stone of scandal which could knock people over. And Pascal has not forgotten the "machine" hidden in the Greek *skandalon*: the deadfall of a trap in which bait has been placed. It is the scandal-as-objective that one is tempted to distinguish from the scandal-as-subject, in the sense of the troublesome explosion caused by the case of a bad example. To create a scandal and to be shocking. But Scripture negates the distinction subject-as-objective through the curse: the eye, the foot, the hand that offend us, we must tear them out and cut them off. A body mutilates itself: the carnal subject cuts off the object that is scandalous to others and inevitably to himself. For there are those terms to be distinguished between but not separated: he who denounces or dramatically proclaims; the others, victims of the bad example; and the situation, the words, the act, or the member, everything localizing that which is scandalous. Another example furnished by Pascal: a monk taken unawares in a place of ill-fame wearing his monk's garb. Or a Greek who says horrifying and ridiculous things. But the site of the scandal, its own space, is made up of a dual motion, repulsion and attraction. One points the finger, one becomes outraged, one makes a scene in order to eloign, to put a distance between oneself and others—between oneself in the eyes of others—that very thing by which one is in danger of being attracted, seduced, or trapped. Like a double bind whose hieroglyph would be one hand cutting off the other.

In propounding as subject the vile, the abnormal, the repulsive, and whatever makes it shudder with abhorrence, the new Mythology reveals this dual motion wherein that which repulses is also that which attracts. A sign that its disquisition manufactures the scandalous, in speaking of it, in arranging it, in setting its limits. For in the new Science there exists a series of divisions of which it is essential to give an account to see how mythology is circumscribed and how far its dominion holds sway.

The school of Fr.-Max Müller resorts to an expedient method. Denouncing mythology as the curse of Antiquity it adopts Draconian measures. Everything that seems contaminated by the disease of an encroaching manner of speech is condemned, cut off from thought, recognized as illusory and reduced to nought. The most reasonable of peoples are cleansed of the suspicion of having imagined so many indecent and immoral stories. But this time the Greeks or the Aryans, deprived of their mythology, are in grave danger of losing their deities and the roots of religion as well. A new differentiation is urgently needed: between mythology and religion. The gods of Greeks and Aryans are a direct result of intelligence: the man of reason discovers them quite naturally in contradistinction to the myths imposed on him through oral communication, against his will. The apprehension of Zeus as the absolute god must not be confused with the immoral stories that circulate about him. Especially since religion, whose minimal essential is the recognition of the godhead, is a good which certifies the

rationality of the human species. In the Introduction to the *Mythologie de la Grèce antique*, Decharme carefully distinguishes between
religious feeling "which was never lacking in Greece" and mythology "which often debases and dishonors the divinity."[71] We must
take notice: "When the Greeks stop using the language of mythology, their conception of the deity does not differ essentially from our
own."[72] And the accusations of immorality sometimes leveled at the
religion of the Greeks can only be explained by misunderstanding or
lack of information. Is it not self-evident that mythology is not
religion and, furthermore, that the "thoughtless and involuntary
products of the human imagination have not, in themselves and by
reason of their origin, any moral character"?[73] No interpreter of
Scripture—Protestant or Catholic—can then dispense with this distinction which is imposed by the system comprising Christianity
itself whence derives the very question of religion."[74]

Those presuppositions are brought vividly to light at the beginning of the next century by a scholar in religion, destined to make a
decision concerning some theories that could not be disregarded
either by the interpreter of the Bible or by the historian of Semitic
societies. To M.-J. Lagrange, founder of the biblical School of Jeru-
salem, it is the moral requirements that determine the nature of
religion.[75] No more than any other member of the human species
can the Savage, even if he marks the end of an evolution that has
failed, worship natural objects for the sake of themselves alone.
Even the most primitive intelligence is capable of "a rational concept
of the deity." Is not the idea of "making things" enough to guess at a
great maker of things? And with this "duty" becomes established:
the superior power for whom the human being feels dependent
demands of him certain acts by opening up to him the possibility of a
relationship with supernatural powers. God is only "a type of
spontaneous abstraction which derives from the nature of man."[76]
That latent monotheism exploded more or less spontaneously and
probably everywhere. But if some people have failed to recognize it,
being seduced by the animistic theory which posits the development of the concept of spirit, that is due to having sought the "best
beliefs" in the mysteries into which strangers are rarely initiated.[77]
But in wanting to aim the proofs of the earliest Heathen religion in
the direction of mysteries—as stated two centuries earlier by Father
Lafitau, himself very observant of secret instruction—the author of
Etudes sur les religious sémitiques took a twofold risk. First, by taking
for granted a thesis that is largely undemonstrable; and then engaging in a polemic that would be deployed around the Christian
mystery in opposition to the pagan mysteries in such a vigorous

way that for a quarter of a century the hive of the historians hummed with activity aroused by an apparition now completely dissolved: religions that have so-called mysteries. Nevertheless, from the point of view of moral order, there is a sure gain: the savage, endowed with the ability to reason, "has a concept closer to monotheism, more salutory to democracy and to social order than the brilliant Greek mythology."[78] Only one criterion is needed to sort out religion from myths, and a trenchant one: the moral sense. Doubt has no place "where there is taught the existence of a great being, just and good, who has created everything and who does not die";[79] it is there that the realm of religion begins. On the contrary, when the faculty of reasoning is shocked, when the moral sense is scandalized, it is a matter of mythology. Whereas religions, even erroneous ones, have always been the refuge "of the highest aspirations," mythology arises somewhere else pervaded by the spirit of curiosity, guilty of the most elementary need for explanation. Religion flourishes in doing homage to supernatural beings, while mythology, on the contrary, sets out with the intention of deciphering mysteries: "it wants to pierce the veil," derive supernatural powers from the unknown, and explain the world.[80] Other mysteries than those where lie concealed "the best beliefs" reserved for patient historians who evince appropriate curiosity about them. This time, in distant echo of Genesis, it is to the sin of curiosity that the dearth of "true religious feeing"[81] is to be imputed as well as the invention of preposterous and obscene stories produced by mythology.

Even more—because in a more ambitious and systematic project—the same Christian model animates the inquiry, "The origin of the idea of God," initiated by an Austrian missionary, Wilhelm Schmidt of the Society of the Divine Word and founder of the journal *Anthrôpos*.[82] In the undergrowth of the Peoples of Nature which Graebner's method of cultural history wants to cross-rule, the résumé of its technological and institutional criteria attempts to mark out "the most primitive" civilizations: the Tasmanians of Australia, the Negritoes of Asia, the Negrilloes in the forests of central subequatorial Africa, the reindeer Eskimos west of Hudson Bay. Sanctuaries of History where survive intact societies at the most elementary state of agriculture, equipped with scant tools but, despite material destitution, disclosed as being privileged witnesses of the religious feelings of earliest mankind. They worship or respect, more or less separately, a Supreme Being, the Great God: eternal, omniscient, creator of earth and sky and of faultless morality.[83] Carried away by the well-being gained through volume upon volume of proof of an original monotheism, W. Schmidt could not restrain himself from praising over and over the Supreme Being who played an essential part in the history of mankind and the growth of civilization. Is it not He who gave to primitive man "the capacity to work, the firm hope of subjugating the world . . . and the aspiration to reach goals existing beyond and above the world"?[84] Qualities especially rare since the original belief in one Great God is as precarious as is man's first oral communication in the theory of Fr.-Max Müller. Monotheism is already threatened, and great inroads upon it are looming by virtue of technological inventions and cultural innovations. The progress of evil which the work of W. Schmidt undertakes to describe clinically. The first signs of decline appear with the civilization called "the minor culture of maternal law" when woman begins to cultivate plants and the shadow of the Earth Mother lengthens. A certain feminization of the Supreme Being changes its great stature as father, along with substitutes for prayer such as revolting rites like blood sacrifices. Second phase: totemic hunters under paternal law introduce magic and the cult of the Sun, causing the downfall of the one and only Great God, soon to become senile and reduced to impotence. The void left by his disappearance is filled by demons and the powers characterizing polytheistic systems. And the disquisition about mythology begins.[85]

As regards W. Schmidt, the most ancient religion, *Urkultur*, is untainted by any kind of mythological fable. The idea of God implies logical thought only, and discovery of a Supreme Being proceeds from intellectual activity only. Ever since the time monotheism first showed evidence of mythology, indisputable proof is at hand that more recent cultures have already debased and contaminated it. The concept of a great and only God as the vital element of Religion is fundamentally "a-mythic": absolute creator of earth and sky but indifferent to human progress, the Supreme Being does not have to understand either events or motivations. He maintains his distance from actions, is aloof to what is going on. And so extreme is this dichotomy that Adolphe E. Jensen, the ethnologist and W. Schmidt's zealous disciple, denounces as an aberrant mythological figure within Christian monotheism the mishap befallen the Son of God put to death and crucified.[86] A paradox in a theory of such devout inspiration which pushes to its extreme the logic of a separation between the natural rationalism of Religion and mythology, carrier of the irrational which leads to the decline of true religious feeling by deifying "the immoral and the antisocial."[87]

The Science of myths entails a tailor's art, sometimes the art of

cutting. Each individual evinces more or less skill. Lang begins by
making two parts: one, with the myths of civilized peoples; the
other, with the rest. The first part is in its turn cut into two pieces:
the one, rational, the other, irrational. The division is clear-cut:
"Rational myths are those that reveal the Gods as beings endowed
with beauty and wisdom." Example: the Artemis of the *Odyssey*
who enjoys hunting wild boar while the savage Dryads frolic with
her is a "perfectly rational mythic representation of a divine being."
It is an idea full of beauty and natural-ness. It demands no explanation. But the Artemis of Arcadia, metamorphosed into a bear, or the
Artemis of Brauron for whom young girls danced a *dance of the bear*,
is "a being about whom one feels the myth is not natural and
requires explanation."[88] It is the second Artemis who engrosses
mythology-science: she is not natural, one feels that; she is even
indecent; definitely ridiculous and barbarous. As for the first, she
needs no explaining, it is enough that she belong to the Religion
which is a natural one.

The Anthropology of Tylor and of Lang does not, at the outset,
wish to exclude or show the illusive nature of the irrational which is
everything mythologic. It only wants to establish that the nonra-
tional in the mythology of the most civilized ancient societies marks
the appearance, both fleeting and temporary, of another kind of
rationalism, as yet crude and very uncivilized since cannibalism,
magic, and the most atrocious cruelties seem quite natural.[89] An
uncivilized state of thought but so well-suited to the primitiveness
of earliest times that, while still convinced of its *unspeakable filth*, the
Anthropological School will be induced to recognize in mythology
as shared by the Peoples of Nature a way of satisfying a rudimentary
form of scientific curiosity. To such an extent that, in order to rescue
and justify this other rationalism relating to origins, Lang will gradually be led to attribute to it the only conceivable basis: the idea of
God which is to erase Tylor's spiritualism and substitute for the
animistic hypothesis the theory of *a great God*, both creator and of
high morality, who was to have such a brilliant career in the work of
Father W. Schmidt of the Society of the Divine Word.[90]

But surely Tylor is the man who most carefully staked out
the course of the science of myths through the movements that
started it.

There is a sort of intellectual frontier on the hither side of which
it behooves us to sympathize with the myth and, on the farther
side, to study it. We have the good luck to live near this frontier
and to be able to cross and re-cross it at will.[91]

The anthropologist is a frontiersman: between savages and the civilized, between the childhood of mankind and its maturity, between ourselves and our ancestors. But this frontiersman is neither a prowler[92] nor a mere ferryman. The boundary line is his domain and he has delineated the landscape beginning with the day when, as happened to the other eavesdroppers then extant, shameful and obscure words evoked in him the echo of those coarse and repulsive fantasies conceived by primitive man. Even before Tylor there was in existence a vast frontier zone between the most advanced nations and the inferior races. Even as vast as the distance the Civilized wished to see obtain between themselves and Savages. And Tylor reduced it by assigning to the beginnings of the mythology surviving in the higher civilizations the reservation where "millions of Savages and barbarians . . . continue to produce, in their coarse and archaic form, the representations in the form of myths that primitive man made of nature."[93] That frontier can also be crossed more quickly: if we can no longer *feel* the myth in the manner of our ancestors at least we can *analyze* it.[94] Which involves continual goings and comings. There is even—Tylor slyly points out—a byroad, a shortcut: childhood. "In childhood we are at the leading-strings of myth country."[95] But the closer one is to myth country, the more one can supervise it and guard its frontier. For Tylor, son of Quakers, is invested with a mission under the sign of evolutionism: "Ethnography . . . has solemn duties, sometimes even painful ones; it behooves him to shed light on what the coarse civilization of Antiquity has *handed down* to our posterity in the form of lamentable superstitions, and to relegate those superstitions to sure destruction. This job, though disgreeable, is nevertheless indispensable to the welfare of mankind."[96] This business of supervision which is the province of ethnography can most effectively be carried on from a frontier, the best observatory. This makes it possible to control infiltrations, to recognize what has passed from one camp to the other, and to denounce it so that it may be crushed. A solemn duty in which the anthropologist undertakes a virtual policing of morals in a spirit of reform. "The science of civilization . . . is essentially the science of reformers."[97] This is the concluding sentence of Tylor's book and it is also a keynote of policy. An entire venture relating to public safety based on the discovery that "there does not seem to be . . . any kind of human thought so primitive that it has ceased to influence our own thoughts, nor so antique as to have ruptured every link with modern life."[98] To recognize the savage in ourselves but in order to eradicate foreign matter, to uproot an excrescence. For improvement of the lot of humanity and the body social is at

stake. The mythology which takes the scandalous as its subject is
based necessarily on a process of exclusion. The eye that offends us
we must pluck out: is it not written?

To exclude: an act which is basic and ambiguous whose importance has not escaped Tylor and whose results he deplores. Very
often—it must be observed—we find in books on savage tribes
"Religion, see *mythology."* It results that

> in the greater part of the civilized world, and in most of the
> important religions in history, we regard as sacred all that
> pertains to the religion or the sect to which we belong whereas
> people belonging to another religion or another sect regard
> those tales as mere legends.[99]

Tylor's lucidity is due to two complementary reasons. Of all his
contemporaries Tylor is the most convinced that mythology is made
up of regular fantasies, subjected to laws and limited in time, the
function of an intellectual state that civilized peoples have finally left
behind them. At the same time, his interior God, freed from all
systematic theology through the good offices of the Quakers, is a
subject of the present morality whose advent seems to him equiva-
lent to a civilized state, superior to the belief in a multitude of
spiritual beings who were the intimates of the inferior races.[100] A
position that enables Tylor, approaching the question with the zeal
of a reformer, to understand the mythology of the inner man and to
oppose divisions of a sectarian kind doggedly maintained by wor-
shippers of a Roman Catholic God as well as by theologians of the
Presbyterian Church.

Indecent, coarse, vile, foul, ridiculous: the vocabulary of the
scandalous is not gratuitous, it is used to convene all the phantoms
of alterity.The Primitives, the inferior races, the Peoples of Nature,
the earliest languages, the state of Savagery, childhood, madness:
so many lands of exile, worlds that have been severed, debarred
images. At the same time, with each of those divisions, mythology
gets out of place, it changes shape and content; it is the unbelievable
that religion places opposite itself; the irrational to which reason
abandons itself; the savage as the reverse of the civilized; it is what is
absent, finished, or forgotten madness.

Circuiting the debate being held by the new science, mythology
is treated in two ways. Sometimes as a relic, sometimes as an entity,
but for other people. Whereas, in our society, mythology no longer
amounts to more than a tenuous debate, in the domain of its beginnings it caps everything with a primary language which is insepa-

rable from it. But at the same time its privative nature which relegates it to the domain of non-being seems to doom it to having no
manifestations except those imparted by so heated a debate, so
motivated by the scandalous. And in the dual perspective revealed
by this cryptic science certain questions arise—our own. The most
urgent of these and certainly the one that such strange beginnings
cause us to ask most pointedly is whether or not mythology with its
semantic double-entry system is not entirely the result of scandal. In
short, the vote of confidence: Is the mythology of the Greeks, an
essential source of reference, more reliable than the mythology-
erudition about myths displayed in its brutality by the men of the
nineteenth century?

Then another field of inquiry opens up: tales, fables, the great
current of tradition where some people try to separate the waters
which mingled these, sometimes by filtering the purest, sometimes
by going up to the inaccessible source. Obviously, all those stories,
scandalous or no, make up a great cultural scene, mostly autonomous, peopled with ancient utterances, inhabited by answering
voices, by tales which echo across continents and from one millen-
ium to another. A culture based on speech, undoubtedly left to
scholars none of whom have been inclined to suspect that it has
more to do with the ear and with memory than it does with letters
and writing. And if the mythologists of the nineteenth century are,
at first, impelled to address readers, their analyses and theories
recognize unhesitatingly that the land of myth, if it exists, is located
somewhere within the borders of the world of memory and forgetting.

Chapter Two
By Mouth and by Ear

For about the last fifteen years the dogma that Greek culture was a written one has been seriously threatened. The works of E. Havelock[1] which extend the surveys of M. Parry on productions of the epic and signs of orality[2] have demonstrated decisively that the Homeric epic could no longer be considered the last remaining islet of an ancient oral culture that since the end of the ninth century was submerged under a civilization recorded by writing. When Plato, at the beginning of the fourth century deals with that in *The Republic* as well as with poetry in general and with Homer, he incriminates not only a production consolidated into a book or a text written for philologists but attacks also the founder of a *paideia*, a cultural system more or less conceived as an encyclopedia of collective knowledge, handed down by mouth and by ear, performed musically and memorized by means of rhythmic phrases. That *poietic* culture induces, in the soul or spirit of those who listen to and experience it, emotions and feelings of which the philosophy of Ideas strongly disapproved.[3] In taking exception to the Homeric *paideia* for encouraging a guilty identification of poet or narrator with the characters of actions being represented, Plato clearly censures the "aural"[4] aspect of an education of which he wishes to be the exacting reformer.[5] Homer's mythology referred to in *Laws*,[6] by means of its words and rhythms, exercises a magical effect; its figments—spoken, charming, seductive—produce an auditory dizziness; they steal into the ears and flood those "tunnels" which let "sweet and soft harmonies" flow into the soul.[7] It is round Homer's epic and the ways the Moderns as well as the Ancients accepted it that the principal ambiguities of a culture halfway between the oral and the written consolidated. For the measures taken by the Moderns with regard to the epic tradition and its cultural identity would not have followed the same course if the privileged position, stubbornly reserved for Homer by nineteenth-century philosophy, had not found precedent in the aristocratic tradition of the ancient Greeks. A start of a literary tradition encouraged by Greece consisted in Homeric poems joined with the first alphabetism as well as the beginnings of the task of interpretation.[8] Obviously the epic is a realm of Greek memory whose sway extends from genealogical lineages to verbose apologues through proverbs, tributes of praise for the living, legends, eulogies for the dead, theogònies or tales of marvelous happenings. Even in its range, in the hands of specialized narrators professionally trained in mnemotechy,[9] the epic narrative continues to bear reference to a common heritage of tales and stories;[10] and no matter how erudite the disquisition about the epic becomes,[11] it remains contributory, continuing to set apart first principles intended to reinforce its special efficacy. In the canto that opens the *Iliad* there crops up, here and there, the fight with the Centaurs, the exploits of Briareüs, the delights of the gods amongst the innocent Ethiopians and the misfortunes of Hephaestus when banished from the heights of Olympus.[12] Whether through hazards of transmittal or misunderstanding it is nevertheless the case that from a *genre* so propagated by oral report only two productions are still extant, which are nowadays readily called "works."[13] Yet both of those render only one version of a story known to all. For the *Iliad* is first and foremost a way of describing the wrath of Achilles just as the *Odyssey* is one way among many others of reporting the goings and comings of Ulysses. But because of having been set down in writing, thus escaping future variations, the epic attributed to Homer, transformed by an élite into a literary monument,[14] stands in the way of any extensive exploration of the realm of spoken memory. Even though it reveals, through its material and point of view, ancient rhythms and vistas, henceforth limited to the sphere of its canti.

The illusions engendered by the literary tradition are so alive that they even impress those Moderns who have worked hardest to establish the idea that the epic belongs to an extraliterary tradition. Two examples show this, and each in its way helps to disclose the obstacles that impede access to Greek reminiscences. In *Le monde d'Ulysse*, published in 1954,[15] M. I. Finley, questioning the value of the evidence in the *Iliad* and the *Odyssey* with regard to the "past," is led to contemplate the role played by Greek poets and chanters of the primitive period, as well as the role of memory specialists in the culture of a society that, since the fall of the Mycenaean world, knew no system of writing before the middle of the eighth century when the Syrophoenician alphabet was discovered. To gain acceptance for his thesis that the Homeric epic tells about an actual society bustling with activity between the the tenth and ninth centuries but still immersed in a world whose only common thought was mythology, Finley is forced to define the status of Homer in terms combining verification and cohesion. As the teller of myths and legends, the poet of the *Odyssey* and the *Iliad* is on the dividing line between the full maturity of mythology—"a social enterprise on a high level" but producing tales that keep changing[16]—and the age of rigid criticism initiated by Herodotus, founding hero of History. Homer and his epic represent "the first stage in the attempt by Greece to verify her myths."[17] Thus, when the Homeric poems speak of wealth, work, and social structures or value systems they neither invent nor spin tales. The poet hands down "with seemingly icy precision the basic materials he received from tradition."[18] An obvious advantage for the historian who is worried, professionally,[19] about whether we should sever the Trojan War from factual history suitable for teaching purposes and from the Bronze Age and, in return, should accept within our body of historical knowledge of the period called "dark ages" the social relationship between Menelaus and Telemachus.[20] The "dark ages," as its name suggests, hungers for "documents." Finley's answer has the virtue of being unambiguous: the *Odyssey* supplies "the documentary raw material for study of a real world made up of real men."[21] The rest is a question of chronology, to be debated with those who believe in Mycenaean truth and for those moderns eager to disclose information about the world contemporaneous to the poet which they find in the epic's narrative.[22] And the historians' convictions do not appear to be shaken by differences in interpretation which lead some of them to find, in the "catalogue of vessels," a scrupulously careful description of Mycenaean Greece, while others, equally qualified, see in the same computation of ships and supplies a very exact record of cities visited in the seventh century by the *théores* of Delphi proclaiming the feasts of Apollo from one end of the Greek world to the other.[23] The point is that there should be no possible failure to distinguish between history and fiction.[24] If, by chance, the account seems to clash with fundamental ideas about myth, it suffices to strip it of those outgrowths, peeling it off like a rind in order to lay bare historical truth.[25]

It is true that Finley's researches do not hide his presuppositions. On the contrary, they are glad to set them forth. For instance, that man's progress can be measured by his command over his myths and his capacity to extend his field of rational thought.[26] But it still remains to be proven that Homer actually exerts such mastery. Here the argument for cohesion interposes. "The poems paint a

picture of the social world which is essentially cohesive."[27] Homer
thus contrasts with mythological thought which has been swayed
by differences of opinion: myths are "hopelessly contradictory."[28]
And others,[29] with Finley or independently of him,[30] emphasize the
consistency in the epic's characters from beginning to end, justifying the existence of distances between their points of origin and the
complete absence of important inner contradictions. Very much
praise which, ever since criticism aimed at decency and indecency
by Alexandrian scholars of the third century B.C., alternates with
complaints about contradiction, doublets, differences of thought
and style as revealed by so-called transitional or amplifying cantos,
all of which establish the merits of the case put by the philologists at
work between the nineteenth and twentieth centuries.[31]

In the absence of any extensive comparison with other
"documents"[32] which would make it possible to establish the "reality" of the history being sought after, consistency is the only guarantee of authenticity, the only touchstone of sociohistoric reality.
Then, too, the argument for consistency needs to be backed up by
verification. But, this time, it is the censor's turn to be censored. Not
only does Homer provide verification for myths in circulation but
now he himself is investigated by an auditor who demands
verisimilitude.[33] That was already the belief of historians of the epic,
like Chadwick, who furnished the pattern for that: poets in the
service of a warlike aristocracy can only reflect a faithful image of
that society.[34] Though the current of tradition rises in the Mycenaean world,[35] as fast as recitations replaced one another palaces
disappeared, collapsed, officialdom was swallowed up, and there
only rose to the surface fragments of the ancient "materialistic
culture" of the Lords of Mycenae, such as the famous cup of the
aged Nestor.[36] In response to his audience's expectations at the end
of the eighth century the Homeric singing poet, dedicated to per-
forming, is, according to Finley, required to describe with formal
exactitude the custom of gift and countergift supposedly central to
the social system of that exemplary world of the tenth and ninth
centuries. Face-to-face with that very knowledgeable and watchful
audience, Homer is called on to check up on his account personally
so closely that it may never betray its sociological pattern—at least in
any important way. And if, by chance, Homer is lured by an
anachronism, such as the idea of a world ordained by divine justice,
a vision well-known to eighth-century minds, he is sufficiently
master of his art to slip in the innuendo by the roundabout route of a
comparison, thus avoiding any contradiction in substance.[37]

Consistency and checking alternate circularly. But Finley's pattern would not be efficacious, that is, would not yield the social reality sought, if Homer could not be recognized in Greek tradition as the inaugurator of the first breakthrough in the practice of reason. Conclusively the first harbinger of rational thought which, by definition, must already be acquainted with the art of writing, of calligraphy.[38] And the discussions about Homer and his work tell how the mastery of graphic symbols is only the natural complement of the pressure of rational thought, witness, with more or less evidence, the writing of the *Iliad* and the *Odyssey*. The historian's interpretation of epic memory is caught in the trap of the fascination wrought by consistency, that false concept limited to the lack of disparity between those concerned with a tenet or an opus, without any surety other than its wretched opposite, inconsistency, almost a "synonym for madness."[39] For all that argumentation, cast at the pathways of memory, always reasserts its literary origins. Ever since the Romantics,[40] the necessary internal consistency is the main postulate of interpretation which must come upon it for fear of being stigmatized as blindness. In its unique and well-considered meaning reiterated in Lanson's textual criticism, lack of inconsistency is the natural attribute of a work in the "literary" category and is thus subjected to being kept within the confines of a written text even if, in the course of its development, dynamics of memory are observed and endorsed.

Inversely to Finley who, to discover historic truth, bases Homeric recollection on conscious reasoning,[41] Havelock, in his 1963 project, *Introduction à Platon*, never wished to derive history from the epic nor to convince himself that the *Odyssey* gives a sufficiently authoritative account to make it possible for a transpicuous society to rise through the foam of the Ulysses's wanderings. His Homer is the eponymous hero of an immense cultural system, forgetful of the past and unburdened by it but deluged by the present. Like a great river dividing the town walls of Mycenae and the remains of the ancient city. This Homer was an answer to the diaspora brought about by the collapse of a splendid civilization and was born of the Greek-speaking peoples' urge toward identity through relating their joint customs and traditions in an unforgettable way.[42] Whether it takes the roundabout approach of the anger of Achilles or the mask of the traveler to the thousand towers, the epic narrative only relates over and over again values and essential practices to a society depending only on memory in order to sing them for everyone with the help of the rhythms and formulary techniques available only to those who can appreciate them.[43]

To Havelock, Homer is no longer a literary genre among others

in a cultural heritage. All of culture is collected in the epic and
transmitted by a language system which, in a musical and rhythmic
form, places at everyone's disposal knowledge and awareness without which the community would be deprived of its beliefs and of a
large part of its social and technical competency. It is to Havelock's
great credit that he rediscovered the strength of tradition in a society
without any means of written communication to record it.[44] The
Homeric epic constitutes the encyclopedia of community knowledge. Not only has Homer declared himself on the most important
subjects: war, command of armies, administration of states, the
education of mankind, but he is also master of all the arts. Detailed
rituals, juridical procedures, sacrificial practices, exemplary models
for family life, relationships with the gods, and even complete
instructions about how to build a ship: the verses of the *Iliad* and of
the *Odyssey* are filled with pieces of information.[45] Homer fulfills a
didactic function that is unequaled. And Havelock finds proof for
this in Plato in the beginning of the fourth century when the *Republic*
demonstrates at length, substantiated by quotations, that poets and
especially the Poet, have the deserved reputation of "being acquainted with all the arts."[46]

But Havelock's interpretation comprises its reverse, precisely in
the same place from which stem his best guarantees: it is from
Plato's *Republic* that he derives his most convincing examples which
almost dictate to him a "tribal encyclopaedia" called Homer.[47] So
much so—another paradox—that by accepting the "platonic" interpretation of the epic, which proves how seductive an archaic culture
of the aural type still was to the Greeks at the end of the fifth
century, the author of l'*Introduction à Platon* is led to delineate the
entire tradition based on memory by means of the epic only and in
its most erudite form.[48] "Aurality" is recognized, but imprisoned,
and only permitted to see a tradition twice scholarly: through two
centuries of modern interpretation as well as through the pedagogic
role assigned to Homer by contemporaries of *The Republic*. Sometimes Havelock's omniscient Homer resembles German philology
like a brother: first and everlasting memorial to the truly Greek
spirit.[49] Confined to the epic now its primordial language, tradition
is as though fossilized in paradigms; from its pedestal it displays
models of socially acceptable behavior. Memories rediscovered but
concluded in the past. As though once the Homeric encyclopedia
was finished, thenceforth, from the seventh century to the age of
Plato, everyone was compelled unconditionally to refer to it, for
essential truth and everything else, whether it were a question of
making a raft or of how to treat aged parents with dutiful respect.

The book casts a shadow of a doubt on the "tribal encyclo-paedia" brought to light by Havelock. All the more unfairly since no one else's research has revealed better than his the swindle of the existence of a "miracle," with respect to writing, in the land of Plato and of Homer. The Syrophoenician alphabet probably appears on the scene about the middle of the eighth century B.C. in Phrygia as well as at the mouth of the Orontes.[50] But the new fact essential for analysis of Greek culture is that the discovery of a technique of alphabetic writing did not entail immediate changes. No break in continuity, no lapse of memory on the part of a narrator recounting the sacred genealogies in his charge which would, in the course of one generation, eliminate forever the great tellers of tales reaching back beyond tradition.[51] In Victor Segalen's poem dedicated "to the Maoris of forgotten time" it is that very Terii, "he who had forgotten the words" because of the palefaced strangers who had come on big ships, who becomes deacon and recites the Book which he learned to decipher in the Protestant Missions school. A civilization based on memory becomes completely amnesiac under the effects of the most virulent poison: the Scripture of a religion sure of the truth enclosed in a Book, its own.

The spread of writing to Tahiti and to the Society Islands occurs opposite to the path of alphabetic writing in archaic Greece. In Tahiti, invasion comes by sea and in thirty years the conquest has been made.[52] The first envoys of the London Missionary Society disembark in 1797, and in 1830 Moerenhout, in his *Voyages aux îles du grand océan*, tells us that an old holy cantor of Raietea revealed the Polynesian cosmogony to him but "he could only recite it spontaneously in declamatory style. . . . If I stopped him in order to write it down he forgot it, could no longer continue and had to begin over again."[53] To annihilate suddenly a civilization so closely engaged with memory that writing a language and teaching children to read seemed ridiculous (for it sufficed for them to read the Gospel just once to memorize it), the unheard-of power of modern colonial enterprise was required. Consolidating in its written symbols the pressure of a mercantile civilization and the imperialism of a religion founded on the holy Book, its partner and its ally. To which the weight of political power was added when the English helped King Pomare I to displace his rivals.[54] The palefaced missionaries shamelessly pretend to be civilizers. Now, "to civilize a people they must first be Christianized."[55] Agriculture, mechanical skills, and commerce will then be revealed to the subjects of King Pomare. Under the circumstances two interdependent characteristics ex-plain the dynamism of the written word which are cumulative. The written record in the holy Book, in the New Testament, knowledge of which is obligatory for the attainment of Truth; also printed script conveyed by the book which has emerged from the Mission press and placed at the center of a system based on the school and scholarly learning. It then becomes a kind of writing readily adapted to the economics of the marketplace. Pomare II, Christian king since 1812, had a house built where he retired in order to write.[56] On May 13, 1819, he promulgated the first code of written laws.[57] And having emulated and soon become the rival of his protégés along with their religious books of regulations for barter and commerce with English ships, he clashed with the missionaries because he intended to keep the monopoly of trade for himself.[58] In 1824 the third Pomare, crowned at age four with a Bible in one hand and a legal code in the other, was sent to the South Sea Academy to receive "a Systematic English education."[59] The whole of the ancient oral culture and its new forms are condemned to secrecy by the unprovoked assault of a culture based on reading and writing, mobilized by a centralized power which leads, hand in hand, commercial transactions and the salvation of souls and has at its disposal that dangerous weapon—printing.

The contrast with the case of Greece is a radical one. In the first place in political organization in which origination of the city and its mental space apparently cannot be separated from mastery of the tool for writing.[60] Whereas Mycenaean writing, called Linear B, cursive and often illegible,[61] serves as a memorandum for high ranking officials and clerks of the palace in their administrative work,[62] the alphabet, with its small number of symbols, vowels, and consonants delineated with exactitude and well adapted to pronunciation, would seem to have been coined for and by the earliest democracies.[63] Its readability as well as its simplicity respond perfectly to the need to publish reports concerning the new state of society. In effect, the primary exploit of the earliest lawmakers was to put the laws in writing,[64] not for the purpose of converting them into codes entrusted to professionals but to place before the eyes of all citizens at the center of the public area. Solon said, I write (*graphein*) laws for everyone, for the good citizen as well as for the bad one.[65] They can be seen by all, and Plutarch as well as Pausanias could still see, in the Prytaneum, fragments of Solon's laws, called "axles," rectangular wooden beams engraved on their four surfaces mounted on vertical frames revolving around their axis.[66] Thus, in principle, both rich and poor could enjoy equal justice.

Many of those monuments inscribed with political writings have probably disappeared with their perishable materials such as wood, slabs of stone, or skins which supported them, and perhaps we should mistrust our epigraphic documentation on stones which bear more private texts than public ones;[67] among the first fifteen documents of Dittenberger's collection of inscriptions—a "classic" work in the proper sense of the word—there exist only two decrees and one treaty between two cities; the rest consist of dedications, of offerings, consecration of statues or valuable objects.[68] But however much we allow for the ravages of time, erosion, and vandalism, it remains true that in the Greek cities political power was never identified with writing. In contradistinction to civilizations such as China and Mesopotamia where graphic symbols, set apart for the use of specialists, constitute an instrument for social codification in the service of a centralized power, the city never adopted the instrument of the alphabet; it did not try to lay hands on a kind of written symbol that nevertheless seems the most appropriate for its political purposes. Such circumspection was all the more remarkable considering that the earliest democracies were established with the determination to make public, through writing, the basic laws of the city.

Several facts make it possible to measure the disparity between writing and power. First, and this is crucial, the city did not inaugurate a system of education. The first schools, around the year 490,[69] were established outside the political domain.[70] Reading and writing resulted from private instruction, and alphabetization is left to the citizens who want it and have the means as well as the leisure for it. Other evidence of relative indifference to the written word is the tardy appearance of repositories for archives.[71] Before the fourth century the cities did not find it imperative to collect in one place official documents such as records of births, marriages, and deaths, of clans, of public associations. Only Aristotle, in his *Politics*, states the importance of such a building for the efficient administration of the city.[72] And when it becomes imperative to record officially transactions that proliferated through economic development, public and private matters intermingled, lumped together in the safekeeping of the registrar, president of the Prytanes. Moreover the documents—tablets of wood painted in white and stored in earthenware jars, or contracts on scrolls of papyrus—even when placed in the Archives are not looked upon as the only authentic documentation.[73] The city seems more concerned to make public on stone and metal the decrees and decisions of the assembly than to register and preserve documents which we would call original. Finally there is the refusal to have recourse to writing on the part of men who, as Plato says, "have the most power in the city." For they are ashamed of transmitting in writing speeches and other texts for fear of the judgment of posterity and of being called Sophists.[74] The orator who speaks in the *agora* on invitation by the herald does not feel the need to have recourse to written symbols: his only tool is speech. "Who wishes to transmit to the neighborhood (*es meson*) wise advice for the city?"[75] It is by speaking that the citizen influences others, that the orator directs the choosing of the assembly and the politician's course of action. Pericles, they say, is to be the first to deliver a speech from a written text,[76] and soon Thucydides is to try to find in a history of politics principles for action not depending on the uncertainty of guesswork. But the author of the *Peloponnesian War*, besides already being a man of the fourth century, is also among those who keep or are kept at a distance from city affairs. Political speech is wary of writing, whether on tablets or rolls of papyrus. In the *Suppliants* Aeschylus proclaims the virtues of the isonomic city called Pelasgos after praising the "written laws" bestowing equal rights on both rich and poor[77] and notes the disparity between a decision by the assembly and a written document: the Argives take Danaüs and his daughters who have come as suppliants into protective custody; "it is an irrevocable decision," a "nail so firmly driven in that nothing can ever shake it out"; and "it is not a question of words inscribed on tablets or sealed in rolls of papyrus. You hear the clear language of free speech."[78] The deciding vote of an assembly cannot be confused with written outlines[79] given to it by registry clerks who are still insignificant. The statistical data of epigraphy confirm that in the city power is not exercised by means of writing. Modern historians have often noted that decrees, the recorded decisions of the assembly, begin to abound around the year 400 and increase until the third century.[80] Writing was also used at a very early date to immortalize names or to draw up the earliest lists of winners in the Olympic games, from 776 or from the time of the ephors of Sparta, 756.[81] Probably, too, tradesmen made use of it for accounting purposes for which its light materials and rapid destructability were well suited.[82] But even in the commercial sector where "writings" seem to assume the most importance, that is, in the activity and operations of the bank, it is still only in the fourth century that the first memoranda (*hupomnēmata*) or bank books (*grammata*) make their appearance with deposits and withdrawals, the name of the depositor, the amount of the debt, and the name of the creditor.[83] And it has long been known that at the same period written contracts are still rare with the exception of maritime loans.[84]

In the realm of the city which puts power "at the center," probably to protect it from the danger of centralization, writing must be more visible than read; it is shown to everybody, evidence of the required publication of information, without ever being called upon to relay speech as a means of communication within the social interconnections of the first democracies.[85] The Greek city makes the best of a state of "limited alphabetization." What concerns commerce as well as crafts is too foreign to its egalitarian system to have disturbed the cautious circulation of written symbols. And the earliest evidence of a commercialization of the book resides in the coffers of papyrus covered with writing collected by the illiterate Thracians on the banks of the Pont-Euxin after the shipwreck of the vessels sent to the Greeks in colonies in the Black Sea. Xenophon relates this in *The Anabasis*, and it occurred between October 400 and March 399.[86] This is the time when writing, hitherto merely sycophantic in content, ceases to be scattered bits and scraps or the mere transcript of efficacious information, is to become more widely integrated in the culture of the city and to acquire mental and social supremacy.

Everything implies that in Homer's land a revolution in writing did not take place but that the use of graphic symbols progressed slowly and irregularly, depending on the sphere of activity. It proliferated in the new fields of learning, philosophy, research in history and in medicine.[87] Man found a way to see tradition in perspective as well as the means of organizing the accumulation of data and opposing observations or theses where schemes could be devised based on cogent reasoning. Writing certainly promoted incipient interpretation and comparison of various versions of the same account.[88] And it is unquestionable that lists of ingredients in the pharmacopoeia as well as daily prognoses must be set down in writing to enable the doctor-theoretician to weigh data concerning the human body and to draft hypotheses for the critical consideration of his colleagues. In a parallel direction, written prose, available to speak of being, nature and basic elements and principles, is first made manifest in the little book costing one drachma in which Anaxagoras presents, at the time Socrates was young, a synopsis whose arrows fly straight to the mark.[89] Still, we must qualify the victory won by writing insofar as the Greek provinces are concerned where books and those able to read were both scarce, by recalling the means of reception accorded written works.[90] For a book is listened to, is read by the ears more than by the eyes. Philosophers, doctors, historians, all engage in public recitation.[91] Herodotus recites his *Histories* to the Athenians and to many others; Empedocles declaims his philosophic poems in the presence of Greeks assembled between the sanctuaries of Olympus, while the authors of what are called Hippocratic writings inform their listeners, probably less numerous, about what the art of medicine can or cannot say about the nature of man.[92] With regard to the spectators of Aristophanes encouraged to laugh, the book held in hand or exciting a hope of an "autistic" reading denotes the intellectual as a type[93] and points out how unusual a man he still is in a big city like Athens which however seems the theater exemplary of a written culture carried on by an élite before the eyes of the multitude. And the book, gradually become a commodity, is written within an ample system of culture which continues to be transmitted by mouth and by ear—even under the windows of Plato.[94]

Thus it would be as ingenuous to believe that alphabetic writing rescued a dying tradition of oral communication as it would be to imagine that a graphic system capable of noting isolable sounds by means of vowels and consonants would have entailed the decay of a culture based on tradition. This had no need of writing to be sustained or recounted for it found in the shared memory of every group of humanity both its principles of organization and its learning methods.

This social memory must be interpreted as the nonspecific mnemonic activity which insures the continuity of human behavior, finding in technical exploits and in words the means of transmitting all knowledge. Memory on which tradition depends and which is biologically indispensable to the human species for whom it plays the same role as does genetic conditioning in societies of insects.[95] But this kind of memory is neither that of biologists nor of cybernetic psychologists who study it as a useful function in communication between two individuals. Social memory is at work in so-called traditional societies, among groups of men whose culture is woven between mouth and ear, that is, in societies with which anthropologists are familiar. Very far from laboratories where alphabetized subjects are ranged in artificial groupings in order to prove the memorability of lists of words or names, more or less long or complicated. That social memory without which there would be no culture in societies "without writing," the anthropologists, when they have not neglected it, have adopted for its study two contrary schemes: the first, oriented toward ethnohistory, favors enquiry into the past pegged to the practice of writing, whereas the second, liberated from obsessions and the phantasms of history, is essentially concerned with the way it differs from the memory of the written work.

Beginning with E. Bernheim's *Critique historique* published in 1889 until and including the work of J. Vansina, published in 1961 under the title *De la tradition orale: Essai de méthode historique*, a project with a dual purpose is formed.[96] On the one hand, traditional societies, including ours, live in history. Not only because they are subject to change in the future but also because the tradition that embodies them, the predominating system of thought, is virtually a scholarly study of the past, a history unaware of itself; a history unknown, just like the historical knowledge dear to Western societies. On the other hand, the tradition the ethnographer tries to file in his archives, tries to transform into written matter, he characterizes with the rigorous nomenclature of "critique of history." Because this past is alive, because it is scattered about among a great many witnesses,[97] any enquiry that undertakes to find the real importance of past events—the history under consideration here is the laborious and stubborn kind attempting to "verify the facts"— convenes those scholars who can, who must, give evidence. The ethnologist confronts his witnesses, questions each suspiciously in turn:[98] according to the rules for good criticism, it behooves him to uncover the reasons that might induce each one to falsify his evidence. His distrust is aroused especially because he is face-to-face with civilizations of mouth and ear where everything is mobile, in a state of flux, continuously muddied by rumor—a type of "source" that manuals for a critique of history classify with the anecdote, the myth, or the proverb.[99] The informants about ethnography are thus disguised as witnesses more or less under suspicion compared with a kind of history that proceeds in the manner of a police inquiry endeavoring to make each of the members of the body social confess the secret reality encompassed by the prestige of tradition which mists it over. That is a strange undertaking which seems to be based entirely on confusing tradition and the historic past, as though human memory had always made history without knowing it. And so it was forgotten that the concept of a past in contradistinction to the present and necessarily to be studied insofar as it is past, does not fully emerge until Ranke's history[100] at the beginning of the nineteenth century. Besides, whatever the merits of ethnohistory[101] may be, the scheme worked out after E. Bernheim's critique of history fails to understand tradition based on memory, since it misunderstands the relation established by occidental erudition between use of writing, its only concept of history, and the workings of memory.

Other anthropologists, less impatient to make history—at least of Bernheim's kind—and more curious about the cognitive procedures, have, from the thirties on, undertaken to analyze the way in which memory produces tradition and changes it in the process of transmitting it from one generation to the other. That is the scheme adopted by a line of British anthropologists, from Frederic C. Bartlett,[102] a contemporary of Malinowski, to Jack Goody, present holder of the chair of social anthropology at Cambridge.[103] Marcel Mauss, of the French school of sociology, had recognized the importance of *tradition* in archaic societies, had analyzed its methods of handing it down, its means of social control, had even shown how its existence is more or less mixed up with the question of handing it down, or again how the knowledge of deeds and of bodily acts passes from one generation to the next.[104] Mauss differentiates between two components: one that is conscious, pure social tradition, the collective memory that must be sought and "found in people who have its secret and its custody";[105] and the other, tradition on an unconscious level, corresponded to the phenomenon of language conveying to those who speak or learn a language a certain common way to perceive, analyze, and coordinate.[106] But paradoxically, after conferring on language the status of rudimentary social phenomenon, Mauss left the study of it to scholars of linguistics and, simultaneously, turned away from orality and its relation to "myths" which he had recognized as unavoidable, unconscious as well as linguistic.[107] In a parallel direction, the work of Maurice Halbwachs, slanted toward collective memory but in the sense in which a group views itself from within for a duration of time not exceeding the average lifetime, excluded our contemporary societies more dependent on the alphabet and remained subject to the narrow experience encompassed by the past of an individual.[108] Between the lengthy period of language established by tradition and the compressed period of short memory, it was necessary to choose a median time span in order to reveal the rhythm of a social memory, to measure its pulsations, and to observe it at work in the exchange between two or three generations. Only thus has it been possible to separate out some essential traits of oral and aural memory, of collective mnemonic activities of societies in which, for reasons simultaneously historic and ethnocentric, the forms of a state or orality were at first only perceived in contrast to written production and to the working of memory in a civilization characterized by the art of printing and general use of the alphabet.

We have long realized that history transmitted by word of mouth, without being entrusted to the Doctors of memory, changes more or less profoundly in the space of a few generations. Without reverting to Thucydides it is equally well-known that before an important event occurs, a war for instance, concerning the life of various groups, each person gives his own version, selects what we call "facts," and produces an account in terms of the way in which his social sphere organizes spoken memory. We have even learned that it would be useless to arrange the successive "deformations" on an axis where the closer the account is to the event the less room is left for the "miraculous."[109] But it was necessary to await studies such as those of John A. Barnes and Laura Bohannan to compel recognition for the concept of a "homeostatic" organization of the uneducated memory:[110] how a dynamic equilibrium functions between changes and survivals in which sorting out new and old pieces of information, if actually performed by the memory of each person, is conditioned by social life; how with each generation collective memory, which is a system of cognitive thought, reorganizes and reinterprets essential elements in social relations. Had there not been mishaps in the English administration of Nigeria, anthropologists would have been satisfied to note that the Tivs, numbering about eight hundred thousand, believed that they were all descended from one man through fourteen or seventeen generations, that their genealogy, often recorded in family trees, served as memoranda to proclaim territorial rights and social relations. But because the colonial tribunals were besieged by plaintiffs who were always genealogists, Britannic Justice decided to fix in writing the abundance of proper names in daily use by every native but which was neither systemmatically circulated nor known to the functionaries of memory. In the next generation the Tivs who had remained "illiterate" refused to recognize the authenticity of genealogical archives; they called them inaccurate and, to the indignant astonishment of the presiding judges, recited others. The rules of the game seemed to be falsified, but there had only been a misdeed. Laura Bohannan,[111] the anthropologist sounded out for unraveling the matter, succeeded in demonstrating that the good faith of both parties was not in question. The records of the English governing body could only report a fixed state of Tiv society, whose genealogical history was in a constant but imperceptible and unconscious state of flux. Thus the normal lengthening of genealogical trees in the course of generations was compensated for by a telescoping mechanism which kept intact its form; just as changes in power structures—the number of chieftaincies or reallocations of land—affected, in an underground way, the equilibrium of whole sections of this architecture of proper names. In searching the archives for phrases of this genealogical disquisition whose sole subject was everybody's spoken word, the written records, robbed of their bureaucratic might, served to reveal—but in the aspect of ethnography—the most fundamental fact of shared memory: that what is memorable, that which this kind of memory remembers, far from being a recorded past or a collection of archives, consists in present knowledge, proceeding through reinterpretations but whose unceasing variations within tradition relayed by speech are imperceptible.

Variation has prompted consideration of another characteristic or orality and its kind of memory. If tradition based on writing had been less importunate, Marcel Mauss would not have repeated the same advice, year after year from 1926 to 1938 in his *Instructions* for future ethnographers: "One will not look for the original text *because it does not exist.*"[112] This other literature, widow of writers proprietary of their texts and bereft of the works expected by our culture based on philological obedience, is not made to be read nor merely recited; it is made to be *repeated.*[113] More precisely, it is through repetition that it is fabricated, taking shape from what we call the variants of an account or different versions of the same story.[114] The world of repetition is also the world of variation. It has often been said, but it is more recently that Jack Goody[115] has taken the trouble better to understand the nature of a kind of memory that combines variation with repetition. Among the Lo Dagaas in the north of Ghana, the *Bagré* is simultaneously initiation rite and the speech arranging it through continuous narration. Some twelve thousand verses that each initiate must learn are transmitted from the elderly to the young without being entrusted to specialists. "The *Bagré* is a unit and yet the manner of its narration varies." Comparison between different versions recorded between 1951 and 1975 leave no room for doubt that the variations between one *Bagré* and another are often great. Not only in the art of the narrator whose nuances are discerned by his listeners but also in sequence, in the length of the deveopment and choice of episodes, all being variations perceived neither by those who listen nor by those who recite. Each version entails new transformations impeded neither by the memory train- ing of a particular milieu nor the forms of constraint that the society could exercise through the intermediary of an initiation rite, the principal referent of the *Bagré*. The variations that ethnographic writing makes possible to observe and to measure yield access to the workings of memory in a society "whose tradition must remain an oral one."[116] And Jack Goody makes important observations. First, as an aide-mémoire. The *Bagré* belongs to everybody. Every Lo Dagaa is familiar with its stories. But this knowledge which rambles and prevents anyone from regulating the reciting of a *Bagré* seems determined by two principles. In the parts where the narration refers to ritual, recollection is based on the parallelism between rites and narrative. In the others, those of simple narration, memory favors "stories," that is, certain narrative elements made up of "a series of events reported or imagined and interrelated by actors in common." This kind of recollection is generative and occurs neither by means of guide marks on the surface of the text but by taking as a guiding thread a plot, a history, and its logical conclusions.[117]

The second comment is more far-reaching. If spoken memory cannot help transforming what it wishes only to say and to repeat, this is because it cannot be confused with mnemonic activity, emphasized and exploited in our society and which consists in stockpiling and reproducing *faithfully* series of statements or pieces of information. In the absence of any system of written notation, the active memory based on oral reports combines knowledge with visual observations, gestures and global situations that render inoperative the pattern of a "mechanical" memory dedicated to exact repetition. This is, in effect, Goody remarks, because this remembering "by heart" can only exist in societies where learning is conditioned by alphabetization and by the combined use of reading and writing. In order to learn something by heart, word by word, as we are accustomed to do, we need a fixed model that enables us to correct inaccuracies. The written text is the indispensable support of a reliable memory of a mechanism that subordinates to the eye, to vision, the word that has become silent. The kind of memory that only enregisters after reading and carefully verifying what it has memorized makes up an integral part of a learning system of which the Sumerian school is perhaps the most ancient form. Designed for vocational training, a system of writing which is a social tool for codification for the convenience of royalty, the remote "house of tablets" inaugurates a system of scholarship wherein the transmission of knowledge occurs simultaneously by means of the literal copy, letter by letter, of lengthy series of texts and in the exercise of word-by-word memory. The break with the learning methods of traditional societies is violent, the more so because "the realm of writing" imposes on future scribes a completely artificial environment that, by removing them from their parents, their background, and their village, deprives them of the environment necessary and favorable to constructive recollection.

No doubt some societies, more than others, are concerned with establishing methods to make firm their tradition without recourse to written symbols, sometimes by entrusting it in part to professionals, virtuosi in mnemotechnic procedures, sometimes by increasing the controls exerted by rituals to ensure regular if not immutable repetition of words, of narratives, or liturgical chants. Having recourse to both methods Vedic India, grafted on a theology of the creative word of which the faintest whisper altered would upset the world order, seems to present the unusual spectacle of memory that is spoken and claims to be infallible.[118] After many years of apprenticeship toward mastery of kinds of recitation called "word for word" (padā) and obsessed by avoidance of the least change in correct pronunciation, the Brahmans, divided up into specialists for some Vedas or others, pride themselves on having carried on to the present time the aggregate of hymns characterized by the phonetic normalization of Çakalya, dated about 500 B.C. Whatever trust the experts in India lore place in the Brahmans who are, however, familiar with writing[119] while at the same time calling it tainted and fallible, it remains true that, lacking a class of mnemotechnic specialists, any tale arrogated to anonymous memory is subject to variations entailed of necessity by the act of repetition.

It is the very need always to repeat over and over that endows orality with its particular manner of creation. Third method of traditional memory, which obviates another comparison with the literature of our contemporary societies. In a system of repetition there can only exist various versions. And, in principle, each version obliterates or eclipses the preceding one whose sole reality lies in an interpreter's voice and in the echo it arouses in his listeners. Roman Jakobson observed this in collaboration with P. Bogatyrev[120] when considering the status of "folkloric" works: the pathway leading from interpreter to interpreter, when it is not cleared away by writing, can only be opened up with the community's assent and with the aid and abetment of the group whose memory is being expressed. There may be seen a specific form of creation which echoes a fundamental difference in the way it is received. In the field of writing where each work involves a "waiting period" and, as it were, bears the image of its addressee stippled by the tracery of the works conjured up by both author and his readers,[121] the very substantiality of the "graphic" or printed manuscript allows a work to wait, for centuries if necessary, before producing its effect and finding readers, almost impossible to imagine. Whereas every oral production, if not immediately received by attentive ears and rescued from the silence that immediately threatens it, is destined for oblivion and instant annihilation as though it had never been spoken. Stillborn from the mouth that gives birth to it, history from nowhere sent back to its silent origins. In order to find a place in aural tradition, a tale, history, or words of any sort must be heard, that is to say, be accepted by the community or the audience to whom it is addressed. It must therefore undergo the "preventive censure" of the group. In the same way as does the word, says Jakobson, in order to become an act of language. For if language is indeed an aggregate of necessary conventions adopted by the body social to make possible exercise of the individual's faculty of speech, every speaker must nevertheless bring to it personal modifications which will only enter the language when sanctioned by the community and accepted by it as universally valid. It would surely be wrong to conclude from this that tradition is "like a language" and that spoken memory stems once again from the privileged skill of linguists. But the comparison is relevant when directed to a form of social control dating from the beginning of tradition that was so cramped as to prescribe a mechanism for producing what should be remembered.

Claude Lévi-Strauss's[122] hypothesis relating to "mythism" reenforces Jakobson's intuition. Let us grant that every "literary" creation, every story told, is the work of an individual. No sooner has it left the lips of the first narrator than it enters into oral tradition, or at least undergoes the test of the ear and mouth of others. What happens to make this story unforgettable? To form a concept Lévi-Strauss suggests distinguishing between levels of structure and levels of probability: the first, resting on common foundations, will remain stable; the second, stemming from approval, will manifest extreme variability in terms of the personality of successive narrators. In other words, in the development of the memorable, that which is peculiar to each narrator, his way of adding or eliminating details, of expanding some episodes or omitting others, would not be the same as that which implants a story in tradition, a tradition that produces it and is in turn produced by it. In the course of oral transmission the levels of probability collide with each other, gradually break down and sift out from the mass of reported speech "its crystalline parts," that is, what gives to a traditional account a more regular structure or endows a story with "a greater symbolic significance." In short and in the words of Lévi-Strauss, "Individual works are all myths potentially but it is their adoption through collective use, if this occurs, which actualizes their *mythism*."

Paradoxically, one of the direct benefits of that theoretical opening at the end of the *Mythologiques* is to cast doubt on the favored position accorded to the category of "myth" by Lévi-Strauss in his *Le cru et la cuit*, universal because Greek in origin. For to discern in *mythism* one of the chief phenomena of memorability in a word culture is to begin to parenthesize the myth as a litrarary genre or as a kind of delimited narrative; to detect the variety of products of memory: proverbs, tales, genealogies, cosmogonies, epics, songs of war or of love. And little does it matter that each society deploys traditional sayings according to its own kind of insights and chosen effects. In carrying on the work of variation within repetition they are all subject to the same decantation: words transmitted and narratives known to everyone are all founded on shared listening; they only retain, they can retain, only essential thoughts, ironic or serious, but always fashioned by the long-continued attention of a group of human beings, rendered homogeneous and conscious of self through the memory of generations who have also been dumbfounded. Perhaps that is one of the reasons why anthropology, since it is an autonomous field of scholarship, has never ceased to question, while more or less spontaneously calling it "mythology," that hidden, secret but essential part of a society or a culture that cannot be revealed either by a technological index, or a genealogical tree, or by any of the obvious forms of social architecture.

Chapter Three
The Mythic Illusion

In instructions for ethnography, edited in the year 1800 for the Société des Observateurs de l'Homme, J.-M. de Gérando is among the first to wish that nothing be forgotten—ranging from lowly sensations and subjects to Religion and its sister-spouse, Morality.[1] When Baudin's expedition headed for the austral lands in the year 8 it brought with it a very precise semiology to enable the observers of the savages "to transmit to us the record of the formation of their ideas."[2] Their last subject of inquiry, and doubtless the most difficult to obtain, is to fathom the "traditions" of savages.[3] Following upon idols, coinage of the Supreme Being and beyond the tomb, "What is a people's cult for the dead and their respect for tombs?"[4] The answers having been duly recorded, the Observers could then apply themselves to traditions, even more hidden than the people who had departed. They are to interrogate the savages concerning their origin, their transmigrations, the invasions they underwent, the important events that took place, the progress they were able to make with respect to industry or politics and concerning their customs. "Perhaps they will only derive very vague accounts, but a small number of facts can cast valuable light on the mysterious history of those nations."[5] Where so many ethnological monographs give space to unforgettable histories of the Others, J.-M. de Gérando demands a history with changes, with important events, invasions, innovations, an origin. Under the rubric "very vague accounts," traditions conceal a small number of facts which suffice for purposes of identification for "our brothers who are scattered to the horizon."[6] Every nation is entitled to a past which is necessarily historic. And since savage peoples live within time, receive visits, experience transmigrations, and make progress in industry, their memory, obviously, also makes history without being aware of doing so.[7] It is up to the travelers enlightened by the Ideologists to apprise them of it.

Nowhere does the questionnaire of 1800 allude to what Fontenelle points out through fables and Lafitau through carnal ideas. As concerns the Observers of Man, savages are quite capable of forming abstract ideas; they have no serious reason to tell ridiculous stories. In a nation that, like others, possesses a historical past, there is no room for a mythology. Fifty years later, when the "Science of myths" confronts the Peoples of Nature, dismissed by History and adorned only with gross and barbarous tales, it is mythology that takes over the whole field. In the obsessive manner of the comparatists, eager to loosen the tongue of scandal, to spy upon its postures, to produce a "scientific" interpretation of its perversions.[8] But today what seems to us the most naively obscene in the Science of myths is the reference, or rather the invocation, to Greece.[9] Let us make no mistake: their precursors are neither Lafitau nor Fontenelle, both equally indifferent to scandal, but rather the earliest Hellenic philosophers, exposing to the light of day a people of statues. Those "pious and thoughtful men," those "delicate and refined" beings chatting under the pediment of archaism—a long time back, say the professors of the middle of the last century—attempted "to explain to themselves beliefs closely allied to religion and yet seeming to be the negation of religion as well as of morality."[10] Trusty and cautious prophets of an emerging science but already in arms. They are shocked and embarrassed by mythic tales and it is religious feeling that dictates their first interpretations. At the same time, those founding heroes of mythology-erudition open up the way, and their rational steps determine the pathway the "civilized races" must follow at a certain time in their history.[11] The inescapable route to intellectual maturity: no civilization can be attained without having first experienced and felt the scandalous nature of mythologic speech.

A proven concept which means to be the salvation of the Greeks even in their mythological deviations. Indeed, are they not the first to be deeply shocked by tales ascribing to the gods "ridiculous and obscene acts" and—Father Lagrange adds in 1905, giving them absolution—also by stories in which the gods evince a nature "in contradiction with that which mankind longs for in divinity"?[12] Correlatively, was not their religious feeling securely enough founded on the censure which, in their wisdom, they apply to such distressing deviations? Model Hellenes in whom are miraculously joined the greatest familiarity with mythology and critical distance from such sinful plots. How could the Science of myths in the nineteenth century fail to recognize itself as embodied in those "pious and thoughtful" men who presage, twenty-five centuries before, the dual movement whence springs a mythology-scholarship; the sudden awareness opening the eyes to the filthy stuff of tales repeated over and over and, in return, the interpretation that inaugurates rational discussion? More than merely precursors, the Greeks, "delicate and refined," are initiators of a project that is enough to take to its logical conclusion with the help of new sciences such as linguistics or anthropology.

This simplification of origins in which everything has been said if not put in writing bears so great a resemblance to the cloudless clarity of those who point it out that such a simple affinity might cause concern. But there is a more urgent quest. Apart from the feverish agitation burning in modern mythologists ever since they have felt compelled to define their position vis-à-vis the Founding Fathers and especially when, with more or less reason, they accuse them of being usurpers. It is imperative to defer the dispute about ordinations and no less firmly to challenge the disquisitions of praise or invective with self-contained secret evidence about myth or mythology. No one would dream of denying that, between the sixth and the fourth centuries the Greek house is filled with a continuous din in which the curses of Xenophanes on the roof echo the indignant whisperings leisurely collected by Plato the prosecutor before he read them out in a famous indictment. A scandalous state of affairs, to be sure, and one that seems to prevail from the *Republic* to the excesses of philosophy as soon as it becomes articulate.[13] But to draw up the official report in those terms is already to have chosen the point of view of an all-important continuity between Plato's severity and the moral judgments of the nineteenth century. A point of view at once too exterior and too cavalier in its abridgments.

Another history is indispensable: an interior history, certainly Greek like the word "myth" which antecedes "mythology," a more roomy but no less unusual nomenclature. A history determinedly genealogical in which analysis of semantics[14] is just the most reliable way to thwart recognition of the obvious, of an intuitive awareness which reconciles differences on the evidence that a myth is a myth. Without there taking place any suspicions of the sheer strength of tautology since it seems to be indigenous and above reproach.

In this polyphonic history with its many diagrams, the strangeness of it prevails at first: with an observable gap, an event that focuses the attention of ancient grammarians and indicates to us there was a primary and very brief schism. Polycrates, tyrant of Samos, was assassinated in the summer of 522. And probably Anacreon[15] had already left the island and his amorous feasts to go to the court of Hipparchus at Athens aboard the great ship with fifty oars, one of the famous galleys sent by the prince to the poet. In 525 occurred the first episode of the revolt against Polycrates: the rebels disembarked and were led by a certain Herostrates at the moment when a white swallow rose up into the sky above Samos, as told in the *Chroniques de Samos*.[16] Anacreon pays more attention to symposiac lovemaking than to episodes of the "class struggle";[17] nevertheless he is, for us, the only contemporary witness of a revolt recorded later by Herodotus in his *Histoires*.[18] A suggesting witness but quoted with marginal notes because of the exotic names of the rebels who "take possession of the heights of the city and its sanctuaries": they are the people of the "myth," *muthiētai*, so-called perhaps on the model of "the people of the city," *poliētai*.[19] Grammarians and lexicographers interpret the word *myth* as rebellion, insurrection, civil war (*stasis*).[20] And the leaders, perhaps the nobles who sided with the transgressors (*halieis*), would have been *mytharchs*[21] just as others are polemarchs or symposiarchs. Anacreon was too close to, too dependent on, the master of Samos not to have called the rebels by the nickname given them by Polycrate's entourage.

Fishermen or fishmongers are people who talk loudly in a city especially if discontented and angry. And the word *myth* is part of the vocabulary from the epic to the middle of the fifth century. A concrete term, as they call it in an assembly, in a council or between interlocutors but without having a necessary division between public and private, political and what is not. When Peleus entrusts Phoenix with the education of Achilles he asks him to make of his son a good "giver of advice" and a good "performer of heroic deeds." The "giver of advice" is, literally, the "orator of myths" (*muthōn . . . rhētēr*):[22] neither the professional orator of the fourth century nor the mature citizen when he takes the floor and discusses projects in the Prytaneum[23] but a man who knows how to express his opinion and to speak appropriately and when necessary. In this category as well as in many others *muthos* is a synonym for *logos*, throughout the sixth century and even in the first half of the fifth. But at the self-same Samos Anacreon's rebels are neither simply givers of advice nor citizens exercising a right to speak, however discreetly. More likely, it is because they lack the right to express their opinion that the lower classes, earning their living from the sea, rise up against the citadel and the domination of the tyrant. It is another meaning of *myth* inherent in this epithet, derisive because of the title of citizen (*poliētai*) that Polycrates took away from them along with their power. *Myth* as a subversive word, a rebellious voice, seditious, but less in content that is empty than in the form others bestow on it from the outside, ever since the existence of sancta of "eunomy." The "myth people" are not endowed with a message or a tale listened to by some and rejected by others. They are the butt of a belittling ruling. Excluded from political discussion they are limited to a space that is empty and unidentified. A kind of insignificant otherness which it would be laughable to subvert.

In the semantic history of the "myth" Samos makes no point of departure; at most, a change of direction, the beginning of a curve, the outlines of another kind of speech whose characters only become legible due to retouchings throughout the fifth century. At first the unwonted image of "mythic people" reveals the dichotomy between what we are accustomed to recognize as "mythic" and the use of a word that archaic Greece does not differentiate from the semantic import of *logos*. The scholarly work of philosophers from Xenophanes, around 530, to Empedocles, about 450, belies the opinion of our contemporaries who attribute to "rational thinking" the purpose of eliminating any other form of thought such as "myth" in the sense of sacred narrative or discourse on the subject of the gods. In his so-called banquet elegy Xenophanes lays down rules for addressing the deity; men should sing "with auspicious texts (*muthoi*) and pure words (*logoi*)."[24] "Myths," combined with *logoi*, are bearers of reverent intentions in contradistinction to other irreverent tales in which the gods have disagreeable experiences such as the wars against the Giants and the Titans.[25] *Muthos* has the same neutral status in the philosophic work of Parmenides. The foreword to the discourse on Truth and the doctrine of Being is a *muthos* in progress whose course, at the advent of the erroneous opinions of mortal men, is interrupted by the solemn words: "Here I stop the discourse, the *logos* of certainty on the subject of truth."[26] New Homer of philosophy, Empedocles, against the grain of the period, intoxicated by the epic, commands his disciples to listen to the *muthoi*,[27] the words of the master permitted by the Muse to hear the word of Truth: the "myth" of an erudition able to escape the error and deceit of the others.[28] And parallel to the reasoning the earliest philosophy unconcernedly calls *muthos* or *logos*, Aeschylus conjures up *logos*, the word transmitted by the stories, by the *muthoi* of Aesop[29] whom we are in the habit of calling the fabulist but whom Herodotus calls "maker of tales," *logopoios* as, in the same *Histories*, is Hecataeus, author of the *Genealogies* and a *Periegesis* at the end of the sixth century.[30]

They all bear witness to the illusory nature of mythologic ideas about the creation and show how foreign to what was going on in Greece in the archaic age the concept of a closely interwoven,

homogeneous system of myth really is. *Muthos*, widely disseminated, lacks the content that moderns attribute to myth with such
zeal without noticing, for instance, that in *Works* Hesiod tells the
logos of the ages of gold, silver, bronze, and iron and not a
"mythic"[31] tale. In a historical tale in which *logos* and *muthos* are
interchangeable, the revolt of the people of Samos is a deviation,
perhaps the first one, but so clandestine that it would appear
accidental were it not perpetuated by both Pindar and Herodotus in
the first half of the fifth century.

They both envisage *myth* as the same empty space, the same
white area, but also as a land of exile eroded by hardship. In the
Histories of Herodotus as well as in Pindar's Victory Songs, that
which stands out among words and sayings is the rarity of *myth*. So
extreme as to endow it with a sort of identity. Only three mentions
of it in the vast corpus of the *Epinicians* amid the hymns and odes to
the glory of the winners in the Games: charioteers, wrestlers, and
runners swift as the wind, all vested with light bursting from exploits evoked by the song of the master of Truth. For the panegyric
repeated by the chorus includes the celebration of the games and the
deeds of heroes. It extends to the poet who rips apart silence and
forgetting to erect, with his voice, a memorial, to build the new
memory on the site of another more ancient by reminding the
forgetful of a hero's strength, a king's triumph or a god's dazzling
deed. Every victory in the games of the rival sanctuaries evokes a
traditional recitation, a paradigm necessary for pronouncing the
true word, the *logos* of Truth.[32] Neither the voyage of the Argonauts
nor the cup of the Sun nor the castle of Cronus belongs to the realm
of "myth." Face to face with the singularity of the poetic *logos*,
"myth," dispersed and increased in number, denotes exclusively
rumor which threatens the word of praise, the voices of envy which
stand in the way of the rise of Truth.

Twice, in three events hinging on Ulysses, Pindar speaks of the
myth, Ulysses who usurped Ajax's fame. There is, to begin, the eight
Nemean,[33] when the most courageous of the Greeks was to have
bestowed upon him the arms of Achilles: Ajax, son of Telamon,
unfairly defeated by a secret vote giving preference to Ulysses. The
glittering deceiver was greatly honored and Ajax, who died by his
own sword, toppled over into oblivion. By the fault of her whom
Pindar calls the Word of delusion, hateful *Parphasis*, the evil pest,
perpetrator of tricks. *Parphasis* the evasive, encircled by deceptive
tales, lying *myths*,[34] crafty and sly as Ulysses when he attempts to be
a seducer and draw his prey into his nets. The *myths* in the train of
the Word of delusion are tales of seduction: through detours,

through unscrupulous insinuations, they do violence to virtue. Dangerous tales, the more troublesome because they work to transfer words of praise to persons unknown, unsubstantial, consigned to obscurity because of their inborn mediocrity. But in another *Nemean*, the seventh,[35] Pindar is not satisfied to denounce the scandal of Ulysses and his unearned reputation; he brings direct accusation against the charm of Homer's narrative: the lies, the machinations which are the reverse side of the sung words of praise. "If the poet's skill had been such as to see Truth, Ajax would not have plunged into his breast the blade of his sword."[36] The tale attributed to the Word of delusion is, in this instance, the poet's cleverness, thief that steals by making use of *myths*. *Myths* which are words or tales known to all but which Pindar loads with everything that is the subject of scandal in the tradition and memory of the Greeks. The force of Pindar's denial bursts out in the first of the *Olympics* when he challenges the traditional version of the feast of Tantalus.[37] Pelops cut up in pieces and served at the table of the gods! Yes, the child had disappeared; his parents, his friends sought him everywhere and no one returned him to his mother; Poseidon had taken him away in his chariot. "And forthwith a jealous neighbor says that in the water boiling on the fire thy limbs, dissected by the knife, were thrown and the guests at table shared the pieces of flesh and swallowed them up."[38] At first a rumor, the voice of a jealous person "because there are many astonishing things and sometimes the assertions of mortal men go beyond the true word, the *logos alēthēs*,"[39] that which is the province of poetic knowledge only. Then, swollen by rumor, the swarm agitates the *myths*, the *muthoi* fashioned like the sculptures of Daedalus and ornamented with motley lies.[40] Idols resembling human beings but poor figurines and ridiculous ghosts of the statue erected by memory in the light of noon.

Tales bearing a deceptive aspect, *myths* spoil the splendor of the *Charis* rooted in the voice of Truth; they are only the illusion of real life inherent in its radiant being. The pleasure and magic they bring with them do not stem from the poet's fallible information but from malicious tongues. Appearing in many guises *myth*, born of rumor, signifies to Pindar the bad traditional narrative; it is the badge of the fictional, the illusory, which must be cast aside, removed from the ranks "of reliable witnesses."[41]

The same dichotomy obtains in the *Histories* of Herodotus where the *myth* is even more unobtrusive than in the poems of Pindar. Two instances among so many tales of the astonishing, the unusual, the admirable. The word *myth* is used twice in the nine books of the traveling rhapsodist who is still considered by historians to be the father of their branch of scholarship; they attribute to an application of ethnography the strange or wondrous stories noted by sterner colleagues who are, however, no less respectful of the Father of History. In his surveys, where he gathers together everything he knows as though he had seen or heard it but without, through that postmortem, discrediting hearsay,[42] Herodotus only writes about *logoi*. And when he refers to traditions that are especially sacred—often without revealing what they are, for that would be out of place—Herodotus calls them "sacred" *logoi (hiroi)*[43] in which our contemporaries can only recognize *"myths"* through extrapolation[44] and at variance with the meaning of the word *muthos* in the *Histories*.

Herodotus does not veil *myth* which, on the contrary, must be laid bare, brought to light. *Muthos* is not a truth revealed only to initiates; it is a maxim or an opinion to be prosecuted in broad daylight. The tales about Egypt provide two examples. Herodotus believes Egyptians to be, of all men, the most strictly religious;[45] their priests are bound by very rigid regulations concerning purity; and their sacrificial practices are differentiated from those of the Greeks by their care in burying the victims in perfect condition: no black hair on the dress, a flawless tail, and the tongue revealing nothing baneful.[46] Moreover, the Egyptians are horrified by animal heads which they curse and sell to the Greeks if they happen to have one of their markets or businessmen located in the countryside. The purity of Egyptians is such that no one, man or woman, would kiss a Greek on the mouth or use the knife, the skewers, or the cauldron belonging to one of those foreigners, or even taste the meat of a pure and spotless ox when it has been butchered by a Greek knife.[47] In these circumstances the Greek gods have no choice but to say a good word for themselves by laying claim to Egyptian origins, and the same applies to Heracles, an ambivalent personage, half hero, half god, but an ancient divinity in the eyes of the Egyptians from whom the Greeks certainly borrowed him. Thus the Greeks are prompted to dedicate their sanctuaries to two versions of Heracles, offering to the one they nickname the Olympian sacrifices as to a god of Olympus and to the other the funeral tributes befitting a hero.[48] Per contra, "the Greeks relate many things thoughtlessly."[49] Apropos of this Herodotus alludes to the story of Busiris, king of Egypt, all the more familiar to his audience because it had been related by two of his contemporaries: Pherecydes of Athens, logographer[50] and an important contributor to the so-called mythological *Library* of Apollodorus, and Panyassis of Halicarnassas, a close relative of Herodotus, in an epic poem to Heracles numbering nine thousand verses.[51]

> They say that when Heracles came to Egypt the local people under the command of Busiris crowned him with fillets and led him in a procession to sacrifice him to Zeus. He, for a time, was quiet; but when, near the altar, they proceeded with the ceremony of consecration, he resorted to force and killed everyone.[52]

Very ill-considered talk but more than being careless and mistaken, this *logos* is a "myth" which is insane and ridiculous (*euēthēs*).[53] Two reasons for that opinion.

> When they give this account the Greeks seem to me completely ignorant of the character and customs of the Egyptians. How could man to whom divine law forbids even the sacrifice of livestock, with the exception of pigs, oxen and old male cattle provided they are unblemished—how could those men sacrifice human beings?[54]

The most religious of the world's inhabitants cannot for an instant be suspected of such a shocking ungodliness. Such a report is unthinkable in the system of values held by Herodotus. It must therefore be rejected, excluded: its absurdity condemns it. To which Herodotus adds another argument reminiscent of the one about the "cauldron":[55] "And, let us add, how is it possible that Heracles, alone and not yet avowed by them to be other than a man, was able to put to death myriads?"[56] The unbelievable is, moreover, improbable, having already been impugned as a fault due to stupidity.

The second opportunity to censure a "myth" occurs to Herodotus apropos of the source of the Nile and flooding of the land an entire hundred days after the summer solstice.[57] When questioned about this, the Egyptian priests keep silence and informants have nothing to say about the nature of the river. That leaves us with the Greeks, very loquacious on the subject. And from the many discourses of those who "want to make for themselves a reputation for high learning,"[58] Herodotus retains three opinions only one of which seems to him worthy of discussion. Of the two others he wishes "to point out"[59]—simply mentioning them does not make them noteworthy—one blames the etesian Winds from the northwest for swelling the river and being solely responsible for preventing it from flowing into the sea; whereas the second "lays claim to explaining the floods through the fact that the Nile flows into the Ocean and the Ocean around the land."[60] The reference to the Ocean betrays the ignorance of the second explanation: "It has, if I may say so, a more supernatural characteristic."[61] Strange and extraordinary, it inspires astonishment or even stupefaction. To such an extent that it cannot be argued: it is an account that can neither be proved nor refuted. As opposed to the theory that bears on the thawing of snow which the Ionian geographers are not at a loss for reasons to raise against it.[62] To blame the ocean is to round the cape of the invisible, to extend the debate beyond appearances, to relate a "myth."[63] Geographic reality is the touchstone here, as much as the religious virtue of the Egyptians in the unbelievable misadventure of Heracles. "As for me, I do not know of the existence of a river Ocean."[64]It is therefore the product of fiction whose presumed author is Homer or one of the preceding poets: the discoverer of the name or the word Ocean, the person who put it into poetry.

But "myth" in the sense Herodotus uses it does not cover names given to divine powers on which the theogony theology invented by the Egyptians is founded. In the opinion of Herodotus those names are Egyptian in origin and the author of the *Histories* gives Homer and Hesiod sole credit, a long time after the Pelasgians, and unacquainted with the names of the gods, for having delineated the figures in the Pantheon and allotted to them their respective fields of competency.[65] The "mythic" status of the river Ocean only has validity within the framework of geographical knowledge and the system of Herodotus. It bears no reference to anything holy. It is a "supernatural" image doomed to be excluded, censured as nonknowledge, a denial of the obvious. Homer or the unknown poet who imagined the Ocean is no more "mythic" in the modern sense than the narrator of a Busiris celebrating the unbelievable sacrifice of the stranger who would turn out to be Heracles. In the opinion of Herodotus the "myth" about Ocean is simply scandalous wherever it may arise, whether in Homer's epic or in the *Periegesis* of Hecataeus, the logographer of Miletus who traveled to Egypt two generations before the *Histories*.[66]

"Myth" is no more a subject for Herodotus than for Pindar in his poems. Sometimes it is a relic, sometimes a beclouded rumor, an illusory word, a lying seduction, an unbelievable account, a ridiculous discourse, an unfounded opinion. "Myth" is still only a word, like a gesture pointing out what it denounces as unbelievable, what it rejects. It is a word-attitude, always evocable at the disposal of any effort to exclude it. Herodotus is proof of this, this time at his own expense. In the fourth century he will be called a "mythologist" by Aristotle, the biologist, in the *History of Animals*:[67] did he not maintain, precisely in his accounts of Egypt, that female fish were impregnated by swallowing male sperm whereas anyone can see that the canal leading from the mouth leads to the stomach and not to the uterus? A foolish account (*euēthēs . . . logos*), which is repeated over and over (*tethrulēmenos*).

Stupidity, fiction or absurdity, the "myth" points out a named place which is still only a delusion to some people. A site both distant and mobile with no landscape other than the successive denials of its existence by the erudition that places it on the horizon of its own particular meaninglessness.

Delusion of others, sometimes seditious, often harmful, the "myth" finds its most intransigeant theoretician at the very end of the fifth century. Beyond the surveys of Herodotus and beyond the sententiousness of learned logographers: in the established autonomy of historical scholarship with Thucydides and the *Peloponnesian War*. This theoretician is also a redoubtable prosecutor: he wants the maximum penalty, he means to sue for the imprisonment of any thought suspected of collusion with what he calls the "mythic" (*muthōdes*). In the genealogical history of the mythic illusion, a history inherent in Greek thought, Thucydides denotes a radical point of schism.

To judge by events, it is of the same order of unusualness as in the *Histories*.[68] But in contradistinction to the casual and accidental custom of Herodotus, Thucydides advances, with equal economy, a concept whose importance is due to his project for a new history. The hard-working tribe of logographers, raised at the end of the sixth century and continuing on, related in writing traditional narratives;[69] Herodotus wanted to give the Greek city a new memorableness.[70] Thucydides invents a model for political action. Neither chronicler nor memoirist, the author of the *Peloponnesian War* is not at all a historian in the nineteenth-century manner of relating what has happened and indicating that this is of interest to the past inasmuch as it is past, that is to say, as distinct from the present. The Peloponnesian war, envisaged as "the greatest crisis . . . affecting the majority of mankind,"[71] is the ideal field for knowledge of future possibilities. On the base of an immutable human reality (*to anthrōpinon*), Thucydides builds a theory of action based on concepts of power and of war. His project is inseparable from Sophistic reasoning and a certain kind of thinking about politics.[72] With regard to the rationalism of the historian-theoretician, truth resides in a discourse based on reason, equipped to furnish methods for action nowadays and in the future in the distinct and understandable space of the city. Truth resides in acts, says Pericles,[73] and history in the science of the useful, even if the Greek city has never deemed it indispensable to accord professional status to the historian.

A conceptual history of the present and at the present, with its paradigms and its strictly regulated relations to time, the *Peloponnesian War* pays little attention to the past and to tradition. It deals with ancient times (*ta palaia*) only to show by means of proofs and verisimilitude how a model of the gradual progress of power functions, one that explains the inevitable conflict between the Athenians and the Peloponnesians. A dynamic of civilizations, centered on Athens, in three forms: Minos and the Cretan thalassography, Agamemnon, and the Greek forces united against Troy, Athens with her fleet and the tribute that supports it. Command of the sea confers command of money which makes it possible to gain power over others.[74] Under the rubric of what is called "Archaeology," Thucydides takes a definite position with regard to "myth," that is, in chapters 20–22 of his first book when he sets forth his project and his method.

Would it were possible for us to subsume that which pertains to myth (*muthōdes*) into reason (*logos*), after being expurgated, and have it appear as history (*historia*). But when the *mythic* so boldly imposes on credulity and has no verisimilitude, we ask the listeners (*akroatai*) to be indulgent and to submit to these old stories (*archaiologia*) with patience.[75]

Nothing is more foreign to Thucydides than this preface of Plutarch to the Life of *Theseus*, the first of his parallel lives, not only in tone but in the intention to mask the myth as rational history. Thucydides' approach is radically different. There is no compromise possible on the subject of "myth." Thucydides goes to war against "old stories," the *archaeology* of good Plutarch. A lightning war or the enemy taken by surprise, defenseless, can only submit to the victor's rule: silence and imprisonment forever. It is in fact tradition based on memory that the *Peloponnesian War* attacks, and case against memory brought by Thucydides, in the broadest sense, is all the more virulent because his conceptual mechanism, adapted to a present without archives with the exception of meager epigraphic documents,[76] seems to operate on the same groundwork as oral tradition.

The first ground for complaint: the memory is fallible. Not only does it have lapses, blanks, but it is incapable of reporting with accuracy, with "acrity"[77] speech that has been heard once. A weakness Thucydides knows from experience. In particular concerning speeches delivered by various men either just before or during the war: "It is as difficult to reproduce their purport faithfully as I have found when I listened to them in person as it is for anyone else reporting them to me from one source or another."[78] The ear is unfaithful and the mouth is its accomplice. Fragile memory is equally deceitful: it selects, interprets, reconstructs. Any report of an event is suspect. "Witnesses to every deed present versions of it which vary according to their sympathies and according to their memory."[79] Without himself, by his presence, being the eye that listens, without blinking, to each event, the historian has no choice other than to take up the inquiry with other people as accurately as possible. Therefore mistrust and a fortiori when it is a question of times gone by (*palaia*). "In this realm, it is very difficult to believe all the pieces of information as they appear."[80] Thus it is that at Athens it was commonly thought that Hipparchus, after being killed by Harmodius and Aristogeiton, was tyrant, but it was not known that Hippias, eldest of the sons of Peisistratus, was in power. His brother Hipparchus, busy arranging the procession for the Panathenaea, paid with his life for the panic of conspirators convinced that Hippias had been informed about the plot.[81] But "there are still other deeds—contemporaneous and unobliterated by time—about which the Greeks develop wrong ideas in the same way."[82] For instance, the idea regarding the Lacedaemonians to the effect that every king has two votes instead of one or that they have a "Pitane battalion" which has simply never existed. Ready-made ideas[83] that Thucydides censures severely for being lacking in information. To those often unconscious defects are joined others, less involuntary, wherein memory is caught in the *flagrante delicto* of subjective interpretation. 430 is the year of the great pest; Athens "had men who were dying within its walls and, outside them, territory which was pillaged."[84] A time of trial and of reminiscence.

> People recalled memories, naturally, and the verse according to the eldest among them was recited once upon a time: The Dorian War will occur and with it an epidemic (*loimos*). In fact, there was disagreement. The word employed in the verse might not have been *epidemic* (*loimos*) but rather *famine* (*limos*). However the prevailing opinion was, as it happened, that the word was *epidemic*, naturally. For people's memory was influenced by what happened to them.[85]

The memory is even weaker in suffering. And Thucydides ends with a comment: "If, I imagine, another Dorian War ever takes place after this one and that there happened to be a *famine*, it will naturally be referred to in that form."[86] A phonema wavers, the mouth is disturbed, and already the ear fabricates another verse, a mouth murmurs another account.

How could hearsay not be discredited when it falsifies the present under our very eyes? Impossible to rely on it and even less with regard to olden times. Thenceforth, silence is in order. And that is the behavior Thucydides ascribes to the Athenians when they have come to explain to the Spartan assembly their disputes with the Corinthians: "Of what use is it to speak to you of very ancient events when they are averred only by rumors that circulate (*akoai*) and not by what those who listen to us have seen with their eyes (*opsis*)."[87] Second ground for complaint, directed to the ear as much as to the mouth: credulity. People prefer "ready-made ideas" (*hetoima*)[88] to searching for truth. Thucydides grows indignant: "Even when it concerns their own country, people accept without examining them the traditions (*akoai*) that have come down from the past."[89] It is not possible more radically to criticize tradition as process of transmission and transformation.[90] Nor is it possible to criticize tradition in a more inhuman way since Thucydides calls on everyone to check all information carefully, each event, the faintest rumor before repeating it: in other words, he is "historian" in the new style.

But the indictment is not yet finished. The real culprits must be denounced. Time is at work: the "ready-made ideas" are just so many "unverifiable facts," but with the years they finally become aligned with the "myth," with *muthōdes*, toppling down in the unbelievable (*apistōs*).[91] To Thucydides there exists a sufficient relation between credulity and the noncredible: the one produces the other. But the situation worsens through the fault of poets (*poiētai*) and logographers (*logographoi*). That which is no longer credible becomes totally unbelievable when the poets begin to sing "endowing events beauties which aggrandize them," whereas logographers put together unverifiable facts "looking for the pleasure of the listener more than for truth."[92]

Adorned like idols, borne by enchanting voices solely for the ear's delight, the accounts of poets and of logographers exploit the weaknesses of memory and the credulity of mankind. And that is Thucydides' third ground for complaint against mnemonic tradition: the "mythic" denotes the masterpiece of artisans skilled in "producing a show for an audience at a given time."[93] Comrades in orality, logographers, and poets compose speeches for an occasional audience. Their public recitations only expedite, in a more or less established form, the unchecked circulation of words interchanged between ear and mouth.

A radical breach, even with his contemporaries. At the beginning of his history of Italy and of Sicily, Antiochus of Syracuse, between 430 and 410, informs his readers he "has written, in this book, the most credible (*pistotata*) and the most knowledgeable (*saphestata*) according to ancient tradition, according to accounts of yore (*archaioi logoi*)."[94] For Thucydides, the useful, the only goal of the new history is the excommunication of old stories. "If one wants to be able to view past events clearly and also future ones which, due to their human nature (*to anthrōpinon*), will bear resemblance and analogies,"[95] it is necessary to give up the pleasure of "myth," to reject the whole tradition based on a means of communication that radically falsifies thought and conceptual analysis. The *Peloponnesian War* is "outside myth"; it begins where, by decree, the action of ancient memory ends.

On this plane and in this perspective there is a rift between Thucydides and Herodotus. The *Peloponnesian War* ushers in a policy concerning memory which relegates the scholar of Halicarnassus to the multitude of "mythologists" long before Aristotle's remark about it. This must be emphasized because the cleavage directly concerns the status of the "myth" at the beginning of the fourth century as much in its relation to remembrance as in its relation to writing. Before Thucydides struck the blow there are three ways of telling stories, *logoi*. That of country folk who have a better memory than others and who like to tell old stories or to put new ones in circulation. It is among them that Herodotus meets or enlists supporters he calls *logioi andres*, probably people of leisure rather than peasants or workers.[96] Besides these casual narrators there exists the category of logographers, more or less "professional" tellers of tales, the authors of tradition. With a repertory extending from genealogies and theogonies to accounts of the foundation or the experiences of a city. Their realm is "archaeology" as it was then called, around the year 430.[97] With regard to their means of communication, it is halfway between recitation and writing. Like Herodotus's which represents the third way. Autopsy, travels, investigation: to do research, to tell about distances covered, to see with his own eyes, all new procedures placed at the disposal of a project which intends to break, but only partially, with traditional memory. To the Greece of the cities in its new political space since the wars with the Medes must be added another kind of memorableness: centered on the unforgettable glory (*kleos*) of the great and miraculous exploits in the confrontation between Greeks and Barbarians;[98] consolidated around the "Hellenic" (*to hellenikon*), that which the cities opposed to the Medes and the Persians have in common.[99] There, writes Herodotus at the beginning of his narration, is what must not be erased from the memory of men.

But the new kind of memorableness of Herodotus, though including the glamorous epic and the ancient Trojan war, is not radically different from tradition based on memory. On the contrary, Herodotus's accounts integrate into the texture of the unforgettable a series of memorials already set up in familiar landscapes or in the distances covered by the investigator across populated territory. Everytime Herodotus halts when he comes upon those who, like Darius, wish to leave "as a monument to themselves" something no other person had accomplished before.[100] There exist "monuments" in the material sense: the meat skewers of Rhodopis the courtesan amassed at Delphi;[101] the canal Xerxes pierced through Mount Athos;[102] the labyrinth of the twelve kings near Lake Moeris;[103] and the statues erected to glorify their owners in Egypt or elsewhere.[104] Monuments in narrative form, recited as exploits, as admirable and noble deeds: admirable things, grasped and explored by the eye with searching look and by the ear which picks up their glory and praises. But there are other memorials which are neither constructions nor offerings: those are famous acts or sayings. For instance, a witty remark when all seems lost. The rumor reaches the Thermopyleans that the arrows let fly by the Barbarians are so numerous that they obscure the sun. "We shall fight in the shade," exclaims Dinarchus the Spartan.[105] Unforgettable, says Herodotus. Or when, at Marathon, Miltiades tries to persuade an indecisive officer: "It depends on you, now, Callimachus, either to enslave Athens or to ensure its liberty, and to leave behind, for all time men exist, a *monument* such as neither even Harmodius nor Aristogeiton have left of themselves."[106]

Those memorable impressions among others are chosen by Herodotus. They do not pertain to an archivist obsessed by the duty to record everything. He "mentions" what is worth mentioning. "To mention," in Greek, is "to remember" (*mnēsthēnai*) or "to give a name to" (*epimnathai*). That is to say, simply to speak of it. Because mentioning it is an inducement to recount it. Thus he says about the Egyptian oracle: "I have mentioned this several times: it deserves amplification."[107] And that which the historian recalls is very often already renowned (*kleos*) in tradition. Whereas "to point out" (*sēmēnai*) is in contradistinction to "mention," more neutral, deliberately discreet. That is not worth speaking about; it is already half erased, like a faded color or a vanishing form of the same hue as the word *exitēlos* in the poem in the *Histories*, when Herodotus explains that his research aims "to prevent that which men have done from being erased from memory (*exitēla*) by time," from disappearing, from becoming *sans kleos*, nameless, anonymous. The distinction is particularly clear and operative in the part about the Nile floods. Of the three explanations current two are worth merely *pointing out*: "I do not think they are worth *mentioning*."[108] And it is the second of those shades of *logos*, evoking the Ocean, that Herodotus condemns to the darkness of "myth."[109] In a way, to erase it from tradition. Pointed out as unbelievable, "myth" is allocated to the opposite of the memorable but without fanfare and only derogated in passing. Hearsay, that which is murmured from mouth to ear, hums and circulates from one account to another. Besides what he has seen, Herodotus gives an important place to what he has heard. "As for me, throughout my account (*logos*) I propose to put in writing (*graphein*) just as I heard it (*akoē*) what different people say." The traveler is always on the road between the oral and the written. Thucydides, on the contrary, is purposefully engaged in writing, conceptual writing which makes it possible to "see clearly," "accepted knowledge forever" (*ktēma es aiei*). Instead of a chance audience Thucydides demands a reader who will avoid time and its surprises; a reader in the mirror of the finished book, permanent and immutable. The truth of effective discourse, of "useful" history, is a written truth. But it is also another kind of memory, sheltered from rumors, purified of the falsifications of hearsay, saved from the temptations of the pleasure of listening and of telling stories.

Here, in reading Thucydides, it is needful to relate the story of Nicias, of his letter to the Athenians and his peculiar harangue before the defeat.[110] Two episodes of the Sicilian expedition in which the author of the *Peloponnesian War*, on the subject of that same military commander, admits his hatred of "archaeology" and subscribes to a Jansenism of written rationalism. In the summer of 414, Nicias wishes to inform the Athenian assembly of the problems of the expeditionary force. His report, written down, is entrusted to reliable men who have received instructions.[111] The letter is extraordinary. Thucydides recalls that Nicias had the habit of communicating events one by one, sending messengers by sea.[112] To write a letter "was, in his eyes, the best means to ensure that the Athenians, informed of his position without its being clouded over by the messenger, take sides in full possession of the truth."[113] After questioning Nicias's envoys—and "winter had begun"[114]—the secretary in charge gives the message a public reading before the assembly. An unusual procedure, the reasons for which are given by Thucydides: Nicias feared "that his envoys, by virtue of a lack of a gift for oratory or lapse of memory or a wish to flatter the people, might not report things accurately."[115] Not only is memory weak but speech is exposed to the temptation of pleasure. In the *Peloponnesian War* speech is always under suspicion of looking for satisfaction of its desire, *terpsis*.[116] There is but one exception: Pericles, intelligence in Power, "the only one who could address an assembly without speaking with a view to giving pleasure."[117] To yield to pleasure is, for Thucydides, to forget the welfare of the city, to adopt an irrational motive, or to make a choice based on the immediate future.[118] Pleasure must no more interfere with the city's decisions than with the writing of history. And Nicias's letter ends with praise for writing which is proof against the sinful cravings of mouth and ear:

> I might have other more flattering news to impart to you but none more useful. . . . Since, at the same time, I am acquainted with your nature, interested in language which above all is pleasurable to hear (*ta hēdista akouein*) but which becomes incriminating when the outcome of events does not correspond to the words, I have found it more reliable to confront your eyes with the truth.[119]

Sight instead of hearing, and to the analytical examination demanded by the historian, in the shadow of the clerk reading Nicias's letter aloud, comes a reply from the silent reader who alone deserves the strict accuracy of the *Peloponnesian War*.

The best thing for the productions of memory is the same as applies to women: that they take care to be talked about as little as possible. To be quiet or, better yet, not to exist. There is a kind of delirium in Thucydides' treatment of the earliest culture: when he rages against country people who are incontinent, babble their recollections, recounting traditions in circulation about the past without bringing to bear any criticism of them! It is necessary to write carefully not to curtail "human nature." In the theory of the intellectual qualities of the man of action memory does exist, the kind that overcomes fear and fosters the application of lessons learned;[120] it is at the command of practical and technical knowledge (*epistēmē*), it helps intelligence (*gnōmē*) to make a complete analysis of the situation.[121] It is perfectly controlled mnemonic action imparted to politicians beyond reproach. As for the rest, the city, Athens, considers memory superfluous, at least that of "monuments" or of "memorials." Pericles says this in the funeral oration: "Alone of all existing cities, Athens, when put to the test, proves better than its reputation (*akoē*) . . . ; by our daring we have forced all the sea and the land to open up and everywhere we have left imperishable monuments (*mnēmeia . . . aidia*), memories of evil and of good."[122] Not ephermeral constructions but actions, choices, decisions. Truth inherent in acts (*ergōn . . . alētheia*)[123] is so powerful it has no "need of a Homer to glorify it nor of anyone whose tone of voice may charm momentarily but whose interpretations must suffer in light of the true facts."[124] The dead of the field of honor are served notice: in giving their bodies to the city they receive for themselves "praise that does not deteriorate and the most distinguished sepulcher."[125] But their real sepulcher, like that of the illustrious men who have the whole earth as their tomb, is carved, buried in memories rather than on steles and mere inscriptions.[126] Memory strictly governed by the truth of acts and constantly reactivated by reasons and actions pertaining to the city which are forever correct.[127] A memory that can dispense with engraved signs and concrete monuments because it is directly located beyond hearsay no matter whence it comes or whence it arises.

That kind of memory, without risks, without setbacks, is the exact counterpart of that revealed by the misadventure of Nicias but, this time, prey to the most incongruous utterances. Judge for yourselves. The Sicilian expedition is almost over; the Athenians are surrounded; the only solution is to do battle at sea but in conditions foretelling disaster. Nicias is sick, out of control. He sees the gravity of the danger, but he is already more than defeated, impervious to reality and behaving strangely. On finishing his harangue, instead of proceeding to act, the generalissimo begins to speak again but in a most deranged way.

> Saying, that as happens at the time of important engagements that there was much yet to be done, that everything that ought to have been said to the men had not been said, and he began again to call upon each trireme commander adding to his name the name of his father and of his tribe: charging them personally, if they had performed some brilliant exploit, not to betray it nor the great deeds of their fathers, if they had famous ancestors, not to tarnish their glitter: invoking their country, the most free of all countries . . . ; adding, finally, that at such a decisive moment one is ready, without fear of seeming to hark back to the same old story (*archaiologein*), to say trite things that people always say: they speak of women, of children, of the country's gods, whatever in that crisis, seems useful to invoke.[128]

It is the fall of the Athenian empire, the end of the maritime supremacy of the great city: Nicias drivels. Thucydides uses only once the
term "archaeology," but this lone instance suffices to make clear the
misinterpretation that turns inside out a similar misinterpretation
toward the beginning of the *Peloponnesian War*. It is with the exercise
of great care that Thucydides chooses to say "driveling" where
others among his contemporaries—particularly those passing
themselves off as "historians" but who are merely vulgar logographers—are more likely to speak of "a speech according to
tradition."[129] The verbal incontinence of a general in senile decay
indicates a break in the lode whose underside reveals memory
mastered by a rationalism of politics and the historian: the irrational
world of the "mythic."

From insular revolts to the senile chatter of a routed army
commander, mythic illusions do not cease to grow among the
Greeks. But what strengthens and ripens them is, in part, the blow
struck by Thucydides. The rationalist historian no longer has anything in common with tellers of tales who are logographers and in
the same category as poets. To delimit the realm of the new historical erudition, Thucydides must close off the territory of "myth" but
along the entire length of the frontier which, despite him, connects
it with the land of memory. And through the expedient of that huge
fortification encircling without his knowledge him who built it, the
Peloponnesian War puts an end to the desultory and scattered history
of myth, that will-o'-the-wisp that amuses Herodotus or the landmark for short Pindaric anathemas. The word of others becomes an
empire peopled by the fables of nomads, by long barbaric narratives
which the mares of memory gallop through, of memory fertilized by
the wind, the wind of words which are windy words. "Myth" is
always a relic, but one completely metamorphosed into a great
explosion in which the scraps detonated by the historian who is a
specialist in public health resemble fabulous riches: all that is told in
verse and in prose by dumbfounded poets and logographers. When
Thucydides calls to mind works of the imagination depicted by
poets and told by logographers with aim to please, he speaks the
same language as Fontenelle, that of Enlightenment.[130] With the
difference that the rationalist history in the fourth century does not
intend to light up the pathways of error from earliest man to the
most recent storytellers. Neither—but here Thucydides is again in
agreement with the author of *De l'origine des fables*—does it intend to
explain or to understand from within. Ancient memories threaten
everywhere; it is imperative to exorcise the thought that lives, to
excommunicate it from the body politic. The light of concepts will

not be deflected in order to make legible accounts founded on
hearsay. There is no room for hermeneutics to express the usefulness of "myth." Just as "monotheistic" religion, once dreamed of by
a missionary of the *Société du Verbe divin*, must be purged of all
mythology, the order of reasons determined by Thucydides must be
asserted from the beginning "outside of myth," *mē muthōdes*: intact,
untouchable, and no fiction, nothing miraculous, must graze it even
with their shadows.

A closed and dark world where ancient fictions wander forever,
"myth," at the same time it ceases to be a landmark missing from
every map, is transformed into nebula where "archaeologists,"
poets, and others still more numerous intermingle in the same
darkness. Thus the solitary historian has decided who, the better to
distinguish himself from the species of logographers more or less in
contact with writing, reminds us regularly of his capacity as authorized writer, of *suggrapheus*.[131] Echoing his official title of "drafter" of
laws,[132] a title perhaps tinged by the name of a written document in
use in commercial law in the fourth century: the contract, *suggraphē*,
which specifically provides for the terms and conditions of its
execution.[133] *Praxis* in writing that vouches for "fact accepted forever" and that legitimizes, by virtue of its visual nature, the exclusion of all "emotional" memory, memory based on hearing, the
most impressionable of the senses, according to Theophrastus.[134]

Chapter Four
The Earliest Interpretation— and a Smile

Whoever goes hunting without the excuse that the wild animal is shy should remember that in spring before the perfume of flowers disturbs the dog's sense of smell, the tracks of the hare are clear but intermingled.[1] Not as a result of the ruse which induces the hare when fearing pursuit to retreat through the same places by leaping together and placing "tracks within its tracks,"[2] but because, partic- ularly at that season, the hare's mate and "roaming together . . . make similar tracks."[3] However confused he may be in choosing between trickery and vagabond pleasure, the "myth" hunter will not be surprised to find that in the land of beginnings, at this season in History, the "pure" tracks as they are called in *L'art de la chasse* are mingled with others, mixed up and so faint that the scent, the technical term used by hunters, seems to have vanished. He will be even less surprised to find that his hare makes its form in the sites of illusion.

The straight and long track which runs between the "people of myth" to the anathema of the rationalistic historian meets a winding path more dense in time where the voice of the earliest philosophy alternates with that of interpretation when this intersects one of the beginnings of the writing of history and of histories. A less visible path which meanders between Xenophanes, philosopher of Elaea, and Hecataeus, the logographers of Miletus. For the word "myth" is missing in its explicit form but indicated by various synonyms opening and marking out the field of tradition. A tradition that is questioned, attacked sometimes, but beleaguered by those who write about it while questioning it and who always change it; this time according to the methods of interpretation and in terms of new practices in the field of writing.

Having haughtily declared himself to be scandalized never yielded Thucydides a place, even a modest one, in the pantheon of the avant-garde established by the nineteenth century. True, his

verbal violence, a serpent's knot of reason, does not immediately
single him out as one of those "pious and thoughtful" men who
painfully endured the divorce between the morality indispensable
to religion and the lewd accounts perpetuated by tradition. A century before, philosophy had taken an intransigent stance, beginning with the anger of the Eleatic school and continuing on to the
severe restrictions of the *Republic*. And it is from those vigilant
philosophers that modern mythologists have taken their instructions, confidently fitting new knowledge in the science of myths
into the rediscovered footsteps of the Ancients. Foremost among
those "delicate and refined" men, Xenophanes, philosopher and
poet who came from Asia Minor to Magna Graecia, gives all the
assurances of thoughtful piety. And without having awaited his
mature years which our chronological short-sightedness place
around 530 B.C. With Xenophanes—and this is new—begins criticism of tribal stories. Boldly, and in a tone to get all the attention of
Fr.-Max Müller and his contemporaries. "Homer and Hesiod attributed to the divine powers everything that is harmful and blame-
worthy in men: stealing, committing adultery and deceiving one
another."[4] The matter is more serious than a commonplace rivalry
between a sixth-century poet and his overly influential predeces-
sors. Homer and Hesiod are in the vanguard of a storm of accounts
no less scandalous and condemnable. And Xenophanes states his
case when he praises good memory: "Amongst all men the one who
deserves praise is he who gives proof of a noble character after
having drunk, using his memory and his strength towards moral
goals. It is he who sings neither of the Titan's combats nor the fights
between Giants and Centaurs, ancient forgeries (*plasmata tōn pro-
terōn*), nor of the violence of revolutions (*staseis*) for therein is nothing profitable. For the gods, one must always have good
intentions."[5] The tone is no longer invective. The melody which
ornaments those solemn words is heard in a banquet hall and is
described in the first part of the elegy sung by Xenophanes. Is the
banquet reserved for a philosophic thiasus?[6] The floor is clean,
hands and cups are purified: no spot of blood, no odor of grease,
and from the middle of the room there arises the perfume of
incense.[7] As if in another agora, built upon the first one, to teach the
ceremony of a new branch of knowledge without any renunciation
of the world or the city or its workings. For, to Xenophanes, it is a
question of good government, of the *eunomiē* inherent in political
space. "Our wisdom, our *sophiē*, is worth more than the strength of
horses and men."[8] It is wisdom that enriches the city's treasures and
not the winning race of an athlete who has left for the springs of

Pisa, "a small stroke of luck" awaited by a community no better governed therefor.[9] It is the philosopher who should be cherished at the Prytaneum and not the winner at wrestling or pancratium, the caricature laughed at by the singing poets,[10] the choristers of victory who bask in the sun on the Helladic earth from Olympia to the most insignificant of cities. "Sophiē," the wisdom of the ancients with its memories of violence and of unholy wars, that is the opponent, that is the internal enemy which threatens the eunomiē of the city and of world order, the cosmos of which the philosopher is henceforth the sole cartographer.

Titans, Giants, Centaurs: kingdoms of earth and fire, Warriors forever adolescent, Hybrids hungry for raw meat, all of them emblematic of immoderation, of hubris, sung in a tradition at once epic and figurative which exalts without respite violence and revolt.[11] Xenophanes does not differentiate between "revolutionary songs"[12] and the behavior of Titans or Centaurs. All tradition is one: it combines the revolts of the present and the theomachies of the past. The anonymous writers scattered between the friezes of sanctuaries and forgotten songs are convoked and heckled, convened under the rubric of Homer and of Hesiod, leaders of tribal history. But Xenophanes does not mean to show them respect for having given the Greeks a pantheon or a theogony as Herodotus will do, for have they not depicted the gods as thieves, liars, and adulterers? Of the two accomplices the real culprit is the poet of the Iliad and the Odyssey for the very reason advanced by Xenophanes: "From the outset the Greeks derive their knowledge from Homer."[13] Not so much Homer the writer secure in the indefeasible rights on his "works" but the nomenclature designating a mode of existence, of circulation and functioning of certain accounts within Greek society.[14] No doubt this is, in part, the Homer recited officially "word for word," first to the Panathenaeans, then in Syracuse where Cinesias, the rhapsodist, introduced him around the year 504.[15] But in addition to that account fixed by the city's decision at the center of its paideia, of its educational system and thus presented to the pedagogues privately entrusted with teaching reading and writing, there is the influence brought to bear by one name upon the countless more or less anonymous stories familiar to everyone both through having heard them always and seen them on vase paintings and sculptures, on Doric friezes on pediments. The bands of Centaurs and the troop of Giants join the powers of Olympus, and the Titans rise in the shadow of the ancient gods who have been betrayed. Is it not blasphemy to believe that one of the Olympians rules the others in the role of despot?[16] And what is there to say about those gods thus fashioned except that they have the equine form given them by horses skilled in painting or marble cutting?[17]

Whatever the true nature of his "*sophie*" inscribed within the city's space may be, Xenophanes of Elea brutally attacks the scandalous characteristics of ancient memory. Tradition which is rife in the city, whether it comes from Homer or elsewhere, threatens the whole body politic like gangrene. Without prompt intervention no good government or *eunomiē* can exist. The city's ancient stories must be amputated. And the form of that exclusion, outlined by Xenophanes's discourse between the iron discipline in his anathema and praise for good memory quite faithfully follows the contours of the "myth" as it appears at the same period by way of an Anacreontic song.[18] The same subversion is at work in the civil wars that tear the city apart and in the deceitfulness of the gods, the combats of the Titans, the immoderation of the Centaurs. Revolutionary violence is nurtured by the "forgeries of the Ancients." And, reciprocally, the fictions of the past nurture words of sedition which identify the "people of myth" as was said in Samos, whether they are called Homer and Hesiod or whether they are concealed in a Battle of Giants.

The thoughtful piety of Xenophanes marks the beginning of the utmost severity, and in his fundamental rejection to traditional culture spread by "the people of myth" is encapsulated the whole of the first progression between the word exploit of Samos and the enraged policy of containment decided on in the *Peloponnesian War*. Certainly Xenophanes would have liked to share the spectacle observed by Pythagores in a catabasion of the Hellenistic epoch: "The soul of Hesiod tied to a bronze column and howling, and that of Homer hanging from a tree and surrounded by snakes."[19] A just punishment in Hades for their blasphemies against the gods. But, in deciding to erase from the memory of citizens so many ancient and familiar stories Xenophanes, in fact, chooses a revolutionary position. And the riposte promptly issues from the most threatened social milieu, if not the most reactionary: the brotherhood of Homeric rhapsodists. A riposte all the keener since the philosopher of Elea once again rivals them by reciting his own works rhapsodically: his Invectives, his Elegies, and also his poems on the founding of Colophon and the colonization of Velia, certainly addressed to an Eleatic audience.

Fictions, those great fundamental accounts? Indecent, immoral, the adventures of gods in poems officially declaimed by rhapsodist actors magnificently appareled before a great conclave of people? In the city of Rhegium in Magna Graecia the narrators of Homer reply to the accusations of Xenophanes. Theagenes, their spokesman around 510, is one of the *Iliad*'s first apologists. His system of defense is based on what Porphyrus calls allegory but which Plato calls "insinuation" (*huponoia*). When Homer shows the confrontation of the gods—facing Poseidon, Apollo and his fletched arrows, against Hera, and Artemis the Noisy—he does not mean to say that the Olympian powers are at war, give battle divided into two hostile camps. His "theomachy" evokes another meaning; it must be understood as a way of expressing the opposition of basic elements recognized by the philosophy of nature: between the dry and the humid, between the hot and the cold. They only among Homer's listeners can be shocked who are so limited as to wish to hear a "literal" account, in its primary meaning, and are so uninformed of advances in the new physics that they still confuse bronze with Hera and the moon with Artemis.[20] In counterattacking on the very field of his opponent Theagenes not only gives proof of cleverness but also how and where the philosophic debate is linked with the scandal of tradition: surrounded by the most official "fictions," those most firmly established in the cultural and political space of the city. For the apology for Homer, improvised by rhapsodists impelled to save their livelihood, is made in the realm of reading rather than of hearing. Theagenes' arguments presuppose a text fixed in writing, the official Homer of cities which, following the example set by Athens, consign to virtuous cantors the task of reciting an epic conforming exactly to the model chosen by the authorities. And among those Heraclitus disdainfully calls "the cantors of important villages"[21] Theagenes represents the literary element, the narrator who doubles as interpreter. In Greek tradition is he not the first of the "grammarians" by virtue of the attention he pays to the correct usage of a word[22] as well as data of biography,[23] on the family, on the period and activities of the poet propagating the first *Lives of Homer*, written due to the piety of Homer scholars in Chios, Samos, and Smyrna?[24] Rather than seeking to interest listeners of whom very few were concerned by fights between the gods, Theagenes addresses readers who without a written text would have trouble distinguishing the second meaning from the first, in so short a period of time, within a work whose continuous recitation could take three days.

In this dispute two notable facts emerge. First, that it centers around Homer, whereas Xenophanes aims at ancient memory, all the tribal stories. One of several signs that in the sixth century Homer is still midway between popular aurality and the alphabetization restricted to an élite which discovers the delights of hidden meaning. And then, and this is most important, the scandal which evokes the first philosophy engages, without using the word "myth," the procedure that is to play a determining role in the elaboration of "mythology": the decision to interpret. This time, with regard to tradition in the widest sense of the term: all the old stories and some more recent ones. It is the field where writing, through the techniques of interpretation, opens up unknown pathways, finds new directions, keeps unprecedented books of records.

As for interpretation, it has certainly no definite beginning. But it would be of little use to define it, out of fidelity to Aristotle, as the decision to "say something *about* something."[25] Likewise, to lower the level to the extent of infringing on a "principle of relevance," universal and immanent in any statement made in a "conversation" as some suggest[26] would presume that everything is equally interpretable, which is perhaps true, but would erase the partition between the societies of aural memory and the civilizations based on writing. The distinction posited by certain anthropologists between exposition and interpretation seems to be more feasible.[27] No living culture, including our own, can refrain from commenting, expounding on, and adding to what has been said in the continuum of its actions and exploits. The exegesis is the unceasing and also immediate commentary that a culture arrogates of its symbolism, of its practices, or everything that makes up its living culture. A parasitic word, seizing everything it can evoke, exegesis proliferates from within; it is a word that nurtures and fosters the growth of the tradition to which it attaches itself and from which it derives its own substance. There is no living tradition without the rumbling of the exegeses it arrogates to itself and which inhere in it, which are incorporated in it. Whereas interpretation arises when there is distance and a perspective from without on tradition based on memory. A distance not due to just any statement made in the course of a conversation in which "incoherence" would be an inducement to seek the allusion and would generate interpretative activity. For interpretation to begin it is essential to have a discussion, to begin to criticize tradition. With the exception of the implicit and unconscious censure of the group which refuses to tell and to repeat,[28] the distance necessary to criticism has no place in the ranks of memory, in the bosom of the tradition of mouth and ear. "One does not discuss the myths of the group," writes Lévi-Strauss, "one transforms them in the belief one is repeating them."[29] That is precisely what changes with regard to the contemporaries of Xenophanes. There appears a distance that is either a wish to throw out material or a feeling of discontinuance but always that which makes possible criticism of tribal stories: that is, writing, like something alien, like another place whence is spoken and written the discourse on tradition. From this point of view the censorious judgments of Xenophanes stem from interpretation as does the apology for Homer from the ancient city of Rhegium.

Once the distinction between exegesis and interpretation has been defined, another becomes necessary to recognize the progress of hermeneutics. At least in its major choices which are located between a radical distance and another which is minimal. In the space where hermeneutic activity is deployed, the first philosophy chooses the extreme position: it assigns to tradition the status of "fiction" and forces the rhapsodist interpreter to detour by way of the *other* meaning, the "allegorical," if he wishes to salvage the discourse of Homer. A divided procedure under the circumstances and adopted by philosophy only when it has discovered that one of the advantages of indirect meaning is to open the shortest way to the primary meaning, to the literal meaning. For is it not a matter of returning to one's own discourse without knowledge of the other one, not falling into the trap of its misunderstanding of the truth? Contrary to philosophic discourse, driven to alterity by being secure in its own knowledge, there exist forms of interpretation so subtle that they go unobserved. Hermeneutics so proximate that the only gap is in the writing and has to do with the effectiveness of its spontaneity.[30] It is a kind of interpretation which would be at the boundary line of exegesis if, in its cultural context, it did not bear the potential of "speaking about" by means of the practice of writing. Padded hermeneutics which begin with usage but also with the decision reached almost contemporaneously with the vehemence of Xenophanes to put in writing, to relate the elements of tradition by writing them down. It is here that the minimal distance of the written is marked out and is emphasized more or less by the procedures adopted by one user or another.

There is no question of ascribing a primary status to writing, as though, endowed with a transcendental anonymity, it emerged progressively from the forgetting to which it was consigned by a millenary and unceasing repression. In Greece writing, in its beginnings, exerts an undeniable critical function. But only in some of its developments. Never when used as engraving on the base of a statue placed in a sanctuary or on the rim of a cup or drinking vessel. Even less when emanating from the pen of a businessman registering a ship's cargo or on lead tablets recording debts as early as 500 B.C. It is small groups, intellectuals—philosophers, doctors, logographers, practitioners of prose—who make use of the assets of writing as criticism. And it is in the practices of the "fabricators of accounts" that is best revealed the effectiveness of the activity of writing where the interpretation is so intermingled with the narrative as to melt into one. The "fabricated accounts" (*logopoioi*) write *logoi* and Thucydides calls them logographers,[31] whereas Herodotus ranks with them, side by side, Aesop the "fabulist" and Hecataeus of Miletus,[32] the traveler and surveyor of the inhabited world who some moderns, in collusion with the Ancients, like to classify as an authentic or primary historian. Therein lies a special field for inquiry, through written material, into certain divisions between thoughts about history, the art of telling old stories, and methods of hermeneutics.

Questions introduced by the preamble to the *Histories* of Hecataeus: "Hecataeus of Miletus speaks thus (*mutheitai*). Those accounts I write (*graphō*) as they seem true to me. For the accounts (*logoi*) of the Greeks, to my eyes, are many and laughable."[33] This narrative writer is not unknown on the main square of Miletus at the end of the sixth century. In 499 the Greek cities of Ionia revolt against the Achaemenidae, against the empire of the Medes. Before engaging Miletus in a rebellion which was to end in the destruction of the city in 494, Aristagoras, the temporary "governor,"[34] held a council with his followers. "All of them urged revolt excepting Hecataeus the *fabricator of accounts* (*logopoios*)."[35] Hecataeus alone advises against the venture. First he enumerates (*katalegein*) the peoples over whom Darius reigns and the forces at the command of the Great King. Then, since his "catalogue" does not succeed in dissuading the followers of Aristogoras from their suicidal project, the "fabricator of accounts" changes tactics, enters the insurgents' camp in order to advise prudence: to ensure their mastery of the sea. The armies of Miletus are derisive, and if the Miletians can lay hands on the treasures consecrated by Croesus of Lydia in the sanctuary of the Branchidae, they can enjoy unparalleled naval power. A strange counselor is this teller of tales, sufficiently influential to have a say in the meeting but without being in any way an "official historian," a personage of whom the Greek city will never, it seems, have need. His advice did not prevail, Herodotus remarks. Nothing is more commonplace than for a wise counselor to be ignored. What is less so is to argue according to a branch of knowledge that singles him out as a "fabricator of accounts," the author of *Genealogies* as well as of a *Periegesis*.

The Ionians wish to revolt? Well and good, provided they can raise new money. They need ships, a fleet, to ensure mastery of the sea if they do not wish to succumb to the coalition of countless peo-

ple who comprise the terrestrial empire of Darius. The solution of
Hecataeus, a realist, is to constitute a war treasury. That is why it is
necessary to "secularize" the riches of the great temple of Apollo, to
use for political ends the sacred offerings deposited in the sanctuary
of the Branchidae. But to misappropriate the money of the gods in
order to increase the power of men is, quietly, without fanfare, to
break with the most traditional values.[36] And it is the same break
with tradition that makes Hecataeus's first argument so unusual: a
catalogue, a long list of peoples. Recited not by an erudite genealogist but by a geographer who suddenly introduces cartography into
a political discussion. And Aristagoras, the strong man of Miletus,
at once profits from the lesson: when he arrives in Sparta to form an
alliance with Cleomanes and the Spartans, he carries under his arm
"a bronze tablet on which were engraved the peripheric outlines of
the whole world (gēs . . . periodos), all the seas and all the rivers."[37] A
space to be read but which can only be recounted by an experienced
traveler, able to draw a map of the world as well as to write a
Periegesis.

During this short political interlude a new man makes his
appearance; he masters graphic space and thus deals with original
and surprising subjects halfway between common and traditional
knowledge and a new form of thought doubtless more revolutionary than the rebellion of the Ionians, deaf to the arguments of the
"maker of histories." The blending of recitation and of writing
occurs in the preamble to a logography which comprises a Periegesis
and Genealogies. Two routes which seem to diverge, since the one
appears to stem from the study of geography and from the curiosity
of a navigator hugging the coasts, discovering distant cities and
exploring the limits of the inhabited world,[38] whereas the other is a
series of traditional accounts of events from Deucalion, the first man
after the deluge, to Heracles through what we call heroic legends.[39]
Nevertheless it is the same written and narrative project: to narrate
by writing, to write while narrating. Two steps elucidated in the
introductory discourse where the verbs to say (mutheisthai) and to
write (graphein) conjoin. A discourse that outlines the draft of a
writer, called Hecataeus of Miletus, proceeding from the third person to the first in the course of a text in the form of "signature,"
according to custom affixed to the beginning of the book. "Thus
speaks Hecataeus of Miletus (mutheitai). These accounts I write as
they seem to me to be true."[40] It is a seal, a sign of propriety.[41]
Hecataeus of Miletus is the maker, the authorized "poiete" of these
accounts just as, at the same period, a potter makes a cut and a poet
constructs a poem.[42] The "I" is inherent in the proper name. And

among the accounts mentioned knowledge of periegesis is displayed as extensively as of genealogy. These are the homologous
discourses of the very same cartographer. With perhaps the slight
difference that explains why the *Periegesis* creates the illusion of a
catalogue of words in contradistinction to the accounts in the
Genealogies. To "catalogue"—in the Greek sense of reciting an exhaustive list[43]—the cities and peoples of the inhabited world, Hecataeus keeps his eyes fixed on one of his maps, devised by his
compatriot, Anaximander.[44] Enclosed within the circular course of
the river Ocean, the world with its continents, its rivers, its cities, is
deployed in a space orientated by corresponding and symmetrical
relationships: the graphic space whose visual image resides in the
memory of Hecataeus and enables the geographer to travel through
the world as well by writing the series of place names as by describing the customs or peculiarities of groups of human beings.
Whereas, in an account of a genealogical sort, the cartography is
more subtle and lies in the writing of the account simultaneously
with, on the chronological plane, taking the form of a tablet on
which proper names are arranged about a vertical axis.

In what respect is the genealogist also a cartographer? The
answer is given in the preamble of Hecataeus in his project for
writing the narratives of the Greeks. "As I see them, they are numerous (*polloi*) and absurd (*geloioi*)."[45] Hecataeus discovers many versions of the narratives, *logoi*, which circulate in Greece.[46] Not in the
form of a plural immanent in a tradition that is narrated and does not
cease to produce variants or versions forever new. But as a multiplicity of sayings suddenly made apparent by their juxtaposition in
the graphic space that attempts to relate them and, at the same time,
to challenge them. And the laughter that overcomes Hecataeus is
more of amusement than moral shock and is the sign of the work at
interpretation to which a "maker of accounts" at Miletus devotes
himself when he begins to narrate the stories of the tribe in writing.
At the beginning of the third century A.D., Aelian the Naturalist
discerns in Hecataeus a "prosewriter of ancient myths," *muthōn
archaiōn sunthetēs*,[47] an arranger of narratives of yore. Aside from the
anachronism of the word "myth," Hecataeus is indeed a prose
writer who deals with stories placed side by side for the first time
which, he thinks, cannot be regarded without laughter. For instance, Heracles going to Geryon to steal a herd of cattle guarded by
a dog with two heads, no less redoubtable than his master with
three bodies. Hecataeus records the different versions: one of them
locates the expedition in the country of the Iberians, another in an

island beyond the Pillars of Hercules.[48] Obviously, these are accounts whose contradictions can be read when they are juxtaposed on the same tablet, enclosed in the same graphic space. But the interpretation does not wither in a smile. Yes, to be sure, the accounts given by the Greeks are ridiculous for if it is improbable to imagine Heracles bringing back a herd of cattle from old Spain to Mycenae, how much more unlikely is it to locate the theft in the Red Sea, mysterious Erytheia on the banks of the Ocean.[49] Nevertheless, Hecataeus remains the narrator (*mutheitai*) and does not reject similar stories of fables in the distant past. Heracles accomplished the deed with which tradition credits him, but it is more plausible to think it took place in the region of Ambracia where Geryon reigned over the Amphilochians. For it is no mean task to bring back so many cattle from the barbarous lands of southern Epirus.[50] "Probability" writes a new version that is added to tradition without censuring it, without seeking to erase Hesiod's account about Heracles in the foggy grounds beyond the circular Ocean.

An interstitial sort of writing, unobtrusive as the smile of someone who is not yet a logographer but a plain "maker of accounts," writing stories "as they seem true to him (*hōs moi dokei alēthea einai*)." The interpretation begins with the graphic space that reveals multifariousness; it continues with the narration of the probable. The "I" refers to the opinion, the *doxa* of the Milesian. From among the multiplicity of accounts within tradition it is certainly necessary to make a choice, to decide what seems to be true. This is the critical glance directed at Greek tribal stories: the narrator, Hecataeus, makes use of knowledge based on conjecture of the same order as opinion expressed in the course of political deliberations. And it is again one of the labors of Heracles that induced him to write "an account of suitability," a *logos eikōs*, as Pausanias calls it in his *Description of Greece*.[51] At Taenarum a statue of Poseidon is erected in front of a sanctuary in a cave: it is there—Pausanias says—that, according to some Greeks, Heracles would have brought the dog from Hades. In any case, the cave does not contain a pathway that goes downward under the earth, and it is not easy to believe that the gods inhabit a subterranean place where the souls of the dead are assembled.

> But Hecataeus of Miletus found an account which conforms to this, saying that a redoubtable snake haunted Taenarum which was called the dog of Hades because its bite and venom caused a lightning death. And it is this snake, he said, that Heracles had taken to Eurystheus.

Several years ago a papyrus from Cairo reestablished the indirect discourse back to the first person:

> I believe (*dokeō*) that the snake was neither so big nor so monstrous, but it was more poisonous than others. And that is why to bring it back might seem to Eurystheus to be a labor impossible to accomplish.[52]

Hecataeus does not mean to produce a new memory with regard to the confrontation between the Ionian cities and the power of the Medes or arise from an "archaeology" of Miletus. He is writing a discourse which is probable within the framework of tradition based on memory. And the opinion, the *doxa*, it must be remembered is neither for Hecataeus nor for Xenophanes an illusory word nor a superficial one.[53] Just as, on the agora, according to the formula for opening a decree "it has seemed proper to the people" (*edoxe tōi dēmōi*), so Hecataeus thinks that the version of the poisonous snake is better suited to the ear and eye of his contemporaries than that of a dog with fifty heads whose brazen voice frightens the shades residing in the depths of the earth. To write stories so that they seem to be true is to give a credible account to the hearers at Miletus, curious as they were about the adventures of Heracles as well as about invisible cities brought to ports by the first cartographers of the sea.

If writing, by making the multiplicity of stories visible, prompts the new "maker of accounts" to undertake the task of interpretation, so also it brings to bear its critical function on another point on which discussion of the most widespread stories will center: through genealogy as a pattern of thought and method of narration. When writing the *Genealogies* in which the Argonauts travel with Parthenopaeüs and the daughters of Danaüs, Hecataeus employs one of the most universal genres in the cultures in which tradition partakes of the mouth and the ear. Genealogies of heroes and of gods, of princes and potentates, of families and peoples: litanies of proper names, some of which are lost in the backcountry of memory while emerging into narratives the size of epics or into the learned constructs of theogony. Noble houses recognize each other through their genealogies, and each one knows the relatives of the other even before hearing the great names borne by those in "the famous accounts of mortals"[54] which the poets sing. When Diomedes questions his identity—"who are you then?"—Glaucos recites a genealogical tree of sixty-six verses, relating the marvelous exploits of his grandfather, Bellerophon, as famous as Sisyphus, son of Aeolus, the eponym of the Aeolians.[55] And a poem such as the *Catalogue of*

Women, attributed to Hesiod, deploys an ensemble of heroic traditions centered around local genealogies: armorial of a nobility that
evokes names and alliances to the ends of prestige and of power.[56]
Between the eighth and fifth centuries birth (*geneē*), within these
accounts, changes in meaning and orientation: more synchronistic
in Homer's epic in which the word generation designates a group of
contemporaries, of men born and reared together, with, in horizon-
tal order, the "time of life," as Hesiod says, it becomes, at the end of
the sixth century when verticality is emphasized, a unit of computation wherein each proper name, instead of evoking cohesion based
on high exploits performed in common, carves out in the same
chronological anonymity a slice of time, 30 or 33½ years of human
life.[57]

In that story Hecataeus is witness at the same time as actor.
Witness, first of all, to the ancient practice of reciting one's genealogy. Herodotus, who is careful not to use the same light touch,
relates in his accounts of Egypt how Hecataeus, in passing through
Thebes, shows the priests of Zeus his own genealogical tree, "deriving his family (*patriē*) from a god as sixteenth ancestor."[58] After
which Hecataeus is courteously escorted into a temple big enough
to contain more than 340 wood statues, each representing an important priest. And the priests of Zeus patiently enumerate them to
show their guest from Miletus that each of those personages is the
son of a father included in the series.

> They began with the one who had most recently died and went
> through the whole gallery until they had given proof for all of
> them.[59] . . . It is previous to those men that they who reigned in
> Egypt were gods living in company with men. . . . And the last
> of those kings would have been Horus, son of Osiris.[60]

For Herodotus there is no doubt that Hecataeus is confused; the
Egyptians, of all men, are those who most exercise their memory,
the only ones to have kept count for all time of the passing of years
and to have put it down in writing.[61] It is apparent to Hecataeus, by
the end of his genealogical walk along some 340 human generations, that his own genealogy is at variance with that of the Egyptians. A contradiction rendered all the more sharp because it is
pictured simultaneously by the spectacle of hundreds of statues
lined up next to one another and by the disclosure of a world in
which memories are entirely written on stones, covering walls and
filling books. Did Hecataeus smile at his family of sixteen ancestors?
Did he foresee, through the commemorative writing of the priests of

Thebes, the widening of what Herodotus is to call the "time of the human generation"?[62] Did he then discover that the catalogue of names could be written as far away in time as in space?[63] His Theban experience, in any case, made of him an essential agent in the process of the arithmetization of genealogies of which Herodotus's accounts already give an indication and which are to motivate the first attempts at systematic chronology on the part of the logographers of the fifth century.[64]

A new form of comparison in which visual experience again cuts into the practice of writing, genealogy defines the ambiguous boundaries of the modernism of Hecataeus: between writing and telling, between "making accounts" and deploying tradition in the space of writing, which is still so near shared stories that to state his preference for one rather than the other based on the probability of the situation is the sole foundation for Hecataeus's criticism. For Hecataeus there is no deliberate break with tradition: those who speak from anonymous memory are called upon to prove that once upon a time all *Hellas* was, so to speak, the home of Barbarians;[65] and writing, at this juncture, tells of the invention of the vineyard in Aetolia through the etymological relationship of the Vine grower, born of the Planter, himself born of father Mountain dweller, whose names reveal the true motives of each, arranged in a narrative written in the same way it could be told verbally.[66] It is a question of setting in order the tales of yore with the amused smile of the person who discovers with his own eyes the multiplicity, unseen until then, of tribal stories, but without meaning to proceed to a distinct separation between discourse based on probability and the test that would be censured as fiction or only denounced as improbable. For Hecataeus does not put any distance between his own *logos* and the category of a *muthos*. Exactly like his contemporary, Xenophanes, but with the difference that the philosopher's erudition entitles him to excommunicate the memories of others, whereas his opinion never incites the modest "maker of accounts" to cut himself off from a tradition his writing continuously embodies, even as he shapes it in his own way.

By choosing a prudent course midway between telling a story and writing it down, Hecataeus has only succeeded, it seems, in making the same mistake as the other interpreters, the moderns as well as the ancients. For some, he is only a short-story writer, a common "mythologist" who cannot lay claim to the dignity of a historian; for others, he is the precursor of a new rationalism or a model memorialist, an archivist so scrupulous that his writing faithfully records the ancient and earliest memorials. That strange theory is defended, in the first century B.C., by a Greek historian with the career of teaching rhetoric: Dionysius of Halicarnassus, author of a *History of Roman Antiquities* in twenty volumes but also of an essay on Thucydides in which he presents his views on the beginnings of historiography. "There were many historians in antiquity in various regions before the Peloponnesian War. Among others, Eugammon of Samos, Deioces of Proconnesus, Eudemus of Paros, Demonicus of Phrygia, and Hecataeus of Miletus. Besides, Acusilaus of Argos, Charon of Lampsacus, and Amelesagoras of Chalcedon. There were others before the events of the Peloponnesian War and living until the epoch of Thucydides: Hellanicus of Lesbos, Damastes of Sigeum, Xenomedes of Chios, Xanthus the Lydian, and many others. Those historians adopted the same principles in the choice of arguments and had more or less the same talent, some presenting the history of the Greeks, others those of the Barbarians without connecting them but separating them into peoples and cities and publishing them independently of each other thus pursuing the same single goal: *to bring to the knowledge of everyone the memorial traditions (mnēmai) which were preserved by the natives, by peoples and by cities, whether they be written (graphai) traditions deposited in sacred or profane places. Those written traditions-memoirs they brought to everyone's attention, just as they received them and without striking anything out.* And among those traditions were certain fictitious accounts (*muthoi*), subjects of very ancient belief, and certain unexpected events such as are represented in the theater and which seem very senseless to our contemporaries."[67]

A view of beginnings, in two settings. A monumental kind of writing, divided equally between peoples and cities; a written memoir, hoarded in sanctuaries and public places, posted in a profane space and in a sacred one; local archives that combine with very ancient "myths" the account of daily events. And, moving about in the midst of the natives, two generations of historians, between Hecataeus and Thucydides, who devote themselves to the entire publication of written monuments without adding or deleting, with the same discipline as a squad of epigraphers working silently at the stamping of documents that would evoke neither commentaries nor conjectures. Dionysius of Halicarnassus is emphatic on this point: his spontaneous local historical tales stem from both memory and writing.[68] Written memorials: they are traditions (*mnēmai*) identical to "those children receive from their parents,"[69] but captured in writing (*graphai*), entirely related in writing just as they came from the mouths of the Ancients.[70] It is not useless to mention this: no element in such a theory of the beginnings of history is verifiable. Until the present, at least, archaic Greece has yielded up neither local chronicles nor sacerdotal archives of the type of the famous pontifical annals of Rome.[71] In *The Ancient City* Fustel de Coulanges could dream of a local history, religious in origin and drafted by holy priests. We are obliged to state, nowadays, that there is no more of a priestly caste in the Greek world than we find Roman chronicles or archives fashioned by Mesopotamians.[72] One of the most ancient "temple chronicles," that of Athens at Lindos, on the island of Rhodes, was ordered by the city in 99 B.C. from two local scholars, Timachidas and Tharsagoras: under the supervision of the secretary in charge, they drew up the catalogue of offerings beginning with the founding hero, Lindos, and commemorated the miraculous interventions of the goddess, for the greater glory of the sanctuary.[73] And if, at Miletus, the list of eponymous priests begins in 525/524, it cannot have been engraved on the stone before 335/334.[74] Moreover, it is only a plain list of names neither in the form of an account nor of a chronicle.

Two aspects of the theory of Dionysius of Halicarnassus reveal its atopical nature. First, the presence in antique "memoirs" of fabulous tales, of myths as unusual to a reader of the first century B.C. as were some reversals of plot in the theater. Carried forward due to very ancient beliefs, the "myths" inserted in memorial writing guarantee its authenticity;[75] they bear witness to the fact that the natives related them like the traditions that "children receive from their parents." "Myths smacking of the soil," marvelously told without any research into old histories:[76] a spontaneous sort of archaeology which would naturally be "graphic."[77] Without, therefore, being commensurable to the earliest "local myths" (*muthoi . . . epichōrioi*) that toward the beginning of the third century B.C., are entrusted by the cities to poets to record in writing (*graphein*).[78] By conferring on earliest history the right to access to "native myths," Dionysius of Halicarnassus effectively does his part to foster the illusion, long indigenous to Greece, that myths belong to the language of earliest times.[79] But there enters the scene of those fabulous tales, written down exactly as spoken, the major phantasm of the origins of history: that there is perfect continuity between living memory and the first writing of history. An oral tradition is etched on stone, it becomes metamorphosed into a chronicle as though, all of a sudden, a kind of silent writing seized upon and immobilized all that is said by men to each other. No breach, no discontinuity between the writing of history and the autochthonal word. It is the exalted paradigm of Egypt, with its learned priests having at their disposal at one and the same time the most highly trained memory and the writing which is most reliable because the most ancient: do they not enregister in their temples all that is beautiful, good, or remarkable in the world and without interruption since the most faraway times? To see all and to say all, like a living eye which never blinks and whose alchemy transforms into written archives all it has seen. A dream of a complete history which would combine both voice and presence in writing, a dream so persistent that a fortuitous discovery will revive it. A few years ago a strange document was exhumed in Crete: half decree, half contract, in which a city, about 500 B.C., decides to employ a specialist in writing. In exchange for food, exemption from taxes and great privileges—fifty jugs of new wine and "ten portions of cut-up meat" in the collective banquets— a certain Spensithios will be archivist for the city "for public affairs, concerning gods as well as men": to write in Phoenician letters (*poinikazen*) and to be a living memory (*mnamoneuwen*).[80] The matter is surprising, to be sure, and for more than one reason, were it only for bringing out of obscurity a "professional scribe" working in the Cretan mountains. But in the ghost of that public writer we find the shade of the historian accountable for events,[81] and dedicated to the task—how thankless, for Herodotus never obtained such a good contract—of enregistering and remembering everything that, were it not for him, would be doomed irrevocably to oblivion.[82] Phantasm of a History that conceals in the writing of it even the greater part of the interpretation, of the continuous choices made, and of the labor of writing it.

Hecataeus, archivist, irreproachable historian? Dionysius of Halicarnassus has not convinced everyone. For those moderns, the greatest in number, who agree about the existence of a mythic thought, autonomous and homogeneous, whose decline coincides with the rise of an enlightened rationalism, the fate of the Milesian "maker of stories" oscillates between two kinds of representation. Either he opens the way to demytholization,[83] by teaching the Greeks to recognize in their tales if not an immediate past at least the part played by men, more probably than that of the gods. Moreover, along the same lines, Hecataeus initiates historical research, he devises rational criticism of the old genealogies, he introduces the enlightenment of the earliest "scientific spirit."[84] Or else, to the contrary, he is guilty of aiding and abetting the most traditional mythology, he fails to recognize the historical nature of his own genealogy "of fifteen generations subsequent to the end of the heroic era." In his Theban excursion and his questions to the priests of Zeus, there is even revealed the proof that he "emerges from history"—which is very awkward just at the time it is a question of

entering it: actually when Hecataeus tries to find out the date at
which the history of the Egyptians begins, does he not choose as
reference point Heracles and the Heraclids?[85]

But it is on the generation immediately succeeding that Hecataeus's smiling attitude produces the most appropriate results.
Does he not provoke the laughter of a certain Herodotus of Halicarnassus which is excusable since he has not yet been informed of his
dignified status as Father of History? Hecataeus smiles on discovering the multiplicity of stories told by the Greeks, but when he draws
a map of the world and when he recites the list of peoples paying
tribute to Darius, he is no doubt very serious. Now another cartographer, approaching in his wake, begins to laugh: "I laugh"—
Herodotus says in his fourth book—"when I see that many people
have drawn pictures of the earth (*gēs periodous grapsantas*) without
any of them having given a rational commentary (*exēgēsamenon*);
they represent the Ocean as enveloping the earth which is entirely
round as though machine-turned and Asia as equal to Europe."[86]
The circular Ocean of Hecataeus assures him of a good position
among the irrational expositors who draw and describe the contours
of the earth. Can one cartographer meet another without laughing?
But more is to come. In his tales of Egypt at the time of the Nile
floods, Herodotus is ironical about the discourse of those Greeks
"who wish to make for themselves a reputation for erudition of a
high order." In particular, by explaining the floods by river Ocean
which seem to stem from the "miraculous" but a privative miracu-
lousness: precluded from the field of debate, originating from far
outside the observable world. This is one of the two occasions when
Herodotus in his *Histories* has recourse to the word "myth."[87] Fifty
years after the *Periegesis*, Hecataeus is called a "short-story writer,"
a common *logopoios*, as they say at the time of Theophrastus: Does
he not invent subjects and facts and try to give them credence?[88]

Hecataeus smiled; Herodotus is shocked. Discreetly, to be sure,
but Herodotus cuts short his investigations whereas the "maker of
tales" sees no reason to finish them off. Interpretation gains
ground, and soon Thucydides will take a position completely outside myth, bringing the same charge against both the logographer of
Miletus and the historian of the Median wars. Very harsh treatment
but one which repeats, within another discipline, the denunciation
already made by Xenophanes. The only difference being that, between 530 and 420 B.C. tradition has been enriched by new tales,
added to the Titanomachies, such as the genealogies and tales of the
Egyptians or of the wars between Greeks and Barbarians. A philosopher in a rage, a logographer who smiles, but both closely en-

twined in the initial interpretation; Xenophanes's anger at the old fictions is no less decisive in its influence on tradition than the smiles of Hecataeus making up his Tales at his writing table. For it is certainly the question of writing that comes up in relation to hermeneutics. Extrinsic writing as viewed by the philosopher denouncing the revolutionary violence of the forgeries infesting the citizen's memory. But always in the wake of a kind of knowledge more or less committed to its own strict rules in the practice of writing. An inward writing imbued with the richness of tradition conveyed delicately by scratches of the logographer's pen with subtle tattoos of verisimilitude without ever yielding to a wish to cut or mutilate. And it is within this logographic activity, intertwining the *muthos* and the *logos*, the writing and the telling, that the graphic nature of what in Plato's time is to be called "mythology" makes its most distinct appearance. Before being thought over, before being discussed, the Greek myth is written down; and "mythology" that is supposed to be as old as memory is, on the contrary, young and new, so faint in outline and so fragile that at the end of the sixth century, in order to be held up to view, it will need the work of Plato, a would-be *accoucheur* caught red-handed and, a few steps away, of the historian Thucydides, also in a rage but for other reasons, it is true, than the "pious and thoughtful men."

Chapter Five
The City Defended by Its Mythologists

In referring to "sensitive and refined" men of ancient Greece, apparently their precursors through their spontaneous reaction to the "foolish, barbaric and absurd" stories which have always been told, the men responsible for the initial Science of myths have more in mind the prosecutor of *The Republic* than the old man from Colophon and his far-off rhetorical assaults. The "ancient fictions" blasted by Xenophanes are censured at length and in detail by Plato in an indictment that draws up the list of crimes of which all practicing "mythologists," poets, or prose writers are guilty, from Homer up to the most unpretentious makers of tales, driven out of ambush in the city and even in the silence of courtyards and houses. A retrospective version of the subject, led astray by the anathema of the keepers of *The Republic*, but a version whose bias does not conceal the fact that the moral judgments of the nineteenth century are sanctioned by the righteous severity of the ancient philosophers. A severity all the more reasonable because it seems to entail a dual trend whence emerges mythology as a branch of knowledge: a sudden awareness of the loathsomeness of traditional tales and, as a result, a kind of interpretation introducing the rationalism needed.

In the genealogical foray into questions of tradition, of memory, and of writing, Plato occupies a strategic position. First, by reason of semantics,[1] since he is the first to make use of the term *mythology*. Then, because Plato's work marks the time when philosophy, while censuring tales of the ancients as scandalous fictions, sets about telling its own *myths* in a discourse on the soul, on the origin of the world, and on life in the hereafter. Original myths characterized by learned fiction used as proof at the philosopher's whim; *myths* so carefully integrated in the philosophic dialogue where they serve to organize autonomous reasons that they seem, when thus moved out of place, no longer to have anything in common with the discourse of others, in verse and in prose—that is, the *muthos* in contradistinction to the philosopher's *logos*. For, in Plato's philosophy at its most obvious, there is an exaggerated way of sanctioning the schism caused by others, since the beginning of the fifth century. There is the separation that Herodotus and Pindar affirm between their own discourse and that of the unbelievable, the ridiculous, the lies, stigmatized by the word *myth*; and that other, more violent and so definite, that motivates the historian of the *Peloponnesian War*, in the name of a kind of writing contemptuous of seduction by the miraculous, to break deliberately with everything woven between mouth and ear, those ready-made rumors and ideas which encumber the Greek's memory.

More than once Plato has recourse to the word *myth* to designate at one stroke the foolishness of an argument or the ridiculousness of an opponent. If it so happens that a *logos*, undermined by its internal contradictions, destroys itself by falling into the ridiculous, into *alogiē*, it is derogated as *myth*[2] in the form of a ready-made idea. It is thus that the rhetoric in fashion at the time will become a means to influence the masses by telling stories, "with the help of a *mythology*" and not by teaching them (*didachē*).[3] Or again, consider the Sophists who appear before large audiences in big cities like old women who tell beautiful stories to little children just to give them pleasure:[4]

> You fill their ears with bewitching words which convey to them spoken fictions (*eidōla legomena*), word phantoms which delude them into thinking that what they are hearing is true and that the speaker knows more than anyone else.[5]

That is the practice of excluding data, a very commonplace one, but not without consequences because they give *mythology* a character that is profoundly heterogeneous. But if a historian of the present time, such as Thucydides, is free to cut himself off completely from tradition contaminated by what he calls the "mythic," Plato, because of the nature of his project, finds himself compelled to busy himself with unbelievable tales, stories known to all including the faintest rumor circulating in the earthly city.

"Do you believe that this talk about myths is true?"[6] Question by Phaedrus to Socrates. They are following the course of the Illissus river and Phaedrus is undecided between two tales on the abduction of the nymph Oreithyia by Boreas, whereas Socrates points out to him that the altar of Boreas is situated farther off, in the direction of the Agra sanctuary. For a long time unbelievers have had their scholars who were clever at interpreting that which is unbelievable and who know how to "straighten out" the impossible concept of the Hippocentaurs, or to make the peculiarities, the *atopiē*, of the Gorgons and the Pegasuses seem probable. Doubtless it is possible, like Socrates, to dismiss so many strange stories and to "refer to tradition concerning them."[7] But henceforth unbelief is common-place. The Boreas brought to mind by the altar so familiar to the Athenians, the Boreas who abducted Oreithyia is no longer a well-known personage about whom the only question would be the sequel to his adventures. Boreas and the Chimaera are exiled to the realm which lies beyond belief. No one believes in tribal stories anymore, and in the space between atopical figures and the plain citizen of Athens the field is open to clever interpreters, men of leisure who abandon themselves to the refined pleasures of exege-sis. The affliction of the interpretation which grows like couch-grass among data that is hinted at, where is revealed the normal state of a society bereft of its most fundamental beliefs.

> How can one, without becoming angry, assert that the gods exist? Because we must hate and find unbearable those who, today as in the past, due to having refused to allow themselves to be convinced by the *myths* related to them since earliest childhood by a mother or a nurse giving them the breast, have obliged us, and still do so, to develop the arguments which take up our time now.[8]

It is here that Plato innovates. The project of reforming the government of men requires him to pay the greatest attention to the slightest word of those who, near or far, philosophy was want to depict as deceptive.

Among traditions are some determined voluntarily. For instance, when a small group of men of a little Christian sect undertakes to authorize canonical books and calls to bear witness those who have seen the Apostles and conversed with them. Face-to-face with the gnostics and against those who choose their own means of transmittal, magisterial men, on their guard, wish to uphold what has been believed everywhere, forever, and by everyone. Their victory is assured when, for the discussion of fundamentals which must always take place and be repeated over and over, there is substituted the authority of gestures, of acts, of behavior to which everyone is accustomed. What Jansenism calls *memory*, that is, authority, pedestal of religion, and underlying rationality. "So many concurrent and permanent measures that nothing more certain exists in society."⁹ Anonymous and necessary, but without being under any compulsion other than to be the only possible model. That is how Plato imagines it, powerless as he is in the face of unbelievers: nevertheless those *myths*, poured into nurslings along with the milk, were repeated by mothers and nurses "like incantations (*epōidai*)."¹⁰ While prayers accompanying sacrifices were repeated to their ears and their eyes saw the spectacle the most agreeable for a young human being to see and to hear, that of their parents officiating in the most solemn manner and addressing prayers to the gods whose existence is the most certain of all.¹¹

Plato is no exception to the rule that speaking of tradition always refers to the present.¹² If there were no crisis in the city and its value system, it would not be necessary to conjure up, more than the *paideia* or the scholarly transmittal of knowledge, accepted truths (*ta nomizomena*), custom and ancestors (*ta patria*), that is to say the "aural" (*akoē*), what is said from mouth to ear but comes from the ancients. "It is they who knew truth. If it were something we were able to discover on our own would we really concern ourselves with the beliefs of mankind?"¹³

Whether it is a matter of delineating the model of a city according to the true philosophy or of reforming the government of men in the society of his time, Plato's project opens up the rethinking of tradition. And it is then that in Greek language and thought there arises the realm christened "mythology" by its discoverer who, no longer seeing simply a place with a name, undertakes to explore its plains, its peaks, and the most remote valleys. Because it is a matter of having a discourse on tradition by mobilizing, in the interest of the future city the most effective techniques for persuasion, "mythology," land of exile, is transformed into a huge conformation in which, for reasons of State, it is advisable to take stock systematically of the forms, the types of tale, the minor and major genres. The invention of "mythology" by a daring traveler defining by his footprints the boundaries of unknown territory. And it is in the course of this trip around "mythology" and starting from a plague-stricken city that, thanks to the lucidity of a philosopher, some of the most surprising words were spoken—words thrown up by an unprecedented upheaval: the will to tradition within a breach of memory.

With Plato, *mythology* is a new word but without being, however, a neologism. The verb "to mythologise" (*muthologeuein*), attested in the *Odyssey* by one incident, affords him a precedent which is perhaps such as to outline the horizon of his semantics. In Phaeacia, where the poet Demodocos sings in the presence of Ulysses of his great deeds and the Wooden Horse, the hero recites his odyssey, he tells of the return from Troy.[14] Cyclops and Circe, the Land of the Dead and the Oxen of the Sun, Charybdis and Scylla. Point by point, he tells his story (*muthon . . . katalegein*);[15] he is his own poet. Until, having returned from Calypso who had tried to keep him with her because of her love for him on his arrival in Phaeacia,[16] Ulysses breaks off and ends his tale with the phrase: "Why take up once more yesterday's story? Why 'mythologise'? (*muthologeuein*)?"[17] Without so much circumlocution: when the story is known, I hate to "repeat" it (*muthologeuein*). What has been already said marks the limit of the performance of the singing poet. When, surrounded by the assembled suitors, Phemius, the faithful poet, tells of losing their way back and the voyage of death, Telemachus springs to his defense before the mourning Penelope and recalls that, inevitably, success crowns the song that is newest.[18] A good poet does not repeat himself; the paths he follows have no ruts; he refuses to "mythologize." As though, in the vocabulary of professional singers, the verb *muthologeuein* already meant what Plato repeatedly is to point out in the tradition of mouth and ear: its repetitive character from the ancients until our time. Stories told since the beginning of time and always taken up again; everyone has heard them and remembers them; "they were told in time gone by and they will be told again."[19]

It is surely not by chance that the charter regulating the education of the guardians of the *Republic* opens on the *myths* told to little children by nurses and grandmothers.[20] The earliest species of makers of fables, *muthopoioi*, in the sociocultural inventory that will go on from the beginning of the *Republic* to the end of *Laws*. The fables told by nurses are of an equivocal kind. They are stories without head or tail. Without significance and only good for interesting that creature who is perpetually restless and who mumbles and wails and who is, of all the wild animals, the most impudent and the most wily.[21] A dangerous animal who must be curbed by the excellence of the "fount of rationality" which is not yet under control. And precisely because the wily little beasts will be metamorphosed into citizens of the *Republic*, it is imperative to pay the greatest attention to everything that nurses and old women whisper in the ears of nurslings.[22]

A basic mythology: stories that come from nowhere; anonymous tales that owe their existence to interchangeable narrators; stories emerging from obscurity, to which well-read Greeks paid no attention, whereas they sought wisdom in proverbs and in philosophy. At the other extreme, as though at the facade of the edifice "mythology," stand the artisans of myth whom Plato describes as "collectors."[23] Not anonymous but great names: Hesiod and Homer. It is by virtue of emblematic names, rather than through the writers of finished texts, that the songs and tales become classified. The story of Cyclops is "mythology,"[24] like the return of Ulysses or the fearful and terrible name, Styx, "which makes everyone who hears it shudder."[25] Abettor of all "poetry," mythology comprises literary genres as varied in written culture as tragedy and epic poem, the dithyramb and comedy, as well as the tales in prose by those the Hellenists and Thucydides call logographers but who "mythologize" as much as the others.[26] An extensive territory as measured by the culture already written and always spoken where, for convenience, Plato sets down certain guide marks. Sometimes with the help of scholarly and didactic classifications. For example when, in *The Republic*, after so many anathemas uttered against the makers of myths, he halts in order to organize the five kinds of discourse (*logoi*) which constitute "mythology" by classifying them according to a hierarchy deriving from worship: gods, demons, heroes, dwellers in Hades, human beings.[27] And tales about man in general are in the category of "theology" with its types and models. Sometimes—and the horizon extends still further out—Plato boldly delineates the paths that lead to great prospects within tradition. Two of the most important, *genealogy* and *archaeology*, open up with the account Critias gives on the subject of the Athens of nine thousand years ago, at the time of Atlantis, which is now engulfed and has almost been erased from human memory.[28]

One day Solon, the wisest of the Seven Sages, had a peculiar experience. It happened in Egypt, the land of Amasis, a philhellenic pharoah.[29] During a trip for sight-seeing but also for a purpose that was "theoretical," in the Greek sense[30]—as a spectator who wishes to see and to understand—the eminent law-giver with time on his hands could not resist the pleasure of conducting "ethnographical" research on the spot. No anachronism: his informants are the most learned priests and, appropriately, Solon wants to induce them to speak of "olden things," of their knowledge of what is most ancient.[31] Perhaps this should be reviewed. It is not in Paris, in 1799, betwixt and between Institute and Museum, that the first "Society of the Observers of Man"[32] was founded. Obviously, it is in Greece, some twenty-four centuries before. Solon had barely begun his research when one of the eldest priests, treating him like a mere boy, courteously began to explain to him why the Greeks are children forever:[33] they have neither writing nor tradition. What could they know about *mythology*?[34] Ever since the most ancient times the

Egyptians have kept in their temples records of all that is good, great, or remarkable in the world and without interruption due to their especial location on the Nile. Whereas the Greeks, like all other peoples, are victims at regular intervals of disasters when the gods decide to purify the earth with water from the sky.[35] In olden times, says the old priest, Athena and Hephaestus, who received Attica as their allotment, placed there as expert artisans men who were virtuous, autochthonous, and organized in cities. But, in the course of successive floods, towns and their inhabitants are swept by the rivers into the sea. The only people to escape the cataclysms, every time, are the ignorant (*amousoi*) and the illiterate (*agrammatoi*).[36] And in the hazy memory of survivors in the mountains who, Critias recounts, are untutored people, only proper names remain from the time of the autochthons of the plains, borne by rumor and with which they regale their children without knowing anything about the virtues and exploits of their forebears other than vague tales.[37] A time of poverty when all the things necessary to life are lacking: their minds are only bent on satisfaction of their needs to the point of devoting all their talk to it.[38] In this mountainous landscape where many travelers will go to discover the vivid memorable of intact and almost unchanging ancient societies, Plato only finds forgetfulness and an absence of legitimate descendants. A dead tradition and the only remains of that great corpse of scattered and unrecognizable bones are names stripped of flesh, separated from the living genealogies which joined together the tales of great deeds performed by princes of the plain.[39] A society so deprived that for many generations men live and die unable to express themselves in writing: silent, "voiceless" as to letters, to the symbols of writing (*grammata*).[40] In those conditions, it is understandable that, on the mountain peaks, "no one paid attention to previous events and stories of the past."[41] Actually, "*mythology* and research in ancient traditions (*anazētēsis tōn palaiōn*) only appear in cities along with leisure and when certain individuals ascertain they have collected everything that is necessary for survival. Not before."[42] Mythology is a luxury only enjoyed by people free from material want, who have become capable of conversing through written symbols.

Of this last point the Egyptian priests seem to have no doubt: "You Greeks, you are forever children."[43] The lesson in ethnography revolves around the error of Solon who had begun to recount the oldest stories known to the Greeks.

> He told them about Phoroneus, him who is called the first man on earth, of Niobe, of the flood at the time of Deucalion and

Pyrrha, he recounted (*muthologein*) their lives and recited the genealogy of their descendants (*genealogein*), while making himself reckon how long ago the things he told happened by remembering their age.[44]

If the Egyptian priests are to be believed, it would seem that there is no true mythology unless there exists exhaustive memory and the labor of writing. From Critias's work which is, in its way, a discourse on genealogy,[45] it may be deduced that "to mythologize" begins beyond just proper names and can also take the form of an inquiry into past events or ancient times. *Genealogy* and *archaeology*: the two genres in which Hippias the Sophist acknowledges brought him his greatest acclaim as lecturer in Lacedaemon.[46] The families of the nobility recognize each other by means of a book of heraldry which is enriched by the singing poets recounting the exploits of some; it ascribes to others a rank according to their descending from heroes of divine origin. The genealogies are the focal point for a whole segment of the first interpretation of the logographers; a generation is its unit of measure.[47] From the time of colonization on, tales about the origins of cities are added. Discourses on *archaeology* which whole cities enjoy listening to with as much pleasure as children gathered around an old woman to hear some beautiful "mythology." And Plato has no dearth of reasons for suspecting the Sophist archaeologist of being at least as dangerous as a mythologist nursemaid.[48] It is in the category of "archaeology," paraphrased by "quest for ancient traditions," that is evidenced a will to tradition, unprecedented and as yet unreliable. It is necessary to find the means to emerge from the obscure zone of hearsay and confused reports. In very ancient cities *archaeology* is founded on search for an identity and by way of inquiries concerning the past, usually the immediate past. Therein resides an active memory, connected with the new practices in politics. In the middle of the seventh century, the *Archaeology of the Samians* was the work of the poet Semonides who was preponderant in the founding of Amorgos with his co-citizens of Samos.[49] And the "archaeologies" will follow hard upon one another, especially in the historiography of the Athenians[50] who demand from those tales the same narcissistic pleasure experienced by the Spartans on listening to Hippias.[51]

Besides the genealogies, which can be transformed into theogonies and archaelogies, old stories whose lesser form would be the nurse's song, the Platonic inventor of tradition based on memory does not forget either proverbs or rumor. Maxims are a part of *myths*, and the law-giver refers to them in *The Laws* apropos of

various rules and regulations. For example, someone places in trust
treasure for himself or for his descendants: neither you nor I have
the right to touch it. The money that we could gain will never equal
the sum of spiritual profit gained by not touching it. "The famous
phrase *not to move the irremovable* is, in actuality, right in many cases
and, precisely, in the circumstances." Proverb applicable to the
pillagers of tombs but to which the law-giver adds, "that which is
repeated over and over," the *myth*, "ill-begotten, does not profit."[52]
Or else, consider murderers, guilty of the most heinous crimes in a
city where they are not expected to arrive. To divert the citizens
from such atrocities there is a myth (*muthos*) or a tradition (*logos*) or it
is called by another name: "It distinctly says, through the mouth of
the priests of bygone times, that Justice watches over the blood of
the relations . . . and decrees that the perpetrator of such abuses
will suffer the same injuries that they inflicted."[53] In the same
category of violence, the "ancient myths" about the souls of the
murdered in purgatory should discourage citizens from becoming
murderers, even involuntarily:

> They say that the victim of a violent death, if he has lived free
> and proud, as soon as he has been buried is angry at the person
> who killed him; and, full of fear and terror as a result of the
> violence suffered, he cannot bear to see his murderer live as he
> had done just a short time before without feeling overcome by
> dread; and the dead man being very agitated tries as hard as he
> can to frighten his murderer by recalling his deed in order to
> terrorize him in his soul and in his acts. Also the murderer must
> go away from his victim for every season of a whole year and
> leave all the places he called home, in no matter which part of
> his country that might be.[54]

An old tradition to add to the number of stories "we do not cease to
repeat and about which everyone is in agreement."[55]

Like other stories, more suspect, that frighten little children: in
the night certain gods move about disguised as strangers or in other
guise;[56] and Lamia, who no longer sleeps, goes from house to house
wishing to abort pregnant women.[57] Dreadful stories that nurses
and grandmothers are forever repeating, threatening to call Lamia,
stories that meet with the approbation of all, like the famous tales
about Deucalion and the deluge. For, in the "mythology" recorded
in *The Republic* and *The Laws*, there are "myths" devoted to mortals[58]
and not only to the earliest representatives of the human species
such as Niobe and Phoroneus.[59] Who is there in Attica who does not

know the "myth" of Melanion, the hunter who went far off into the mountains to flee women and marriage? "I heard it myself when I was a child," says an old man who believes the story to be sufficiently convincing to be used immediately to oust the female tribe installed in the Acropolis.[60] But from the entrenched camp came a prompt reply to Melanion, another "myth" in the manner of women: there was a certain Timon, homeless, who could not be seen anywhere. He withdrew from the world out of hatred after uttering a thousand curses on the wickedness of males (*andres*). . . . He bore evil man a hatred without measure, but he liked women very much![61] After a rejoinder one story invented another: Timon's misanthropy is no less "mythic" than Melanion's misogyny, it is correct enough for people to take pleasure in telling it over and over, here and there.

Obviously, the "mythology" discovered by Plato in the course of his long and complicated journey does not at all resemble the collections of dull images or the carefully tended herbarium of the eighteenth century where the adventures of heroes continue the well-mannered stories about the gods. The forms of "myth" are innumerable: they escape all attempts at classification. They go back to the practices of tradition based on memory: silent, unconscious, persistent, that Plato undertakes to study in the region, to listen to attentively. The faintest whisper, the slightest rumor, can be transformed into one of those stories "we do not cease to repeat and about which everyone is in agreement."[62] As though one of the most important properties of the realm of mythology was that every rumor was metamorphosed into "myth" as the mysterious result of repetition alone.

When hearsay so openly penetrates a mythology fraught with the most anonymous voices, it is the very nature of culture that changes meaning. The *paideia*, the culture of education, the transmission of which is conscious and voluntary, is regulated in *The Republic* to the extent that it is indispensable to the guardians of the city. And its rules of conduct, its hierarchical scholarship, its strict program apply to a tried and tested scholastic system. But if tradition is too broad to fit into the house of the pedagogue, if it listens to too many strange voices in books and writing, then it does not suffice for the poet-mythologists, invited by the city's administration, to make up poems that reflect the image, the *icone* of "good conduct."[63] For

> is it not to be feared that our guardians may not grow in stature in the midst of images of vice as in a bad pasture where every

day they may pluck and graze on the poison of some venomous grass, in small but respected doses and thus accumulate great corruption in their souls without even noticing it? On the contrary, would it not be better to seek out gifted artists to copy what is beautiful and well-made so that, like the dwellers on healthy soil, the young may profit from everything and, from no matter where the emanations from beautiful works reach their eyes and ears, they may welcome them like a healthy breeze from salubrious regions and, from childhood on, imperceptively learn to love the Beautiful and to resemble it and to establish a perfect harmony between themselves and Beauty.[64]

The cultural borders on what is cultivated and promoting growth means to educate as much as to bring up. First there is a dietary regimen: that of the human herd, the band of young people put out to pasture in a perfect meadow where colchicum does not grow. The same example in *The Laws*: the city's established practices are like wheat but it is essential to know the effect they have and the way to make use of them—which can be eaten and in what form.[65] With the difference that, in *The Republic*, instead of cereal there is rough grass put forth spontaneously by an excellent meadow.

But culture is not limited to what is eaten. It is also in the air. Climatic conditions vary according to the waters and localities, as is taught in Hippocratic medicine. There is the breath of air and of water, all that penetrates and transforms the living through their eyes and ears. *Paideia* is not in books and mythology is not confined to a Homer whose censured verses[66] could be easily deleted. Like the air in motion, culture is everywhere: in the song of an old woman, in the "counting out" rhymes of children's games, in rumors that circulate. And if, like tradition, culture is formed by hearing and sight, an old man's babble is as important as the genealogies of a Hesiod. Whoever wishes to reconsider tradition and memory held in common is urgently bound to legislate on rumor. Or at least raise questions about the strange power of what the Greeks call *phēmē*. "She, too, is a goddess," says Hesiod.[67] She actually has her own altar, at Athens.[68] "When there are many who have proclaimed her, no *phēmē* altogether dies."[69] Powerful, because manifold. A report that is promulgated, the distant echo of a procession or of a battle, the laudatory discourse which gives birth to the heroic deed of Cleobis and Biton or the unseen voice of a dream or a prophesy— such things are always *phēmē*. Rumor is omnipresent in *The Laws*;[70] it is rumor that insinuates that Dionysus became deranged by his cruel stepmother and, to get revenge, he sent to mankind madness,

St. Vitus's dance and, in addition, wine.[71] He is responsible for
hearsay and ancient traditions, for the golden age[72] as well as the
punishment of Tantalus, the most sorely tried of men.[73] But among
the rumors that infiltrate everywhere,[74] there are good ones and bad
ones.[75] The malicious gossip about Socrates calling him a Sophist, a
meteorologist impiously ransacking both the heavens and Hades;[76]
the empty rumor, devoid of truth, according to which the stars, the
gods of the sky, wander slowly in space.[77] The most base kind of
rumor[78] which flies and runs like sand. Once disseminated, such as
the rumors of painful diseases and of death that Pandora let out of
her box,[79] rumors roam about among men, speaking in silence,
never dying out entirely. Whereas the good *phēmē* comes from the
gods: supernatural voices or signs that the prophetic diviners[80]
interpret or that were perceived by the ancients "who were worth
more than we and who lived nearer to the Immortals."[81]

The most subtle element in the atmosphere, rumor is a fundamental component of tradition. And in the new city, *phēmē* must
guarantee the unanimity of the citizens: it is the rumor of good laws,
of good *nomoi*.[82] To hear her it is not necessary to be a legislator or
guardian of the constitution. For the majority of citizens the laws
penetrate through the eyes and ears. Like the air breathed in the
city. But, the good rumor evoked in the last book of *Laws* echoes the
phēmē of the preamble. It is in Crete that *The Laws* are related in
the course of a journey that takes three old men from Cnossos to the
cave of Zeus and his sanctuary.[83] And the Athenian who leads the
dialogue begins by referring to the origin of all legislation on the
island. A god, to be sure, established the laws: Zeus. But aided by a
mediator, an exemplar of mythic legislators of those who, at the
beginnings of mankind, have already succeeded in promoting harmony within the city. This law-giver close to the gods is called
Minos: "Every nine years he went to meet his father and he established the laws of your cities in accordance with the *phēmai*, his
father's oracular pronouncements."[84] *The Laws* opens with a good
rumor, simultaneously oracular and political: it comes from on high
and spreads through the city.

The whole enterprise of the *Laws* is in the light of *phēmē*. But
Plato the law-giver makes no mistake: even if inspiration is bestowed by the gods, a good reputation requires constant alertness.
For there resides in *phēmē* a simple mechanism which is nevertheless
a very delicate one. In book 8, the old Athenian is concerned about
the passions, particularly amorous desire with its violence, its baneful influence, its couplings of men-women or of women-men.[85] The
wildness of Eros is needed in the city; it can contribute to the

common welfare in the form of controlled desire simultaneously directed to soul and to body. But how to found laws upon it?

> We know that, even nowadays, regarding most men however perverse they may be, there are cases where they faithfully and strictly refrain from all relations with beautiful people not against their will but completely in accordance with it. For example when the beautiful person is their brother or their sister. It is an unwritten law which successfully protects a son and a daughter, so much so that nobody dares to sleep with them either openly or clandestinely or to risk any sensual approach. And the majority of people do not even desire such relations. . . . Is there not *a very brief saying (smikron rhēma)* which snuffs out all such desires? It characterizes such acts as absolutely blasphemous, hateful to the gods, the most unspeakable of all acts. And is not the reason because no one speaks about this differently and because, when the impulse arises, each one of us, always and everywhere, hears the same prohibition whether in farces or tragedies in the theater, the great tragedies in which it often appears with characters such as Thyestes or Oedipus or Macareus who, after having clandestine intercourse with their sisters and this has been found out, voluntarily kill themselves in self-punishment?

That is correct, says the Cretan, "you have put your finger on the astonishing force of rumor (*phēmē*); no one would dare even to breathe differently that prescribed by law."[86] There exists, therefore, a very simple method to enslave one of those passions which themselves enslave men. The law-giver has only to instill that hallowed voice in the minds of all;[87] slaves, freemen, children, the whole city. And in that way he will have established that law most solidly. But, the Cretan says, how to arrange for everyone to share a common parlance on that subject? It is easy to imagine a whole city in which people only make love in order to follow the natural impulse to procreate. "But perhaps a strong young man seething with sperm will rise up in protest and, on hearing this law, will curse the imbeciles who proclaim those impossible decrees and will fill the city with his noisy protests."[88] That is why the procedure that seems the easiest is also the most difficult.[89]

Yet the difficulty stems essentially from the moral state of today's city: the strength of the opposition caused by skepticism[90] embodied in the young man whose violent words bespeak a lust which no one finds fault with anymore. Fortunately, in the city of the *Laws* the citizens have very cultured souls. Even since they were children we have spoken highly of conquering their pleasure "in our tales (*muthoi*), in our discourse (*rhēmata*), in our songs (*melē*), and, in all probability, we shall lay them under a spell (*kēlein*).''[91] The good reputation of the *Laws*, its fundamental commandements, its *phēmai*, all citizens will have them sung like hymns to children.[92] The melody of high principles will rock nurslings in their cradles, so harmoniously that it will not even be necessary to say a single word. And it will alternate with the spellbinding methods instituted by the law-giver so that reports of the Good and the Beautiful may always hum. The nomothete of the *Laws* feels repugnance for the tyranni-cal, he is master of the art of persuasion.[93] All rules, customs, and established practices are presented in the form of a prologue or a preface, often called *paramuthion*.[94] A seductive tale or incantation which, in an obvious way, recalls a tradition, a proverb, an ancient story, some *muthos* that will make it possible to dispense with written legislation or legal regulations.[95] Thus, regarding marriage, between twenty-five and thirty-five years of age, there is only one shibboleth, only one *muthos*: that everyone should seek out the party who serves the city and not the one who appeals to his intimate preferences. And by a sort of incantation in the form of an exordium (*paramuthia*), the legislator tries to induce everyone to enter upon a marriage approved by the Wise men: always choose a party who is slightly inferior. The city will find this advantageous.[96]

To persuade, to charm, to enrapture; that is the only policy concerning myth in the city of the philosophers.[97] To such a degree that the mythology conjured up by the law-giver and spread by rumor which increasingly pervades the model state becomes in-creasingly identified with an absolutely political scheme. A scheme that, from the *Republic* to the *Laws*, becomes increasingly explicit. By means of a great "*mythologeme*," the tale of autochthony, so-called Phoenician or Sidonian. In *The Republic*, which differentiates be-tween the bad imitation and the good *mimēsis*, Plato develops the theory of the necessary lie, *pharmakon khrēsimon*, the beautiful useful lie.[98] It is important to make the city's magistrates and, if possible, the rest of the city believe the Phoenician tale "which has already happened in many places as the poets have been told and made to believe, but which has not happened in our day and which may never happen and which it is difficult to make convincing." There are three types of men and three classes of citizens: gold, silver, and iron mixed with bronze. An attempt should be made to convince them

that all the upbringing and education they have received from
us from which they thought they experienced the results are
none other than a dream, that in reality they were formed and
brought up in the womb of earth, they, their weapons and all
their equipment; that after having completely formed them, the
earth, their mother, gave birth to them, that they must now
regard the earth they inhabit as their mother and their nurse,
defend it if attacked, and consider the other citizens their
brothers, having, like them, emerged from the womb of the
earth.

But that "mythology," Plato adds, will furnish us with a revised
version, that of intermixture. For it can happen that from a man of
gold there be born a child who does not resemble him, an offspring
of silver, or yet again of iron and of bronze. Each generation must be
sorted out: promoting some and demoting others to the lower class.
For there is an oracle that says the State will perish the day it is
guarded by iron or by bronze.

"Do you know of any method," Socrates asks, "to make people
believe this *muthos*?" "None," his interlocutor replies, "at least as
regards the generation of which you speak; but perhaps it will be
possible to make their children believe it and their descendants and
mankind of the future.''[99] The time for persuasion is to come, and
the philosopher of *The Republic*, inclined toward the paradigm
"raised in the bright heavens,''[100] is content to express a wish: "Let
our *myth* go on its way at the whim of the flying report, *phēmē*.''[101] No
doubt *The Republic* is too geometrical to undertake to legislate on
circulating air. It is the *Laws*, more pedestrian, that takes the matter
seriously. For the law-giver who recalled the "oracles" of Minos
assigns himself the mission of winning over the greatest number of
devotees to the right and holy life. From the very beginning his
enormous task consists in persuading the inhabitants of the city that
the right and holy life is really the most pleasant. And to lift the
darkness that often admits the opposite, he sets out a series of
methods: praise, reasoning, habit.[102] The hour is come for the law-
giver to dare to perpetrate his most useful lie, the one that will
enable everyone, freely and without compulsion, to do what is
right.[103] And here it is easy to turn the thing around: the Sidonian
"*mythologeme*," however incredible, is made easy to accept.[104] The
incredible becomes credible. For henceforth the law-giver knows he
has the power to inculcate whatever he wants in the souls of the
young without leaving to the first flying report the trouble of forgetting or remembering a "myth."

By placing itself under the aegis of the flying report, the Platonic politics of mythology, enunciated in *The Laws*, separates radically from the authoritarian system devised in *The Republic*. Where there operates a technical and skilled model of myth that legitimizes a device for surveillance coupled with the apparatus indispensable for fashioning the State's mythology. The city is infested with "makers of tales," *muthopoioi*. To begin with, the mothers and nurses,[105] then old men and old women,[106] inexhaustible chatterboxes[107] who busy themselves around the newborn, gather very young children about them and "pour into their ears bewitching words" and offer them spoken fictions (*eidola legomena*), word-phantoms that give them the delusion that what they hear is true.[108] An entire mimetic emotional structure borne along on a swarm of "myths" and beautiful stories engrosses the eyes and ears of the youngest people, spellbound, fascinated by those spontaneous "mythologists": like Sophists they employ ruses, exaggerate the illusory forms of things and of the world, all the imitations that, begun in infancy and extending throughout life, "turn into character and second nature for body, voice and thought."[109] The foundations of the social structure are threatened by an ash cloud of invisible "mythoplasts" who take part in the underground enterprise of seduction, semi-stagy, semi-pictorial, in which forms, rhythms, and colors seize that part of the soul in which desires and passions go wild and draw it irresistibly to a world of transmutation. Shall we permit our children to listen to the first "myth" that comes along fashioned (*plastheis*) by the first stranger[110] who would thus abuse the enormous privilege of molding the soul of a "young and tender" being, "because it is at that time that is fashioned (*plattetai*) and indelibly imprinted (*tupos*) the desired impression on an individual (*ensēmēnasthai*)?[111]

Unconsciously, in telling stories for pleasure,[112] those humble "mythologists" reveal an activity that is really technical in nature. Mythology stems from skilled craftsmanship, proficient enough to combine the art of molding and of printing.[113] As though the makers of tales produced from a single matrix the figurines that they used like seals whose hollow stamp redoubled the charm of the relief. It is in relation to that model, brought to light by their acumen, that those responsible for *The Republic* decide on the procedure to follow concerning "mythology": it behooves philosophers to fashion the "prototypes" according to law,[114] after which the artisans of the State, official poets, will be commissioned to fabricate the myths to be impressed on the souls of future citizens. And, so that those stories may leave an "indelible and unchanging"[115] imprint, old men and old women will be compelled to repeat them to children, to pour them into the ears of nurslings.[116] From top to bottom, from the philosopher to the nurse, the *"mythologemes"* essential to the welfare of the city will be told over and over. Owing to a division of labor which puts a stop to the confusion between the different operations involved in "mythoplasty" that regulates the hierarchical relations between the three stages of the production of mythology. The weight of erudite philosophy cannot sustain the nightly influence of the first-come grandfather who, like Critias in *Timaeus*, suddenly begins to tell his astounded grandson a story so miraculous that it becomes engraved on the child's memory in "indelible characters"[117] and, sixty or seventy years later, all the details reemerge in a tale exact to the point of passing for "a true story in the opinion of a well-informed listener."[118] In the streets and squares of *The Republic* there will be no wandering teller of tales, no roving mythologist. The only policy at the orders of those responsible for the State's mythology will consist in supervising the official "mythoplasts."[119] Of course they will be called upon to fabricate new stories, long and short ones on the same "model," since they must all produce the same result.[120] But those who tell tales of Hades, for instance, will be very closely watched.[121] Then, there will be the process of censorship; sequences to be expunged,[122] developments to be eliminated, and forbidden names; for example, terrible great names "which make those who hear them shudder."[123] Finally, as a last recourse, undesirable poets will be physically deported.

The machinery is perfect. But from the very first "mythologem" it proves to be ineffective and useless. There is no way of gaining credence for the Phoenician "myth" of three classes of citizens. The apparatus for fashioning a State mythology will perhaps be useful "to the man of the future." For the present, it is purely fiction, a dream of a mechanism for institutionalizing in which everything had been regulated as though the omnipotence of the flying report were meaningless. And it is at a sudden whim that the philosopher of *The Republic* gives up his myth which no one will believe.[124] A disabused act acknowledging the failure of the influence of political authority over mythology.

But if no power exists that can dictate from on high the use of memory based on tradition, nor covertly decide about the content of tribal stories, then it is also necessary to revise the Egyptian paradigm that assigns to written work the prerogative of producing an authentic mythology. For if the land of Egypt marks the apogee of archival memory: all facts converge at this central point where the most ancient traditions are preserved. "All that is great, beautiful and remarkable that has been achieved either in your country or here or in some other place, of which we have heard tell, all that has been written down here in our sanctuaries long since and saved from oblivion."[125] Protected by the Nile, the priests possess unparalleled knowledge; they have before their eyes sacred tales whose uninterrupted continuity establishes an accurate chronology. A huge book without any blank pages: "Your exploits, Athens, from the very beginnings, are written here";[126] a book to be read word for word which tells about everything, every event: "Another time, at leisure, we shall go through all that in detail, without interruption, . . . but we shall make that exhaustive review with text in hand (ta grammata labontes)."[127] A written memoir as envisaged by Dionysus of Halicarnassus in a Greece pending its first historians but which arrives here, through the voice of Solon, to let the Greeks know how laughable is their mythology since the flood, how infantile the archaeology of Hecataeus of Miletus. As descendants of illiterates who left only the heritage of a few proper names in the midst of vague tales, Solon's compatriots are limited to groping for knowledge based on ancient tradition by means of a few half-obliterated traces. A knowledge impossible to attain since it is locked up in the sanctuaries of Egypt and the priests, in their wisdom, only dispense scraps of it, pieces destined for those children who are and will always be Greeks.

But that mythology based on exemplary writing, is it really above suspicion for going so far back in time? For the memory of the Egyptian priests, even if they let nothing escape it, by their own avowal records what they have heard said, what they know by means of their ears, by hearsay, by akoē.[128] And it is through the hearing that traditional reports concerning Atlantis reach the Athenians. Those were transmitted in three tales: the one that confused Solon;[129] the second, confided to his friend Critias; and the last one that another Critias, nearly ninety years old, told his ten-year-old grandson one day. A long oral tradition culminating in a contest of recitations, of rhapsodies, open to children on the festival of the *Apatouries* when fathers usher new adolescents into the various clans.[130] And, surrounded by the child rhapsodists, a very old man begins to tell the story of Atlantis, that which happened once upon a time that Solon found out in Egypt, an episode so miraculous that, if he had had the time to write it down in a finished form, would doubtless have made Solon even greater than Homer and Hesiod. Not only is the history of the beginnings of Athens, the tradition of a society proud of its ancestors, entrusted to a little boy who learns it from the lips of an old man which casts doubt, if not discredit, on the "archaeological" mythology of the cities, but it is only a mythology that can be written and read word for word in a fanciful Egypt, imbued with rumors spread by mouth and ear. The "archaeological" undertaking of logographers is a decoy; the pursuit of tradition fails in the practice of a writing that seemed to be most propitious to it. A mythology cannot be written either in temples or on any tablet any more than it can be instituted by the decree of a tyranny; laboriously to seek out old stories is never other than the symptom of a lack impossible to make good.

It is the hoary law-giver of the *Laws* who devises the astonishing project of domineering over rumor, of organizing its orientation, and of making it circulate via a thousand channels. He will leave no stone unturned so that the community may express constantly and in the most useful way "one and the same voice throughout its existence, by means of its chants (*oidai*), its tales (*muthoi*) and its discourse (*logoi*)."[131] To this end the nomothetic old men, in their wisdom, set up three choruses to direct their incantations to the souls of citizens when they are young and tender. To chant

> while preserving all the beautiful discourse we have set forth and shall continue to set forth but emphasizing the essential: we shall assert that in the gods's judgment the most pleasing life is also the best and so we shall all, together, speak the simple truth, expressing it in the best way by convincing those we wish to convince.[132]

One and the same voice and three choruses in unison corresponding to three ages of man so that the best hearsay may deluge all members of the body social. Children, hallowed by the Muses, will publicly chant exalted maxims in a solemn manner and for the benefit of the whole city. Second chorus: those under thirty will address a paean to Apollo to bear witness to the truth of high principles and to bestow upon youth his grace and power of persuasion. The third group of choristers will be mature men between thirty and sixty years of age.[133] But in this community concert old men fill the most subtle and fundamental role: men over sixty who "are no longer strong enough to sing" will tell stories based on exalted principles and behavior; they will be the "mythologists" of the city, "inspired by a flying report emanating from the gods (*theia phēmē*)."[134] The very one entrenched in the cave in Crete when, every nine years, Minos, the first law-giver, went there to listen to the oracular voice of his father, the flying report from Zeus. Old men who have passed singing age have reached the age of mythology. They are the dialecticians of silence in whom wisdom and experi-

ence pare down the voice so that through them there is only heard
flying reports from the gods, the unceasing and important one of
the Good and the Beautiful. As mythologists they assume for the
whole city the secret and essential function that the old women
fulfill spontaneously with respect to nurslings.[135]

By assigning to old men the task of administering the common
memory, Plato rediscovers a natural function of old age: telling
stories or acting as mythologist.[136] At the same time, despite the
suspicious attitude of the public prosecutors of *The Republic*, he
restores the privileged relation that mythology insists on fostering
between old men and children. For it is the youngest, with the help
of the Muses, who relay the word of mythology in the city and begin
to bear the whole burden of the chant. Paradoxically, the politics of
hearsay mobilize the two extreme ages of people in the city: without
doubt, those farthest removed in time from human life but also on
the verge of political space, barely participating in activities of the
citizenry. The children because they are "unfinished," not inscribed
in the register of the civil state; the old men because, being "super-
annuated," they are relieved of all political responsibility.[137] As
though being together at leisure qualified them to promote in the
shadowy light of semi-silence the mythological reports without
which the city could not be well educated. And throughout *The Laws*
there is recounted and set up sequentially the trio of old age which,
advancing toward the cave of Minos, devises belief in the charm of
the tale and which, from seductive tales (*paramuthia*) to incantatory
words (*epōidai*) claims to be child's play, entertainment (*paidia*)
round the best education (*paideia*) but of which the only subject
remains this "unfinished" creature apparently so close to men of
over sixty years of age. Moreover, it is not the quintessence of
education to induce the souls of the youngest citizens to conform to
those of the eldest,[138] to bring about that harmonious accord
(*sumphōnia*)[139] with the help of magical spells (*epōidai*) which, by
virtue of the inability of a youthful soul to imbue with gravity
(*spoudē*), are, in fact, simultaneously entertainments (*paidiai*) and
chants (*ōidai*)?[140] The pleasure accorded to eyes and ears by the
narrator to the listeners justifies the transmission of ancestral customs, of unwritten laws,[141] of customs handed down from father to
son of all that, from long ago,[142] builds the framework of the edifice
of society "which supports its center but remains hidden to sight."[143]
There is no effective education without the pleasure of telling and of
listening. To such an extent that because the charm of "myths" casts
a spell on them too, old men succumb to the seduction of their own
incantations and become like children. Abandoning themselves to

"wise entertainment" (*paidia emphrōn*),[144] playing the game of laws appropriate to their advanced age (*peri nomōn . . . paidian pres-butikēn*),[145] the law-givers reveal themselves to be "old children" (*paides presbutai*)[146] as they call themselves. The enchanter becomes the enchanted and, through the enchantment exuded by "mythology" both heard and recounted, the disparity between the two ages of man is eradicated. The same words circulate unflaggingly down the generations without ever changing. And if *The Laws*, in their entirety, do make up a vast "mythology,"[147] as the old men say, it is because they function like a spell whose power is so astonishing that the spellbound city throughout its existence speaks with one and the same voice, from the child to the old man, who act in collusion to the extent of identifying with each other which seems to abolish the gap between mouth and ear.

As a force uniting the words and writing of Plato at a time when, in the diseased city, it becomes unbelievable, mythology occupies the entire field of politics. There will arise no new city without the creation of an extraordinary political system based on mythology which aims less at the uprightness of the inner city monopolized by the philosopher of *The Republic*[148] than at the like-mindedness of thought, the shared knowledge indispensable to the harmonious functioning of the city of *The Laws*. Mythology is not the silent empire of which a certain philosophical trend of thought, conforming to knowledge of history, liked to define the boundaries with the excuse of encompassing its own demons. And it is illusory to seek it in Homer's epic or to come upon it in the adventures of gods and heroes. Because it belongs to the silent tradition which is whispered in proverbs and anonymous sayings outside the realm of the written word incapable of conveying it and beyond any deliberate research into the past. The quest for a tradition that must remain an oral one, inherent in which is the "dirty word" never to be uttered, is undertaken by Plato like a voyage to the very end of memory which ends with the fixity of a white-haired child engulfed by the whole city in an ageless rumor of voices all mixed up with one another.

Paradoxically, it befell a philosopher, more perspicuous than others, to teach that the world of illusion was inhabited by memory and by tradition and thus to create, in the most lofty solitude, a mythology lacking common measure with the conflicting concept of reasoning of a rationalistic kind which was for so long to obsess the thinking of modern mythologists.

Chapter Six
Two-headed Greek

In beginning, each year, the course "Lessons in Descriptive Ethnography" for the benefit of administrators or of colonials bereft of professional training,[1] Marcel Mauss, the nephew of Emile Durkheim, never failed to remind that "the young ethnographer engaging in fieldwork should know what he already knows in order to bring to the surface that which he does not know yet."[2] And, in compliance with knowledge already known without which no one could map his course or fill out one after the other "descriptive forms," the newly elected member of the Society of the Observers of Man was invited to make an extensive collection of "religious representations," classified properly within the social physiology coming after "still very materialistic"[3] aesthetics but of a higher order than the economic and of the juridical and moral phenomena that encompass it. It would be ideal, said Mauss, if no expedition left without its geologist and its botanist, its indispensable experts. Fortunately, every ethnographer was born a mythologist. Was it not enough to appeal to cultural intuition? To be sure, "our way of conceiving of mythology, as illustrated by *Orpheus in Hades*, is only one possible way and not the only one. It is important to know how the natives think."[4] Therefore, no haste, and above all no exclusive recourse, for such an inventory, to the list of categories current in philosophy classes. The "individual beings" who make up the population of mythology are divided into spirits: there is the double soul, the phantom spirit within the living being, the protecting spirit, the soul of the voice, the concept of duality, the soul of the eyes. Once in possession of those lists of individual beings, drawn up in every possible way, "the mythology of each god can be written."[5] For the myth, it is known, is the story of the god. Fable, morality tale, but unlike the legend or the fable—no one is obliged to believe it—the myth belongs to the system of compulsory religious representations. "It is obligatory to believe in myth."[6] Subjects for belief, myths take place in eternity. To neglect collecting them and putting them in writing, Mauss says, is serious, very serious: that leads to disfiguring the facies of a religion.

Instructions so clear, uttered authoritatively, certainly made urgent the gathering and writing of mythology. No observer worthy of the name would have considered leaving the field thus entrusted to him without having filled the file labeled "myth" of chapter 9 of *Instructions, sub verbo* "religious phenomena, *stricto sensu.*" And every year the libraries of the great colonial powers, responsible for the development of ethnography, indexed new "mythologies" which, placed next to the old ones, confirmed the knowledge that everyone already knew but whose specifications remained the subject of more or less courteous disputes among experts, among those the eighteenth century would have called "mythologists" to distinguish them from "antiquarians" devoted to making inventory of exhumed documents.[7] At the same time it seemed obvious that collecting myths, even intensively, did not make it possible "to bring to the surface that which is not yet known." The ethnologists become impatient and, in 1928, Mauss disclosed confidentially in a stage whisper to the French Society of philosophers: "It is not enough for us to describe myth. According to the principles of Schelling and the philosophers we wish to know what aspect of existence it interprets."[8] In other words, the question being by nature a philosophical one, it is from philosophy the answer must come. Schelling has made this clear long ago: philosophy of mythology is the real science of mythology. And Cassirer, in *La philosophie des formes symboliques*, published in the twenties,[9] pays tribute to the intuitions in *L'introduction à la philosophie de la mythologic* (1856). Speculative idealism has discovered in mythology a primary orientation of Spirit, a process essential to consciousness, uninvented. It required reconciling in a rational mythology the monotheism of Reason and the polytheism of imagination. Primeval man must be the one who posits God through his nature and the mythological route the only conscious one through which God becomes progressively manifest as the real God. To this theogony of the Absolute, constructed and enunciated by Schelling, the critical philosophy of Cassirer respectfully contrasts the necessity of departing from the "given,"[10] those facts empirically ascertained and verified by cultural consciousness, that is, the matters and pieces of information recorded by comparative mythology and by the history of religions since the mid-nineteenth century.[11] The innumerable collectors of myths are rewarded for their trouble. And Neo-Kantian philosophy also puts an end to Mauss's anguish: it assumes the burden of expressing the "pure essence"[12] of the function of mythology.

If the unity of mythic productions is not questioned by ethnologists in general it must remain an enigma, writes Cassirer, so long as mythic consciousness is not recognized as a kind of autonomous knowledge, a particular method of spiritual formation of the human species, a dominant thought with its categories of time, space, and number. A primary form of spirit, myth is a concept of "concrescence" whose temporal and spatial insights are concrete and qualitative: a concept that amalgamates and welds together all its components. Seduced by intuition, it is a concept fascinated by the immediate sensuousness of the universe whose charm is so powerful that no other can be exerted. Captivated by intuition, it does not heed representation and conceptual action. The ego of mythic concept, attacked by fright or the desire for every momentary impression, stammers out differences; it separates, it differentiates, but without ever really tearing itself away from undifferentiated and primary intuition. And the forces that haunt mythic experience in its fetal state are still only shadows of powers yet unborn.

In this form simultaneously rich and confused, mythology binds to herself the primary virtues of speech and belief. Through the images it creates, mythic thought is the homologue of the earliest language, and in the belief at the root of its unity of experience mythology is already a religious idea. Like language, myth is a specific way of seeing and the mythic image an intuitive way of envisaging produced by reality and making a sensual universe. Just as every phoneme has meaning in itself, just so does each image convey a god of the moment who presages the clear and active powers of the great well-known mythologies. "Myth and language," writes Cassirer, "are two modalities of one and the same drive toward symbolic formalization."[13] And the pantheon resounding with words and phrases is built on the same spiritual driving power as the enormous palaces of mythology. Besides, insight into myth does not occur without a belief, more pathetic than logical, but at work in the midst of affects. Since its beginnings the myth has the force of a religion and, in its most rudimentary forms, mythic concepts conceal all the riches that anticipate the highest ideals, those that are slowest to take hold in history. For religion does not arise with the individual ego aware of itself through absolute subjection to the divine; it is already wholly present in mythic experience. Concomitant with language and religion, mythology is allotted a central function in theory of the human spirit: it is the native land of all symbolic forms. In it are connected, primordially, practical consciousness, theoretical consciousness, the worlds of knowledge, of language, of art, of law, of morality, including the fundamental models for the community and the State. Nearly all forms of culture are rooted in mythic thought: "All of them seem clothed and enveloped in some form emanating from myth."[14]

In this region where there is neither inventor nor individual nor a people, "the authentic motherland of mythology"[15] discovered by Schelling becomes for critical philosophy the matricular nebula where are already gathered together souls eager for reincarnation, all the modalities of existence and assorted knowledge produced in the course of history. In thus affirming the "pure essence" of mythology, Cassirer consciously took up one of the main propositions of Durkheim's sociology: that myth expresses the totality of the natural being in the language of the human and social being. Mythology, or rather religion, wrote Durkheim in 1899,[16]

> contains within itself from the beginning, but in a confused state, all the elements which, by separating from each other, by becoming determinated, by intercombining in a thousand ways, have given birth to various manifestations of their collective life. It is from myths and legends that science and poetry have come; it is from the ornamentalism of religion and cultist ceremonies that the plastic arts derived; law and morality are born of ritual practices. One cannot understand our conception of the world or our philosophic concepts of the soul, of immortality, of life, without knowing the religious beliefs that were the form they first took. Kinship began as an essentially religious link; punishment, like contract, the gift, the tribute are all transformations of the expiatory sacrifice, contractual, communal, honorary, etc. At most can it be questioned whether economic organization is an exception and derives from another source; although we do not think so, we grant that the question must be held in abeyance.

Eleven years later, in the conclusion of *Les formes élémentaires de la pensée religieuse*, Durkheim reaffirms the nature of religion and of mythology: it is the great incorporator, the thought of thoughts. Simultaneously itself and more than itself. And it has in it nothing mysterious, illogical, or specific which is indescribable.[17] Because it is enough to "lift the veil with which mythological imagination has covered them"[18] to reveal the True realities which will later become subjects for study by scholars. "Scientific thought is only a more perfect form of religious thought."[19] Doubtless Durkheim explains nature by the social order, giving preference to the sociological deduction of categories over the transcendental deduction that enables Cassirer circularly to connect in his concept of mythology the totality of the natural being and the language of the human and social being. But both agree in endowing mythology, or mythological religion, with the power to engender the fundamental concepts of science and the principal forms of culture. And that engendering takes the form of an unveiling without tearing the matricular concept or causing a split between a mythology that is never by nature illogical and concepts clothed in rationalism people would find unprecedented.

Sociologist and philosopher are still better partners. They both turn spontaneously toward Greece and her thinkers. If logic, immanent in the elementary forms of religion, assumes that man has a confused awareness that there is a truth, separate from sensory appearances, and thus conceives of "a whole world of fixed ideals, the common realm of all intelligence," there had to arise, in our western world "along with the great thinkers of Greece," the clear awareness of Truth becoming detached on a higher level from the fleeting impressions of sensory experience.[20] Without them, and above all, without Plato, the reign of Truth would not have seen the light,[21] and the existence of a universe of concepts or a dominion of intellect would have remained in a veiled and obscure rudimentary state.[22] It is thanks to the philosophy of the Greeks that scientific thought becomes, as Durkheim says, a more perfect form of religious thought or of mythology.

Through the medium of the Greeks to whom the sociology of Durkheim attributes the great Enlightenment, the philosophy of Cassirer places emphasis on the sprightly dialogue of the Greek thinkers when deliberating among themselves, not only about the eventual outstripping of mythology but also about the best policy to follow with respect to the "pure essence" of mythic thought. A dialogue staged when the question arises of a "philosophy of mythology" in the introduction to the second volume of *The Philosophy of Symbolic Forms*.[23] And Plato retorts to Parmenides. The philosopher from Elea initiates the concept of Being and his iron idealism makes it imperative to relegate the ancient mythological tales to the desert of nonexistence: philosophy cannot be itself unless it maintains distance from myth; and mythology denotes that in which the concept of being must become absorbed, the obvious meaninglessness of nonexistence. A proud policy which Cassirer's Plato opposes with doubly admirable wisdom. First, by challenging the allegorical practices of the "sophists," the *sophië* of the boors in search of a meaning other than the literal one. But above all, when he shows sufficient perspicacity to discover in mythology a primary concept: that myth is the adequate language to speak to the world of things in a state of transformation. It is the same intuition, rediscovered by Schelling, that the correct interpretation of mythology takes the "tautegorical" route: the meaning of the myth is in what it relates, it cannot be elsewhere.

In paying homage to Plato for a clarity so closely resembling his own, Cassirer means to justify the requirement for philosophy to analyze the concept of myth in itself. Undoubtedly, of its own momentum, philosophy can only withdraw itself from mythology, separate itself from myth which has always been the opposite side of its coin as well as its context. Furthermore: philosophy would be in mortal danger if it called myth illusory, whereas mythology is not only a particular mode of the spirit's formative process but also inherent in consciousness of myth is the origin of all the forms of spiritual culture.[24] The fate of the one is coupled with that of the other so that philosophy can only know itself by *mastering* consciousness of myth.[25] Mastery of a branch of knowledge which knows what it must do: "Thorough examination of myth must depend on knowing and recognizing it."[26] That philosophy would be senseless that treated as a mere shadow the form of spirit in which are wedded its origin and its first counterpart, in which the fundamental obstacle it confronts on the very first day intermingles with the inexhaustible source of all knowledge. It is like a primal scene, narrated and played by a philosopher of Enlightenment sure of having a "historical" point of view and who, without yielding to the temptation of questioning what he calls Greek evidence, never stops averring with unchanging severity: "It is only through confrontation with the concept of myth that philosophy succeeds in defining precisely its own concept and in acquiring a clear awareness of its own task."[27] The pure essence of mythology is only perceptible in relations of closest propinquity, established and formulated by the Greek thinkers. The great Greek philosophers are no longer supernumeraries in sociological discourse; they are protagonists of the true Science of mythology, the first to recognize in myth rich and confused thought which their own abstruse erudition can only master and outstrip by conceptualizing the truth hidden in mythological thinking. Schelling was right, to the degree that another philosopher, a century later, restores the view well-known to Western culture that the masters of *logos* had once had of their *muthos*. Thenceforth the circle is closed: for the benefit of the ethnologists who look for mythological tales in the archaic trusting their intuition only, the philosophers, thanks to their enlightenment,

reveal the meaning of a primordial concept from which stem the
basic forms of all culture, including philosophy and scientific
thought. The unity of the productions of mythology is effectuated
within the theoretical discourse of philosophy. A discourse that
restores Reason with its historic rights and gains distinction by
restoring the otherness of mythic thought. Radically, because
mythology, free from the taint of invention, possesses neither date
nor birthplace.[28] It begins nowhere; and, as primordial concept, it
continues to progress until it reaches the place where it is transformed, has attained the unattainable some say; where it dies, say
others. It is precisely there that philosophy arises and positivism is
founded. Unlike myth, rationalism tends toward a civil state; aware
of its origins, it can thus speak of the Other without being interrupted or contradicted, unless by its own self.

In bygone times those responsible for the Science of myths,
impelled by exalted moralism, solemnly decided which exclusionary methods to apply: to return mythology to its primary status, to
demote it to the domain of inferior races, or to relegate it to the
Peoples of Nature. Or again, when adopting the vocation of "reformers" they entrusted each other with the mission of adjusting
the coarse beliefs that had invaded their society in the form of
"deplorable superstitions."[29] Henceforth it is philosophy that takes
the lead, conceives of stratagems, and dictates choices. Either
mythology has a meaning or it does not. Since, according to Cassirer, philosophic thought censures the idealistic temptation to re-
strict myth to illusion and superficial appearance, it cannot tolerate
meaninglessness. But neither does philosophy wish to revert to the
aporia, denounced by Plato, of a mythology in which the meaning
of "other" would open up the vagaries of allegorization. Therefore,
if mythic concepts have any meaning it seems, it remains blind
through an embarrassment of riches and must yield to philosophy
the task of demonstrating and interpreting it, to reveal its investiga-
tive methods, its forms of logic and types of classification. Thought
of thoughts, mythology cannot lack for understanding whether it
speaks according to its lights—and that is the point of view of those
who follow the "tautegorical" route—or whether it says more that
exact reason can understand—such is the "symbolist's'"[30] hypothesis.

The Greek paradigm is the center around which are built up, in
anthropological thought, the great theories that, from Lévy-Bruhl to
Lévi-Strauss, determine the status of mythology in the intellectual
field. When in 1962 *La pensée sauvage* tries to show that knowledge in
archaic societies proceeds through the understanding, as in our

own society, with categories and contrasts, it seems advisable to recall the opposite steps described in *Fonctions mentales dans les société inférieures*. From 1910 to 1938, in fact, Lucien Lévy-Bruhl tries to prove that the thinking of Primitives, controlled by a law of participation that makes it indifferent to the logic of the excluded third party, becomes manifest in a mental climate different from our own, ruled by affectivity and by mysticism.[31] In a certain way, the discovery of the prelogical of the Inferior Peoples brings with it the solution of the question raised by the scandal of a barbaric element in mythology and in the thinking of the Superior Peoples. The thinking of Savages is radically cleft from our own: neither causal nor logical, it advances reasons to justify its self-confinement. An unobtrusive confinement and, in truth, precarious if we agree with Maurice Leenhardt that it depends on one letter: the *s* in *mystique*, which differentiates it from *mythique*.[32]

To define the limits of the prelogical we must redefine the coordinates of mythology, its position relative to mystical experience and rational thought. In the first pages of *La mythologie primitive*[33] Lévy-Bruhl asks the basic question concerning that which distinguishes the Greeks:

> I admire the perceptiveness of Fontenelle who was able to unravel traits in common and emphasize striking similarities on so many points ["An astonishing conformity between the fables of the Americans and those of the Greeks"].[34] . . . But is it possible to cite that relationship in order to assert that what is true of classic myths also applies to those of the primitives?

A new question, directed toward our categories: must our concept of myth coincide with that of the Australians and the Papuans? But it is even more directly connected with the Greek paradigm and the need to distinguish between two types of mythology: the one primitive, the other cultivated. As many ethnologists have observed, primitive mythologies are crammed with inconsistencies. "If one compares the legends of all the totemic lineages of Dobu," writes Dr. Fortune, "one arrives at an extremely illogical system."[35] Moreover, he adds, no native of Dobu has ever gone to the trouble of doing so. But Lévy-Bruhl does not believe this is due to intellectual laziness alone. Even if the primitive people bothered to compare the different versions, they would not see the contradictions between them; their study faith in myths is exempt from the requirements of logic.[36] Added to the congenital inconsistency of primitive myths is their incapacity to speak in etiological terms.[37] The tales of primitive peoples never correspond to a wish for explanation: the intuitive recognition of the presence and action of the supernatural world excludes all research on secondary causes. The primitive myth does not explain, it legitimizes.[38] True and real, of a transcendental and imperishable reality, it cannot explain nature because it is dedicated to describing the supernatural. This second weakness, as congenital as the first, requires correction of the limits of religion as well as revising the very category of myth. Inseparable from mystical experience, the mythology of primitive peoples stems from a mentality that is not only prelogical but also prereligious.[39] It is dominated by belief in forms, influences, and actions imperceptible to the intellect but nevertheless real. Whereas religion arises and is founded when nature becomes intelligible and subject to conceptualization, only then does it become possible to think of the supernatural, rejected by transcendentalism.

Lévy-Bruhl's division between the prereligious and religion is neither more nor less arbitrary than other differentiations, made at the same time, between myths and religion: for instance, by A. Lang, according to whom the irrational or scandalous element prevails in mythology while rational order appears along with religion;[40] or by M. J. Lagrange who attributes the realm of religion to "moral requirements."[41] As for Lévy-Bruhl, the cleavage occurs between the Greeks and the others, the Primitives, whose mythology is distinguished by two negative traits ascribed explicitly to the positivity of the Greek model. Is it not obvious that the society from which emerges the philosophy of nature is no longer subject to the rule of the affective category of the supernatural? And how could the civilization that gave us the principle of the excluded third party be insensible to inconsistency and contradiction? With her gods, her hierarchical power structure, her temples, her cults, Greece is endowed with institutions that place her in the first rank of Mediterranean societies, a thousand leagues from the "so-called local centers of societies based on the cult of the totem."[42]

In 1910, in *Les fonctions mentales dans les sociétés inférieures* (9th ed., 1951), Lévy-Bruhl had undertaken to consider myth as a category in order "to account for the dichotomy between peoples of Antiquity and such societies as the tribes of Australia and New Guinea."[43] Paradoxically, "the lowest societies" (Papuans and Australians) live under the aegis of a dearth of mythology. As long as the period of mystic symbiosis lasts, myths are simultaneously poor and few. A poverty that is the other side of the coin of wealth: the fullness of communion with the world does not, in principle, leave any place for mythology. Such participation occupies the whole field: being really lived, it has no need to be thought or represented. Collective mental states are of an extreme emotional intensity. And what we read word for word in the Primitive's tales are, in fact, mystical realities of which each is a determining factor: "Simply to hear a myth, from the emotional point of view, is thus something quite other for them than for us."[44] Barbaric mythology is first mystical experience and thought. It is the Sacred History of the lower societies.[45] It is necessary to await cultured mythology for form to emerge along with its positive content. Everything that interests us under the first heading: the interconnection of facts, the thread of the story, the adventures of heroes, only become perceptible with the withdrawal of participation, when mystical communion yields to representation of what has been lived.[46] Myth as plot is a form of mutation from the prelogical to the rational. That is rooted in the only civilization where the separation occurs: neither in India, nor in China, but in Greece.[47]

The problem of mental and logical change which seems to take place in that part of the world is nowhere squarely faced by Lévy-Bruhl. Doubtless it is true that he rejects the genetic point of view which would relegate the psychology of the Primitives to a state of infancy, to a state less advanced but one that every kind of intelligence would encounter in the course of its development.[48] One system does not abolish the other.[49] And the case of Greece is an example. In their intellectual creations, in the works of their new branches of knowledge, we recognize the same mental climate as our own: submission to logic and the requirements of verification and of experience. But in the mythological tradition of the Greeks there remains the semblance of a desire for participation. In order to triumph logical thought does not demand the disappearance of all prelogical thought.

The Greek's peculiarity is still to live on the boundary. As sole evidence of the transition to a new rationalism, cultured mythology has a mediatory function. As the result of religion, the myths change from sacred to profane.[50] But if the myths related in "Greco-Roman" mythology are no longer credible in relatively high stages of civilization, the fabulous and unbelievable elements they convey remain very close to the tales and experience of the Primitives.[51] Halfway between mystical reality and pure fiction. And this ambiguity is within us all, we have internalized it even into the capacity to revive the memory of a remote symbiosis between animals and humans. Beyond and by means of our natural speech which nevertheless implies a vague zoological classification. As Aristotelians and offspring of Linnaeus, we still keep within ourselves the capacity to enter into the spirit of ancient stories about the werewolf.[52]

Insofar as Lévy-Bruhl is concerned, the benefit we drew from Greek mythology is measured in units of pleasure. The pleasure of the myth is directly proportionate to the innocuousness of its reception: its being heard at a good distance from the prelogical where, without the danger of seeing the primitive world invade reality, we can savor in tranquillity, the remnants of thought so foreign to our own but still very seductive to us.[53] To be sure, the mystic mentality has become unbelievable because "of the rational nature of the civilization that classical Antiquity established and bequeathed to us."[54] But rationalism, anchored in the laws of nature and of thought, has never ceased to be a difficult road or to demand strict discipline based on controls and verification. A necessary discipline, asserts Lévy-Bruhl, to help us repress the tendency, always alive within us, to regard the mystical part of experience as being as real as reality. But that "constraint," that "force," renders all the more "voluptuous" the pleasure, at certain moments, of abandoning the rational attitude as, giving ear to fables and tales, we return ourselves briefly "to the ancestral attitude."[55] Then we see live again before our eyes the mysterious and fluid world of the most ancient myths. "If the story of Donkey Skin were told to me, it would give me very great pleasure": those are the closing words of La mythologie primitive which attempted to look at the myths of the lower societies with new eyes.[56]

Cultured mythology well deserves its name. On the threshold between the great "Enlightenment" by virtue of originating the concept and mystical expereince comprising the mythic tale, the Greece of Hesiod and of Plato is also the native land of a frontier knowledge, of a logos discoursing on the muthos, the model for which is so well fashioned, so well constructed by the natives that it seems impossible to get rid of it, no matter what the effort involved. As shown by Lévy-Bruhl. By having separated cultured mythology from the primitive, he raised the question of the mythic "text," underlying the idea that a myth would not be the same for us as for the Papuans. Also by having tried to be unimpressed by the Greeks—for which he is praised by Louis Bréhier[57]—in refusing to follow the process of interpretation, common ever since Xenophanes, which would have reduced others' mode of thought to a state of illusion, denounced since the fortification of rationalism. Such clarity, doomed to a setback from the time the Greeks realize they conceded the prerogative of an autonomous mythological space organized on their own model with respect to which the *mystique* of Lévy-Bruhl is gauged. When Louis Bréhier proclaims the originality of Lévy-Bruhl who preferred structure to genesis, and when he wants recognition for the excellence of the solitary interpreter to whom he attributes the discovery in the psychology of primitives of a different structure "without trying to denigrate it as illusory except for its rationalism, like the Greeks," he seems to forget only one thing: the whole activity of the prelogical, which would thus be termed "tautegorical," internalizes the old philosophic model of the *logos* arguing with the *muthos*. For the *mystic* is always a displaced *muthos*, either ahead of time or in another place.

The system of Lévy-Bruhl made him wary of hypotheses intending to account for the production of myths through logical and psychological activity "similar to our own, even assuming it to be childish and thoughtless."[58] There was no other conceivable unity between tales that were nearly fictional plots and others, absolutely unbelievable, stemming from trivial events in societies which were too impressionable.[59] There is no doubt that under pressure to answer the question to be put by Lévi-Strauss and his opponents— Is there a single explanation by mythology?—Lévy-Bruhl would have answered firmly in the negative.

In the sixties the question became trite. Regardless of its logic,[60] unity of mythic thought is attained when Lévi-Strauss asks if it is not necessary to seek in myths more than "some laws of mental activity operative in society."[61] Thus rediscovering, going beyond Cassirer, Mauss's doctrine of mythology as ineluctable social concept belonging to the unconscious.[62] In fact it was Mauss who, in 1903, had posited that mythology is reduced to a small number of combinations, that the seeming illogic of the mythic tale is actually a sign of its very logic. "Myth is a mesh of a spider's web and not a definition in the dictionary."[63] A symbol by whose means society pictures itself and whence proceed, in archaic civilizations, morality, rites, even economics, mythology demarcates the dominion of unconscious ideas at work; it becomes identified with the system of symbols that makes possible communication and harmony between forms of activity both different and yet the same as our own. Contrary to Lévy-Bruhl, it became essential to predicate a common spontaneous origin of reasoning in the most archaic societies as well as the main forms of science and philosophy.[64]

From the beginning, Lévi-Strauss's project to render an account of the human spirit promotes an effort to prove that the myths related in Greece two millennia before the American tales in the same way give rise to an image of the world already engraved on the architecture of the spirit. In 1955 the hypothesis is formulated: "Myth is language." A catchword in *Anthropologie structurale*[65] which, no sooner enunciated, is installed in the interlocutory network organized a few years ago around linguistics, the only science of man to call itself truly universal.[66] This venture in semiotics, directed toward a narrative grammar, precipitates the unitary aspect of mythology in which A. J. Greimas discerns a "natural meta-language,"[67] that is, a language whose secondary meanings— in the event of *"mythemes"*—are structured by using a human language already in existence. Beginning in 1966 a narratology is roughed out in which myth is defined as a particular type of tale in which the narrative unities seem discernible at the end of a new examination into the research of Vl. Propp on the structure of the folk story.[68] There is a growing belief that the separation between myth and story is reduced, in an identical narrative syntax, to the sole emblematic variation of the "agents": in myths, actors—the dramatis personae—in the story, magic objects.[69]

The Greek paradigm is applied. "The historian," A. J. Greimas remarks in 1963,

> can observe how pre-Socratic philosophy emerges from mythology. It is fascinating to follow the mythologist [in this instance Georges Dumézil; later, Lévi-Strauss] in the performance of a similar task, of seeing how the interpretation of myths gives rise to a new ideological language, that is to say, a meta-language, with its models and concepts.[70]

The semiotician occupies the same position as the historian when studying emergence: the task of interpretation undertaken by the mythologist regarding the concept of myth seems homologous to that undertaken by pre-Socratic philosophy concerning mythology. The only difference being that myth, medium of emergence for philosophic discourse, no longer is so for modern mythologists, if this can be believed. It seems that it is from the Greeks that the major presupposition of mythological scholarship comes—including semiotics—according to which the origin of philosophy is obviously associated with the nature of myth.

In Lévi-Strauss's *Mythologiques*, the Greek model is explicit, without reservations. The conclusion of *Miel aux cendres*[71] reverts to Greece when the complexity of the American myths is discovered, establishing relationships between various codes, exploiting the differentials which are sometimes expressible in geometric terms and sometimes transformable by means of algebraic processes. A concept of myth moving toward abstraction and counting on it alone, drawing from its own self the strength to "transcend itself," and to contemplate, beyond images and the concrete, "a world of concepts . . . whose relations become readily clear." Now we know—writes Lévi-Strauss—where that upheaval took place: "on the border of Greek thought where mythology yields to a philosophy which is preliminary to scientific thought." A scene of dual action: withdrawal of mythology at the juncture where it outstrips itself and the emergence of philosophic thought whose conceptualism prepares for the future of science. A little later, in 1972, the strictures of the same model are repeated as revealed in an essay that gives rise to the thought that the mythology of the ancient Greeks bears a peculiar resemblance to that of other peoples.[72] Ethnology must not only maintain that it is confronted by forms common to ancient cultures and to others wrongly called primitive ones. There is more to it than that.

> The ancient Greeks seem to have considered their mythology in terms of a problem which is analogous to that in use by ethnologists today to bring out the spirit and meaning of the myths of peoples who do not write.[73]

It is fascinating to discover that Greece is twofold and that Hesiod is the true homozygous twin of the archaic philosopher musing on the dry and the wet, the high and the low, at the same time as on being and nonbeing. "The Greeks themselves made the structural analysis of their mythology: that work on myths is skin-deep, so to speak, in Greek myths."[74] The Greek "ethnologists" are the precursors as well as the emulators of structural ethnology. Their astonishing culture presents the spectacle of a mythic concept which, in outstripping itself, attains a formal logic enabling the Greek, sure of his concepts, to consider his own mythology in the interpretative mode.

That step-by-step progression, notwithstanding the distance traversed, was recognized by Tylor. But in the meantime, the spectator has taken the field: the new anthropology, freed from civilizing and missionary prejudices, mediates upon the emergence of philosophic thought whose conceptual rigor presages the virtues of science. And where a certain cultural myopia which Durkheim and Cassirer have in common envisaged the unique and major event in our history, Lévi-Strauss only discerns one form among many others, forgotten or misunderstood, of autonomous progression of mythic concept toward abstraction. The Greeks, to be sure are like

other people but with a slight difference which is not without
significance: they have two heads. More than twins, they are
Siamese twin brothers who are perfectly polite to each other. Each
one rules his territory and the first seems undisturbed by the discourse of the second. Moreover, the philosophic head shows no
intention to dominate his mythological neighbor. No tensions, no
conflicts. Lévi-Strauss refers to the "withdrawal" of mythology to
give precedence to philosophy, as if, having outstripped itself,
mythic thought found its completion in this other emerging thought
which, before making ready the future of science, presented it with
the reflected image of its own wisdom from time out of mind. The
existence of the one thought and of the other requires no explanation. Just as Fontenelle, in his essay *De l'origine des fables* did not
doubt that the Americans, quite a new people when discovered by
the Spanish, if they had had time would have come to think as
rationally as the Greeks.[75] That is to say, he added with careless
impertinence, to say the same silly things as the so-called philosophers of whom we make such a fuss. But Rationalism of Enlightenment ascribed the fabulous to ignorance whereas, since Cassirer,
the mythic, restored to its quality of autonomous thought with its
own logic and its own mode of experience, has become the native
land where philosophy becomes self-aware according as it succeeds
in becoming abstract; and his "abstract" discourse suffices to realize
the transition by making it obvious and necessary.

Outstripping, withdrawal, abstraction, emergence, meta-
morphosis, recognition, all metaphors that evade the question of
change, unavoidable for some more historically minded, quoting as
their authority for the French sociological School and its conceptual
analysis of mythic systems as much in contrast as the Chinese and
the Greek. The sinologist Marcel Granet and the Hellenist Louis
Gernet have in common the hypothesis posited by Emile Benveniste
that language conveys concepts which in turn give rise to institutions. Model of a linguistic sociology outlined by Antoine Meillet:
words must be defined in the context of combinations and their
particular structures; vocabulary is less a lexicon than a conceptual
system; it is organized around concepts which refer to institutions,
that is, to guiding schemata, present in techniques, modes of living,
social relations, the processes of word and thought.[76] And the dominant characteristic of those institutions is that they are long-lived
despite the passage of centuries and changes in way of living, that
they constitute a sort of historical unconscious. Longtime historians, practicing a semantics polarized by fundamental categories,
Granet and Gernet emphasize equally the mode of thought they call

mythic, mythicolegendary or mythicoreligious. That mythic thought, in every civilization, is apprehended in an ambiguous form: depositary of the basic frameworks of an ancient kind of thought, it can be read in the text on monuments in fragments, residual remains, ruins often reused in other constructions. A labor of archaeology, of protohistory, aware of the social milieux in which are entwined "mythic themes" transformed into legends which, in turn, in ancient China, are disguised in historical discourses or in the tales of chroniclers[77]—a survey that aims at finding a common ground for ritual and juridical acts and for philosophic models. Hence a divided but unitary mode of thought, global before being disseminated, dispersed rather than really demolished. With regard to China, Granet finds the crucial points in the fabulization of ritual dramas and religious dances, around distant seigniories who contrive the guiding schemata, who forge the logical articulations and create the great images, principles of thought and action centuries ago.[78] In Greece, it is the peasant phratries and ancient royalties that are at the hub of Gernet's "careful reading" of mythic themes connected with scenarios for festivals. On the other hand, the landowner's background of beliefs and practices in which people have festivities, dispense food, marry, compete in games; on the other, traditions of sovereignty, of royal power with figurative images of gifts, challenges, treasures, trials, and sacrifices.[79] Basic assumptions about myth comprising "a good deal of social unconscious"[80] in which the sociologist is tempted to read a real society mirrored by myth without any confusion,[81] whereas the historian of "prehistoric behavior," inclined toward a social memory that transmits symbols and their emotional value, worries about discovering therein the germ of religious and juridical concepts which are profitable in the city. In 1948 Gernet recognizes in mythology a kind of language with connections between its elements in which every image evokes a similar series.[82] Language in action, for mythic imagination is encased in human behavior and even in certain body postures. But it is also a global language, a total concept "which concerns economics, religion, politics, law, aesthetics,"[83] fields that become differentiated later on but that at the time were more or less intermingled. Another Greece is uncovered through a primordial mythic experience, a unitary language enveloping all the main forms of social and spiritual life,[84] as if they awaited from the course of history and the succession of events a conjuncture favorable to coming to light and progressively unveiling secularized modes of thought, law, philosophy, history, or politics, all the beginning emerging from the depths and awakened from a long mysterious sleep by an accidental change: the "city" or the "law."

Within Hellenism there is a strange change of scene brought about by the seism caused by Durkheim. And this upheaval is made most vivid to us, today, in the works of Hesiod which radically change place and status with John Burnet (1892) and Francis M. Cornford (1912 and 1952). For the former, witness *L'aurore de la philosophie grecque*,[85] scientific reasoning emerges at the end of a long night, streaked with strange tales and shot through by barbaric stories and shocking accounts of the origin of things.[86] But no matter how far one delves into the past of Greece, the old mythology that previously Homer, a man of experience and integrity treated by silence, is a construction destined to fall into ruin.[87] It is a primitive view of the world, made up of bits and pieces, "ready to crumble in the fresh breeze of a broader experience and a bolder curiosity."[88] Paradoxically, it is Hesiod, agitated by the nightmares of the Greek, who marks the decline of ancient mythology. Precisely by succumbing, in his *Theogony*, to systematization. For the myth, essentially a local[89] thing, atrophies; it perishes when it is uprooted from its cultist soil: "A system is necessarily fatal to a thing as arbitrary as mythology."[90] Fantastic teller of tales and suicidal poet, Hesiod makes way for the Ionian cosmologists, to the scientists of Miletus who cease to be "Maoris" when they decide, one fine day, no longer to tell tales about what existed when nothing existed but henceforth to busy themselves with what all things are in reality, now.[91] Realism in science begins with the decision to get rid of the fabulous, the marvelous, and the daydream. For Cornford, on the contrary, Hesiod's theogony, greatly influenced by Near Eastern theologies and thus rooted in impressive rituals, denotes the nodal point of a mythic, homogeneous, rigorous, and cohesive system. In his way, Hesiod the mythologist is as rational as the philosophers of Miletus.[92] So much so that Cornford has been reproached for giving the impression sometimes that the philosophers in the dawn of time were satisfied merely to repeat in a different language that which the myth had already said in the silence of night.[93]

A complete reversal which first signifies the wish of some to give mythic thought the key to the city in the Greek land where, after all, it is at home, if the philosophers and sociologists are to be believed. Subsequently, rather than to remain silent spectors of so great an upheaval, why did historians not look for sociohistorical models which could render an account of it? For George Thompson, adherent of the strictest Marxism, the determining factor of the intellectual imitation of the myth envisaged by rationalism and philosophy is the invention of money, of merchandising, the discovery of economics. Money introduces the abstraction of which philosophy will make use for better and for worse. For Jean-Pierre Vernant, sociologist and historian, more heedful of compromise, the most cardinal element in the advent of positive thought is politics, when the Greek city invents rules of an intellectual game from which the new rationalism derives its fundamental principles. But both hypotheses, whatever the distance separating them, invoke, in order to explain transition or change, a form of thought, economic or political, whose theory about mythology since Durkheim and Cassirer repeats that it is already contained, at least implicitly, in the primordial mythos. Is not this the sign that these solutions, like those preceding them, are subject to the same limits of the closed field and that, if they seem to interpose from the outside a social and economic history, in reality they remain prisoners of the closure set up by philosophic rationalism outside of which all "mythic thought," deprived of unitary principle, is also deprived of every form of existence?

The channel derived from symbolism corresponds to the tautegorical channel which runs dry after spelling out the inventory of the types of logic activated by mythic thought at its different levels of similar meaning. From Frobenius in 1904 to Griaule, confidant of the blind Ogotemmeli in October 1946, the expeditions into the depths of the dark continent bring back in their nets marvelous mythological shapes in the forms of pyramids, erected by the societies of the Niger and the Sudan.[94] Whereas Malinowski, angered by the "Herodotusing" of those who confine their curiosity to man's primordial eccentricities, limits mythology to the social organization whose pragmatic charter it is, the necessary but not autonomous code, Frobenius, in Frankfort, and Griaule, in Paris, devote their entire lives to going over the labyrinths of great symbolic systems of correspondences in steps, dazzled by the halls of mirrors of endless palaces entered into by the stairheads and secret doors. Long and complicated journeys without end in labyrinthine worlds in which the ethnologist, embarked on the discovery of another and more ancient kind of wisdom, allows himself to be guided by native wise men toward a mythology giddily opening onto the inner well of black thought.[95] But also, in turn, of all white thought because, since the twenties, phenomenology devotes in the great *mythologemes* the standpoint of apperception of a primordial reality; what it calls symbols are figments of the transcendental imagination, opening the entrance to the Presence. As revelation of a symbolic language for thinking without counting, for it is imbued with hierophania, the *mythologeme*, code of the Presence, becomes the nocturnal word enunciating a primary metaphysics, antedating and founding that which, since Aristotle, is called "what comes after physics."[96] Wisdom, "sophie," says Griaule, mythology is, in actuality, the deliberate fabulation of governing ideas which cannot be put within everyone's reach at any moment. Primordial metaphysics, so fascinating with regard to existential thought that it goes so far as to consider its own metaphysics as a second mythology. The "transcendence" recalled by Cassirer after Kant is erased and philosophy bows to mythic experiences, the abundance of its experience of life and its boundless advantage in revealing a reality so inherent in every person that it entirely controls his behavior.

Now begins a long steep climb that seems beyond the scope of ancient philosophic reasoning and its fixation on a dead mythology[97] but that emphasizes the impossibility of escaping the presuppositions of that very discourse on mythic thought when, at one of its extremes, symbolism leads to seeking the essence of myth at the most central point of clear thought: in its maturity where rational concept and mythic image are inseparably balanced. Around the seventies Jean Rudhardt, a Genevan religious historian, without renouncing the theophanic experiments, which taken as a whole arise from an immediate contact with the deity, raises the question whether mythology, at its most pure, cannot be grasped in societies where conceptual thought and mythic thought coexist.[98] That is, with the exception of civilizations without writing in which myth is barely elaborated on due to its limitless freedom and where each of the two thoughts becomes aware of its specific nature. A deliberate return to the country of origin of the only thinkable problem: to Greece, where mythology never ceases to confront rational thought. But a return whose peculiarity, compared to others, is to question the concomitance of myth and of philosophy in the same culture, apart from transcendent or decaying models.

To take as point of departure lack of cohesion, mythology's most ancient insignia, even by refusing, like Lévy-Bruhl, to see it as mystical experience or some form of prelogical thought, is not to be innovative straight off. To seek cohesion behind the negation of it through symbolic images meaning something that can neither be denoted nor known except by means of the symbol that expresses it, is still only to give place to "messages" while refusing to be subject to a codified language. There would be a dual specificity regarding myth considered as language. On the one hand, its figures, images, and schemata orientate the mind toward a signification found beyond the representationalism and concepts of linguistic forms. On the other hand, the plurality of tales in a mythology gains credence from an inner cohesion wherein each story refers to yet another, all of them tending toward a final meaning which cannot be codified to which the whole system orientates the mind, the mind of the Greeks and subsequently our own. In other words, the function of the images is to express a part of the lived experience, sufficiently basic to be repeated, to be reproduced, and thus to resist intellectual analysis attempting to break up its unity. This would not be new if it resulted in checking off, in mythic thought, the joint use of images—cosmic, biological, psychological, and social—in the form of immediate unitary experience in contrast to that which conceptual activity will later distinguish by separating a physical world, a psychic reality, a biological activity and a social relation. The peculiarity of Rudhardt's solution is to wish to recognize in the Greek myth a form of rationalism favoring subjectivity, alone capable of rediscovering religious meaning in worldly experience through symbolic images: a rationalism other and wider than conceptual intelligence, the *logos* able to discern if proceeding by sections but amnesic of the meaning of the whole. It is a matter of constructing a dialogue between cohesion and its opposite within the same mythic structure, within thoughts so exalted and deep that conceptual reasoning has to come to listen to the reasoning of mythic experience. To the ancient predominance of Greek culture in having first outlined Western science must be added, more remarkably, the fact of having understood and accepted the special function of mythic thinking. Not, as Cassirer thought, by ascribing to myth the fluid world of becoming but by averring the complete equality, in the same culture, of rational intelligence and mythological wisdom. More than ever the Greek holds his two heads high as the sign of his obvious superiority over the monocephalous crowd. And this time the chosen one surveys with his dual regard the whole field, no longer familiar with the truncated horizon of a Hermes with two faces unaware of each other. Structural anthropology enjoyed looking at its reflection in the mirror of the Hellenic philosopher discoursing on mythology: it was divided between the surprise of discovery and the narcissistic pleasure it felt but convinced that this spectacle presaged the advent of an authentic grammar of myth. Whereas a historian from Geneva, loyal to symbolist inspiration, invites everyone to be converted: to listen today to the meaning and the message of the myth, to take note of our bicephalic nature, is it not enough to listen to mythology in order to live it since, despite Christianity which has never stopped working against it, nevertheless the fundamental experiences in which it is rooted always remain ours?

"It is a question of knowing how the natives think," Mauss kept saying to new recruits to ethnography. That was surely a question detrimental to every effort to collect specimens in the field or to analyze them in the study. A question that had to be asked in the first place of autochthons representing the Science of myths as well as how mythology is thinkable and thought about by those who speak of it from high up in their pulpits ever since 1850. The answer by the whole Western tradition of "mythologists" is, today as of old, a formal one: there is no thinkable mythology without implicit or indirect reference to the Greeks' interchange of ideas on the subject. For Mauss and his disciples could only experience the burning desire to understand the pure essence of the function of mythology in a society absolutely sure about the first manifestation of mythology. One becomes a botanist or a geologist but one is born a mythologist.[99] This should not be overlooked by the young ethnographer entering the field for, if he "must know what he already knows," it is no longer possible to hide from him that the Science of myth, ever since it rages, has always been cast in a Greek mold. It is the great men of the pantheon of philosophers who ensure the necessary comparison with mythic thought, the other side of the coin of rationalism called upon to prove its hegemony through the channels of abstraction. In the same way as the earliest thinkers, obliged to explain to themselves beliefs so obscene, which sanction the scandalous movement which gives rise to the need for scholarship on the subject of myth. To speak of mythology is always to speak Greek or, since Greece, without her knowledge, but at risk of being designated for perpetual residence in that place where the delusions of modern man about mythology redouble the phantoms and fictions produced by the first "mythologists."

Chapter Seven
Untraceable Myth

If *Donkey Skin* were told to us would we really take great pleasure in it, we who have become readers of myths? For a long time has there not been admixed to that pleasure the vexation of being condemned to listen to the spoken word banished to the field of writing and to perceive with our eyes tales now only told in books? There is, in the West, an unfortunate awareness of mythology since the romantics became convinced that the mind's first experience involves a primitive language, that of the myth, simultaneously spoken word and song sprung from common knowledge and immediate contact with the world. And at once they come up against the mythography of the Greco-Roman world: inimitable mythology shrouded in treatises whose erudition stems from a lettered tradition from the Hellenistic age to the eighteenth century by way of Boccaccio and Noël Conti[1] in the Renaissance. From the time the living spoken words of a peoples or a nation are consummated in the verbal expression of mythology, any written symbol imposed on them seems a mutilation. Writing changes the brilliant bursts of grand speech, distorts the voice of myth, perverts mythologic revelation. In the interim between a state of primordial orality and the written form of the mythology unfortunately called classical, the time came to mend the breaks, to account for gaps, but also to find short cuts, to draw a map of hidden paths. Painstaking tasks that engross the nineteenth-century interpreters hard upon the disappearance of those who, like Hölderlin, expected the birth of a new mythology "of the greatest spiritual depth."[2]

For the adherents of a kind of history which only values writing, the discourse of earliest speech has become, in the country of Greece, so inaudible that it is almost illegible in the very place it is delivered by means of written symbols. Mythology, having become inaccessible, reveals only the mask made, in embalming it, by obscure craftsmen of mythology in the form of manuals in the period of Alexandrian scholarship. A dead writing, powerless to hide the contradictions in what are only remains, relics. And those inconsistencies prove to be as embarrassing for modern scholars as they were for the austere and exact minds of ancient times: Xenophanes, Herodotus, or Plato.[3] The Greeks so efficiently achieved the triumph of reason, of the *logos*, that they ruined the ancient system of thought to the extent that only fragments of it remain, unintelligible phrases. The distance cannot be breached between the words of myth true to life and tradition recorded in writing.

For others, more numerous and apparently more active, all lines of approach have not been cut. There exist forgotten or overgrown paths which lead to the border of the land of myths. Tactics are proposed to reduce the split between ourselves and primordial mythic language. The archaeology of language is one of the first: comparative grammar breeds an infallible science of mythology. According to the theory of Fr.-Max Müller, the system of sonorities, controlled by inflexion, is rooted in the human voice whose first sounds, emitted in response to the astonishing spectacle of nature, give rise to a series of phonetic types so potent that they affect the thought processes of earliest mankind, delude and make them err. It is there that mythology originates and thus is born only of illusion. It develops in a superfluity of meaning which cannot be mastered by words and which takes the form of strange, aberrant, and often incongruous phrases. The exacting rules of the science of language explain the formation of mythic discourse. Essentially, the earliest mythology is the aftereffect of a parasitic sickness of language, traces of which are still apparent on the surface written by the most rationalist societies. Comparative grammar leads straight to the country of myths only to discover the strange mirages that language causes in the thinking mind: phantoms, fictions which obsess the earliest speakers; a swarm of lies in place of the transparent truth inherent in the beginning of the human mind and spirit.[4]

Another tactic at the same period, which in turn follows the path of genetics but aided by history and geography, was developed by Karl Otfried Müller (1797–1840), innovator in this field. He believes that mythology is an essential product of the human mind, necessary and unconscious.[5] It is a kind of thought ascribable to the naiveté and simplicity of the beginnings of time, but it is constructed slowly under the influence of events and circumstances, some external, others internal. To have access to mythology is to rediscover the first landscape, recognize its modalities of expression in a well-defined territory, to discover by means of successive landmarks the fund of reality which, between two mountain peaks or in a valley, has suddenly awakened mind and spirit and made it possible to articulate relations in the form of actions in a tale told at the hearth. History enables us to define a limit to the mythopoetic faculty. About the year 1000 B.C. it shows signs of running out even when feverish colonization brings about a renewal of such activity. The erosion begins with writing, in particular, that of makers of prose who contribute to erasing the figures of primitive tradition and breaking up local rights and properties. The advent of writing is itself only one aspect of a vaster movement which, along with philosophy, research on nature, and the awakening of the sense of history impedes, if not the creation of the myth, at least its reproduction within the rank of a tradition. But writing assumes an ambivalent role. Wherever it infiltrates mythopoetic creativity atrophies and only distant lands and mountainous places, protected due to isolation, favor the survival of tales whose archaism becomes clear in comparison with other versions. At the same time writing petrifies the tradition it covers, marking it with what it has erased and pointing out landmarks to be read—proper names and geographic features—enduring charts which encipher for the traveling archaeologist a limited landscape. A hermeneutics is instituted which wants the onomastician to tell it the truth about the meaning hidden in a tale, not through etymology but by recalling a story whose events fall into a course whose bearings have been taken. And the search terminates when there appears at the end of the long and complicated journey the native land of a *mythologeme* whose original property is at last reestablished in its preferential rights.

Paradise lost, the country of myths is a forgotten world; reminiscence about it, rather than an effort to recall it, occurs in contemplating a landscape that authenticates the tale that grew in the same soil. It sometimes happens that a mythologist, taking a short cut, emerges in an isolated village where, in the steps of Pausanias the Geographer, he discovers a "mythic" history neither writing nor culture has yet contaminated. Since the solitary trips of K. O. Müller in the beginning of the nineteenth century, the same route has been followed, even by our contemporaries. Consequently, in careful research on the Giants and their war against the gods,[6] Fr. Vian attempts to "extricate the fable from the accumulated deposits which have made it unrecognizable during the course of time,"[7] in order to bring out the mythic tale which will provide information for an extensive politico-religious debate on the triumph of order and of Olympus.[8] In a second stage, the issue is to rediscover, beyond the work on myth by singing poets or poets, the authentic myth whose truth is authenticated through its oral form: that which another traveler, in the second century A.D., picked up in a remote corner of Arcadia as, at the end of a long journey the ethnographer, coming fresh from the course given by Marcel Mauss, records the extraordinary tale the natives confide to him, more or less spontaneously, furnishing it with references to a cultist landscape and a sacred geography.

Many approaches, none questioning that the real life of the myth arises from living speech. Moreover, does not the earliest anthropology discover that millions of savages or barbarians continue to produce the mythic imagery that primitive man derived from nature?[9] Here come inferior races, Primitives, the Peoples of Nature who give voice to words spouting from the mouth of mankind presently in the world; instead of the fleeting echo of a voice on the skyline, the wild strength of a mythology enveloping everything in a primordial language. The good news spreads that mythology has been lived and is still living, that, in the back country of *homo sapiens*, speech reigns over the body and words reign over the mind, that we are freed from the grand classical myth and ancient humanist ceremonies. But the division of labor imposes restraints: the autochthons sing, recite, narrate; and the ethnographers, as their name implies, write, take notes, record, make archives. As Lévy-Bruhl said to his audience at the Sorbonne: they, they listen, and we, we read.[10] For the natives, primitive listening, intense emotions, full awareness; for us, books, conceptualization of the prelogical, writings on barbaric mythology. The process of writing must be re-begun. The insanity of graphic systems must be given up. "The primary function of written communication is to facilitate enslavement," asserts Lévi-Strauss,[11] to the keen satisfaction of some Marxist puritans. But at the same time structural analysis, operative in the *Mythologiques*, postulates unanimity of all readers in all countries to establish the nature of myth: "A myth is perceived to be a myth by every *reader* in the whole world."[12] The Greeks, who devise a structural reading of their own mythology, become the guarantors of our lettered perception of the myths of the uncivilized; they guarantee a good use of written symbols in behalf of the peoples formerly called "uncivilized" and nowadays described as being "without writing."[13] Paradoxical societies arise in which myths are thought and spoken about among themselves but from one ethnographic book to another, in the silence of a study where no one must disturb the anthropologist at work. Civilizations saved from writing rather than deprived of it for the absence of written symbols assumes a positive value: it exerts "a sort of regulatory influence" on their tradition. A tradition "which must remain oral," it is said.[14] But whence comes this partitioning that an association of readers is asked to sanction if not from the a priori of a primordial orality? As though, at the heart of some civilizations with a history static, congealed and never cumulative, there were a proper way it behooved eye and ear to react. To postulate a tradition "which must remain an oral one" is as illusory as to grant the existence of a mythic trend of thought: like philosophic reasoning Western writing discovers an opposing phenomenon. So persistent that it hides the fundamental source of effective writing: mnemonic activity, the workings of memory, its cognitive quality. Not to raise another contrast, a metaphysical one, with memory with or without writing. But in order to inquire into the modalities of impact exerted by different systems of written symbols on the intellectual activity and, in particular, on the social memory, the mental machinery for producing culture by constantly changing what it must repeat over and again. But the variations of which, the successive metamorphoses engendering tribal stories, remain unseen as long as writing—primarily the ethnographer's—does not play a telltale role copying, at different times and places, the different aspects of a narrated story which appear to be one and the same.[15]

Fleeting voice and living word are part of the creations of mythology, of its lures, mirages continuously reappearing which it takes pleasure in raising up through self-creation in the course of a history that had to be recognized, albeit provisionally. For mythology, in the Greek sense—simultaneously fundamental and assumed—is constructed through the practice of writing, is impelled by it. An internal history riveted to the semasiology of *muthos*, formally gives the lie to the assertion that mythology knows no place or date of birth, that it has no creator, just as myths do not know their author. Genealogical research is redolent of the registry office: "myth" is born illusion. Not one of those fictions unconsciously made up by the earliest speakers, one of those shadows that primordial speech casts on thought, but consciously delimited fiction, deliberately exclusive. A burst of meaningless illusion, idiosyncratic, fragmented and empty; an unbelievable tale, sheer lying seduction, dead rumor. The "myth" closes on illusion. It is also a space appropriated by subversive words, absurd and discarded stories. Abandoned illusion, empty dreams that have been outlawed through new scholarship, philosophy and thinking about history, embodied in writing, and denoting an ignorance about which there is nothing to say. Nevertheless scandal, mainspring of the creation of myth, threatens that stubborn silence, incites talk about the proscribed not as such but as belonging to a broken tradition, to an ancient common memory whose interpretation begins to spread in the distance and through space opened up by the activity of storytellers who this time write them down. When Thucydides' rationalist and violently discriminatory approach to history leads finally to a policy of excluding data, it is forced to categorize as illusory the ways of writing tales of yore or of today simultaneously with ready-made ideas, absurd stories, and scandalously unverifiable reports of past events. In what historical scholarship calls the "mythic," the illusory feeds on ancient memory and fiction feeds on logographers' tales, archaeological research, and the ramblings of genealogists. Whether short, timely, or compiled slowly, mythic illusion seems to have no future, and in this state the "myth" seems only the shadow of a fiction. No truth is asked of it and it is endowed with none.

Until the moment when that hidden and disorderly place fills with strange figures as though the delusions of moderns, like those of the ancient Greeks, had suddenly set free a mysterious capacity to produce illusory effects. Scholarship in mythology becomes inventive, projecting its imaginary figures onto the mirror surface of myth-fiction which apes indiscriminately the obscene talk of the demented, the fabulizing naiveté of the childhood of mankind, or the profundity of primordial thought from which science ultimately emerges by way of philosophy. Reflected images, long journeys lead to the search from an empire of myths whose downfall, rumor has it, was caused by the Greeks' discovery of truth through logic; and the rediscovered Atlantis beaches on our shores, the fabulous riches of a forgotten rationalism, but still the same as our own and of the scholars since the beginnings of this phantom continent. In every shape it creates mythology, is metamorphosed, and its scholarly learning changes; it takes the ephemeral form of the space it inhabits one day. Yesterday, carnal thoughts, the barbarism of the Peoples of Nature, the insanity of an ancient mankind; tomorrow, the song of the earth, primordial speech, a wisdom beyond metaphysics. But whatever the legend may be, the realm delineated by mythology is always a provisional site, an open camping place; like the wrong side of a borderline from which the eye takes in the proximate horizon. In themselves, neither the unbelievable nor the irrational constitute real territories; they are the shadow cast by circumstantial reasoning or religion. And every vision of the world discovers a new mythology adjusted to its own knowledge of it but seeming faithfully to reproduce the old one.

Impossible to locate for it is the moving form of a mirage ever in

flux, mythology, nevertheless, seems to guard an inalienable territory: myth that is at once the unitary principle and elementary unit.
There is no presence more familiar, more obsessive than the mythic
figures ever since it conjured up a story or a tale. It matters little
whether it speaks the language of integration or of confrontation.
Whether it be normative or controvertial,[16] coherent or not, it is
understood that the myth tells a story. And, according to some
people, it is in the story told that its essence is to be found, thus
making it easy to separate this from its narrative form. Whence it can
be concluded that no other kind of tale better lends itself to translation and that either mythic stories are amenable to a grammar or else
that they amount to a sum total of themes and are distinguishable
due to the type of questions raised.[17] According to others—more
rigid semioticians—the myth is a kind of tale.[18] With its own linguistic characteristics: the *He*, not the *I* or the *thou*; the third person
acting in a drama based on a diachronic Tale;[19] or yet in a syntactics
governed by a before and an after; a tale that unfolds with particular
emphasis on time. It is in the same terms that Plotinus once interpreted the "myths" told by Plato: the *muthos* is a tool for analysis and
instruction which can be understood by splitting mixed up concepts; it separates the events in the tale from each other in time,
intermingled individuals who are only differentiated by rank or
power. The tense of myth, said Plotinus, is the imperfect, the mode
of the perceptible world.[20] A Neoplatonic reading which Cassirer
revives when demanding of Plato that he be the forerunner of his
clairvoyance: myth is the language that makes it possible to put into
words the world that is coming to be.[21] Between speculation and
action: the half-truth of philosophers.[22] But will not others, contemporaries of semiology, turn myth into the paradigm of the intempo-
ral and oust the existence of its beginnings in "Once upon a time,"
the turn of phrase in which can be read the mythological in its
simple form?

Delusion about myth glories in making modern inventors of
mythology believe that nothing is more concrete, more real, more
obvious than myth. In sociological research by a native sage in the
country of the *muthos* the myth, on the other hand, is told in its
various forms to such an extent that it uses every means to attain an
end. Does it not cover the ground between the proper name and the
epic, the proverb and theogony, the fable and genealogy? Mythology, comprising *muthos*, is open territory where everything said in
different tones of speech is at the mercy of repetition which trans-
mutes into the memorable, the noteworthy, that which it has
selected. And the myth, far from awarding to mythology the iden-

tity it would seem to owe it, reveals by going from one sense to another that its meaning is at the disposal of everyone who comes along. To such an extent that Aristotle, in the middle of the fourth century B.C., can choose between them in his *Poetics* to define what the soul of tragedy should be:[23] the plot, "the systematic arrangement of actions into a story."[24] From the point of view of Aristotle's *Poetics*, the myth is not a narrative, it is the product of methodical construction. A myth is shaped; facts and deeds must be weighed;[25] the actions arranged according to probability or necessity;[26] the story must be of a certain length so that the memory may easily recall it.[27] The plot must be devised in such a way that, independently of the play, even if they are not depicted "as learning of the deeds which are occurring, one shudders and commiserates with what is going on."[28] The effect of tragedy stems from the myth plot. If, on listening to the story of Oedipus we feel fear and pity, it is because the plot is good, well-constructed, and the author has dealt with it cleverly like a skillful craftsman. Hence the myth is the product of invention[29] but based on traditional stories of which the poets sometimes record the raw material and sometimes select only those pertaining to a few families, such as the Atreidae or the Labdacae.[30] Stories that become real myths according to the *Poetics*[31] only after they have been made into tragedies.

Interest in plot which Lévy-Bruhl, cocksurely, attributed to the mythology of the Greeks—so cultivated they had become indifferent to the dangers of mystical experience[32]—is, in fact, invented by Aristotle on a theoretical basis while considering the nature of tragedy and thinking not at all about the essence of a "mythology," in his eyes nonexistent. "Myth" is so unimportant as module of a system of autonomous thought that the same word applies simultaneously to the illusion of other people and the plot of a story. And this uncertainty continues since, in the view of a "critic" such as the grammarian and philologist Asclepiades of Myrlea, "myths" are "false tales," fictional stories having nothing to do with either gods or heroes, or with famous men whose life stories are all classified as "true tales."[33] Subsequent to mythology bereft of myths we now come upon "myths" without gods and without heroes.

To cite, today or tomorrow, that which everyone agrees to call myth is to endorse an out-of-date faithful acceptance of a cultural model that appeared in the eighteenth century when the sum total of accepted ideas concerning pagan divinities between Ovid and Apollodorus are in the realm of *fable* which scholarly erudition then called *mythology*.[34] But no episode in that long span of time warrants attributing to myth a literary genre or a specific type of tale. Mythology, a fish emulsified in the waters of mythology, is an untraceable form.[35] It thus seems risky to have wished to take it as the subject for a rigidly applied method of scholarly research and to have laid down its rules since the discovery of the West Indies.

What then does a myth-less mythology mean? How to save "mythology" from adherence to rules, once the play of mirrors, of reflexions and illusions in which scholarly knowledge of myths is trapped and concealed from him whom the anthropologists, in accordance with the Idealogists, call the observer? What is its purpose? A certain knowledge[36] of ways of thinking,[37] a particular mode of symbolic activity?[38] To conjure up "tribal stories" seems a pleasant way to dodge the question.

> Oedipus, if I just say his name, one knows all the rest; his father Laïus, his mother Jocasta, who were his daughters and his sons, what is going to happen to him, what he did. And the same is true of Alcmeon, one says his name and low and behold, all the little children cry out that when he went crazy he killed his mother.[39]

Stories that everyone already knows, basic stories: in short, the mythology "of families" comparable to the kind of history of France or England that students used to study.[40] Doubtless it is because they are basic that everyone knows them already; but, beside the fact that this criterion cannot account for them, having recourse to it would lead to reintroducing the category of myth barely disguised as basic tale. To such an extent is it obvious that a mythology without tales is unthinkable. Nevertheless, the man who, a long time ago, went off on his own and discovered the invisible city he named "mythology" because in his language there existed no name more suitable, did not come back with grand and miraculous tales. On returning to his city which awaited him, he did not tell stories of gods forever young nor of the birth of sky, earth, and sea. Not even a winter's tale, not a single "mythological narrative." But all the old men over sixty began at once to mythologize in such a sublime way that enchanted, fascinated children stayed to listen and, little by little, grew old while the old men imperceptibly became like children. The plague had left the city; Plato's city had been saved from unknown evil, and in hushed tones some people diagnosed that which in other disturbed times perceptive minds were to call "broken tradition."

One can speak Greek and so be a master of deceit but perchance discover a stimulating idea. Hence this pattern of three generations, eliminating the middle course with its contrivance of spellbinding rumor whose content and narrative style are obliterated by the principles, maxims, and unforgettable thoughts nurtured in the bosom of a city devoted to the Good and the Beautiful. The dream of a tradition that must be passed on by virtue of "old children" through one and the same voice, from the Ancients to the youngest of the living. But it is also an image of mythology without myths projected by a conceptually ideal duration: the homogeneous span of three generations. True, in the platonic model temporality is eliminated and mythology is as immutable as its very mythologists. Speech transmitted in a circular way must not be altered; furthermore, it cannot be, for the platonic system considers memory in its relation to Being and to the world of Ideas and makes it into mental activity inaccessible to change. Now this is precisely what is lacking in Plato's model which would make it possible to save an exsanguinated mythology, bled of its myths. In the span of two or three generations in societies whose culture has not been recorded in any kind of writing, everything that is said and narrated is subject to unavoidable and continual metamorphoses, no matter what the authority and the number of "memory administrators" there may be. Words and stories remove some little detail and substitute another, perhaps a more pleasing one as Fontenelle suggests, but certainly not the aim of adding the "fake miraculous" to what is already fake. To the ears of those who fashion it unconsciously, the memorable is inevitably the most true. The unforgettable is produced spontaneously, that is, by an autonomous labor of memory of three generations or more, all commingled in that already anonymous narrator who seems to repeat the story or the turn of phrase in which everyone recognizes himself at once. "Stories we never stop repeating accepted by all," the same Greek tells us for the last time. Is not "mythology" just such an unforgettable thing stemming from extraneous memory and proceeding to a kind of teaching wherein writing is invented with unpublished subjects of thought,[41] a memorization so mechanical and word-for-word that the main point, accepted by all, must of necessity be said and come into being elsewhere? Creative memory alone, sister of forgetting, might perhaps save "mythology" or at least rescue it from the deviations where Greeks like ourselves have conducted it by means of such long lectures.

A final story while awaiting the theoretician. They say that in the suburbs of Syracuse, Hieron II or I—no one knows which—had made a sumptuous and magnificent garden. He liked to go there to handle business. Hieron's garden was called "Myth."[42] Was that indicative of irony directed at the audiences the prince granted his guests or was it, in a more commonplace way, his parlor used for chatting in the midst of running water, the delicious shade of the incense tree and amidst the mingled scents of innocence and depravity? Short-sightedness alone prevents us from seeing that the "paradise" of the king of Syracuse, in every season, brought into flower the species—alas extinct—that the solemn Observers of Man, unfortunately deluded by the writings of certain botanists, persist in confusing with couch grass or I know not what other rank weeds.

Notes

Once Upon a Time

1. Fontenelle, *De l'origine des fables* [1724], ed. J. R. Carré (Paris, 1932), 11.

2. Fontenelle, 33.

3. Conversations with Dan Sperber have helped me in this project even though he remained very factual.

4. Aristotle frag. 668 Rose. I should not have noticed this remark without Michel de Certeau, *L'invention du quotidien*, vol. 1, *Arts de faire* (Paris, 1980), 167.

5. Aristotle *Métaphysique* 12.8.1074*b*10–12; *Du ciel* 1.3.270*b*19–20; *Météoroligiques* 1.3.339*b*27; *Politique* 7.9.1329*b*25.

6. Aristotle, *De la philosophie*, frag. 13 Rose; frag. 8 Walzer. On the group of proverbs in the encyclopedic work of Aristotle and his school, cf. K. Rupprecht, s.v. "Paroimiographoi," *Realencyclopädie des klassischen Altertumswissenschaft* 18, no. 4 (1949), cols. 1736–1738; R. Weil, *Aristote et l'histoire: Essai sur la "Politique"* (Paris, 1960), 141–144.

7. Of which Milan Kundera speaks, *Le livre du rire et de l'oubli*, French transl. F. Kéral (Paris, 1979), 10.

Chapter One

1. Claude Lévi-Strauss, *Anthropologie structurale* (Paris, 1958), 232. (I underline the word "*reader*.")

2. Three reference works: H. Pinard de la Boullaye, *L'étude comparée des religions*, vols. 1 and 2 (Paris, 1925); Jan de Vries, *Forschungsgeschichte der Mythologie* (Fribourg and Munich, 1961); B. Feldmann and Robert D. Richardson, *The Rise of Modern Mythology, 1680–1800* (Bloomington: Indiana University Press, 1972).

3. A. Lang, *La mythologie*, trans. L. Parmentier (Paris, 1886), 55–56.

4. P. Decharme, *Mythologie de la Grèce antique*, 3d ed. (Paris, 1884), vii–xxxvii. Same problematic conclusion in M.-J. Lagrange, *Études sur les religions sémitiques*, 2d ed. (Paris, 1905), 34.

5. Fr.-Max Müller, *Nouvelles leçons sur la science de langage*, trans.

G. Harris and G. Perrot (Paris, 1868), 2:115; quoted by A. Lang, *La mythologie*, pp. 20–21, to whom the last sentence is attributed, at least in his letter.

6. These are the words of Fontenelle, *De l'origine des fables* [1724], critical edition of J. R. Carré (Paris, 1932), 30–31. A. Lang, in *Myth, Ritual and Religion* (appendix A) (London, 1887), 2:321: "The disciples of (E.B.) Tylor, Mannhardt, Gaidoz and the others do not seem to guess that they are only republishing the opinions of the nephew of Corneille."

7. References in de Rochemonteix, *Lex jésuites et la Nouvelle-France au XVIIe siècle*, 3 vols. (Paris, 1895); G. Chinard, *L'Amérique et le rêve exotique dans la littérature française au XVIIe et au XVIIIe siècle* (Paris, 1934); M. de Certeau, *L'écriture de l'histoire* (Paris, 1975), 215–248 ("Ethno-graphie: L'oralité ou l'espace de l'autre: Léry").

8. Yves d'Évreux, *Suite de l'histoire des choses plus mémorables advenues en Maragnon ès années 1613 et 1614* (Paris: François Huby, 1615), 105–106. Michel de Certeau's research ("Récits de voyage anciens, XVIe/XVIIIes: Archéologie du discours ethnographique," *Semiotica* 7 [1973], 4, 373) today reveals "the savage, body of sensual pleasure" as one of the products of this kind of dissertation.

9. J.-Fr. Lafitau, *Moeurs des sauvages amériquains comparées aux moeurs des premiers temps*, 2 vols. (Paris, 1724). Cf. finally the resumés of G. Tissot, "Joseph-François Lafitau: Figures anthropologiques," *Sciences religieusses/Studies in Religion* 4, no. 2 (1974/1975), 93–107; and his thesis *Image et origine: Fondements du système de religion de Joseph-François Lafitau* (Ottowa, 1978).

10. M. de Certeau, 188–196.

11. M.-V. David, *Le débat sur les écritures et l'hiéroglyphe aux XVIIe et XVIIIe siècles* (Paris, 1965).

12. J.-Fr. Lafitau, 1:8–9.

13. Ibid., 2:154–157.

14. Ibid., 1:138.

15. Ibid., 2:157.

16. At most, the sorrow caused by the degeneration of an ancient "sacred Tradition," of a "Religion holy in its origins, holy before being corrupted" (ibid., 1:8).

17. The "modernism" of Lafitau, averred by scholars of folklore, by anthropologists and historians of Antiquity for the past half century, from Van Gennep to Brelich, is based on various misapprehensions. One of the most fruitful of these is the *initiation*: focal in the hieroglyphic and mysterious forms where the missionary deciphers the traces of a Religion ancient and consentient, it foreshadows the anthropological "category" of the *rites of passage* and *states of flux* exploited by our contemporaries.

18. Compare what J. R. Carré says about this in the critical edition of Fontenelle, 81–82.

19. Cf. J. R. Carré, *La philosophie de Fontenelle ou le sourire de la raison* (Paris, 1932); F. E. Manuel, *The Eighteenth Century Confronts the Gods* (Cambridge, Mass., 1959).

20. Fontenelle, 12 and 30 (commentary, 84–91).

21. Ibid., 31–32 (commentary, 93–94).
22. J.-Fr. Lafitau, 2:157.
23. Fontenelle, 34.
24. Ibid., 34.
25. Ibid., 35.
26. Ibid., 13–14.
27. Ibid., 20–22: "in some way, men have taken pleasure in deceiving themselves [20]; since accounts of true facts, mingled with false imaginings were such circulated, . . . even slightly remarkable facts were no longer recounted without the ornamentation which it was realized was conducive to pleasure [22]."
28. Ibid., 34: "When poetry or painting have made use of them (fables) to reveal them to our imagination, they only return to it its own workings."
29. Cf. R. Mauzi, L'idée de bonheur dans la littérature et la pensée françaises au XVIIIᵉ siècle (Paris, 1960).
30. Panckoucke, Les études convenables aux demoiselles (Lille, 1749), 2:268–412. In his preface (pp. viii and xiii), Panckoucke insists upon intense study of mythology side by side with poetry, rhetoric, geography, chronology, and history. As for Abbey Banier, La mythologie et les fables expliquées par l'histoire (Paris, 1738–1740), i–iii, everything converges to remind us of those ancient figments which encompass, beneath their embellishments, a part of the history of earliest times. The method is simple (i, 16–17): when a fable seems historical, it suffices to eliminate the supernatural which is mixed up with it. "A poet having events to describe does not only relate them as a historian but includes his own artifice."
31. Cf. J. Starobinski, "Le mythe au XVIIIᵉ siècle," Critique, no. 366 (November 1977), 977.
32. Fontenelle, 11.
33. Ibid., 32.
34. Ibid., 39–40: "Let us not seek anything in fables other than the history of the mistakes of the human mind. . . . It is not a science to have filled one's head with all the wild nonsense of the Phoenicians and the Greeks; but it is one to know who led the Phoenicians and the Greeks into that wild nonsense."
35. R. Schwab, La renaissance orientale (Paris, 1950), 171–204.
36. M. Foucault, Les mots et les choses (Paris, 1965), 245–249, 292–313. Cf. R. H. Robins, Brève histoire de la linguistique: De Platon à Chomsky [1967] (Paris, 1976; French trans.), 137–205; M. de Certeau, D. Julia, J. Revel, Une politique de la langue: La révolution française et les patois (Paris, 1975).
37. M. Foucault, 299. Cf. also G. Genette, Mimologiques: Voyage en cratylie (Paris, 1976), 227–240.
38. A. Schleicher, Die darwinische Theorie und die Sprachwissenschaft (Weimar, 1863).
39. Cf. R. Schwab, 198–202 ("Le langage, arme de guerre: De Klaproth à Gobineau").
40. M. Foucault, 303: "In a language the one who speaks and who does

not cease to speak in a whisper which is not heard but from which comes an explosive burst, is the people."

41. Cf. J. Starobinski, 993.

42. Cf. D. Janicaud, *Hegel et le destin de la Grèce* (Paris, 1975).

43. Cf. M. Detienne, "Au commencement était le corps des dieux," *Critique*, no. 378 (November 1978), 1054–1055.

44. A. Lang, *La Mythologie*, 55.

45. E. B. Tylor, *La civilization primitive*, 2d ed. (1873), French trans. P. Brunet and Ed. Barbier, vols. 1 and 2 (Paris, 1876).

46. Frédéric-Max Müller, *Collected Works*, 20 vols. (London, 1898–). Cf. the analyses of H. Pinard de la Boullaye (index: s.v. Müller, Fr.-Max).

47. Fr.-Max Müller, *La science du langage*, 3d ed., trans. G. Harris and G. Perrot (Paris, 1876). "La theorie de Max Müller" is the subject of a chapter in A. Lang, *La mythologie*, 20–45.

48. Fr.-Max Müller, *La science du langage*, 469.

49. Ibid., 12.

50. P. Decharme, vii.

51. Fr.-Max Müller, *Über die Philosophie der Mythologie*, reprinted in appendix to Fr.-Max Müller, *Einleitung in die vergleichende Religionswissenschaft* (Strasbourg, 1874), 316; quoted by E. Cassirer, *Langage et mythe: A propos des noms des dieux* [1924], French trans. Ole Hansen-Love (Paris, 1973), 13–14.

52. Cf. E. Cassirer, *Langage et mythe*, 13–14.

53. St. Mallarmé, *Les dieux antiques: Nouvelle mythologie d'après George W. Cox* [1880], 10th ed. (Paris, 1952), 15.

54. Ibid., 4.

55. Ibid., 9.

56. As explained in the "editor's preface of 1880" (xi–xvi). The work is dedicated to Charles Seignobos, deputy from Ardeche: "His old friend. Stéphane Mallarmé."

57. St. Mallarmé, 9.

58. P. Decharme, xix.

59. M. Bréal, *Mélanges de mythologie et de linguistique* (Paris, 1877), 163–164.

60. P. Decharme, xxi. The contrast between the two temperaments and the two rival schools is analyzed by Fr.-Max Müller, *Nouvelles leçons sur la science du langage*, vol. 2 (Paris, 1868), 248–249, 271–278.

61. A. Lang, *La mythologie*, 36–38.

62. Ibid., 58.

63. E. B. Tylor, 1:274 ("Langage émotional et imitatif," 189–276). Cf. R. R. Marett, *Tylor* (New York, 1936).

64. E. B. Tylor, 1:347.

65. Ibid., 1:343.

66. Ibid., 1:324–325.

67. Ibid., 1:324.

68. Ibid., 2:574.

69. A. Lang, *La mythologie*, 56–226.

70. Ibid., 3 ("Objet de la mythologie scientifique").

71. P. Decharme, vii.

72. Ibid., viii. In full agreement with M.-J. Lagrange, who considers a distinct separation of religion from mythology to be indispensable (22). "A serious question," writes St. Mallarmé in *Les dieux antiques: nouvelle mythologie d'après George W. Cox,* "is mythology the *religion* of the peoples of antiquity? Yes: insofar as a religion cannot supply certain religious impressions and its followers will be forced to go to another source, for instance the maxims of poets and philosophers which have a moral and sacred influence on life which, in principle, is lacking in Greek theogony. In that way it will form, helped by the human conscience, two distinct currents of ideas: the one, located between religion and fable, is the mythologic, properly so called; the other would be that which today we would simply call the religious" (13).

73. P. Decharme, xxxvii.

74. In *L'étude comparée des religions,* H. Pinard de la Boullaye congratulates the Hellenist, K. Otfried Müller, for having seen "the extent to which mythology and religion are separate entities" (275).

75. M.-J. Lagrange, 2–40. In his reading of "sacrifice" and his way of exonerating the Greeks of "carnal and disgusting rites," cf. M. Detienne, "Pratiques culinaires et esprit de sacrifice," in M. Detienne, J.-P. Vernant, et al., *La cuisine du sacrifice en pays grec* (Paris, 1979), 31.

76. M.-J. Lagrange, 23 ("religion should be founded on simple ideas accessible to the most primitive intelligence").

77. Ibid., 22.

78. Ibid., 23.

79. Ibid., 22.

80. Ibid., 28–30.

81. Ibid., 36. Yet to be explained in the Semitic field, and the Babylonian myth, and his irrational: if it verges in the obscene (like others), it must be because, in that culture, "obscene rites" were supposed to promote fertility (40).

82. W. Schmidt, *Der Ursprung der Gottesidee* (Münster-en-W, 1912–1935), i–vi. Concerning this lengthy survey and its place in the research of his contemporaries, Schmidt has subsequently furnished an expository synthesis: *Origine et évolution de la religion: Les théories et les faits* (Paris, 1931). His theory prevailed in Rome, in Catholic universities, until the sixties.

83. W. Schmidt, *Origine et évolution de la religion: Les théories et les faits,* 323–346.

84. Ibid., 348.

85. Ibid., 352–355.

86. A. E. Jensen, *Mythes et cultes chez les peuples primitifs* [1951], trans. M. Metzger and J. Goffinet (Paris, 1954), 118–120.

87. W. Schmidt, *Origine et évolution de la religion: Les théories et les faits,* 355.

88. A. Lang, *La mythologie,* 3–5 ("Objet de la mythologie scientifique").

89. A. Lang, *La mythologie,* 55–226.

90. W. Schmidt, *Origine et évolution de la religion: Les théories et les faits*, 219–234, has sketched out the evolution of A. Lang in his works that appeared between 1901 and 1906: *Magic and Religion* (London, 1901); *Myth, Ritual and Religion*, 2d ed. (London, 1901); *Custom and Myth*, 2d ed. (London, 1904).

91. E. B. Tylor, 1:363.

92. As does the present-day historian of whom M. de Certeau speaks in *L'écriture de l'histoire*, 91.

93. E. B. Tylor, 1:363–364.

94. Ibid., 1:363.

95. Ibid., 1:325.

96. Ibid., 2:581. We underline the verb "handed down."

97. Ibid.

98. Ibid., 2:580.

99. Ibid., 2:574.

100. Cf. the remarks of G. W. Stocking, Jr., s.v. "Tylor (E. B.)," in *International Encyclopedia of Social Sciences* (1968), 16:170–177.

Chapter Two

1. E. A. Havelock, *Preface to Plato* (Cambridge, Mass., 1963); "Prologue to Greek Literacy," *University of Cincinnati Classical Studies, Semple Lectures*, vol. 2 (Oklahoma, 1973), 1–59; "The Preliteracy of the Greeks," *New Literary History* 7, no. 3 (1977), 369–391; "The Alphabetization of Homer," in *Communication Arts in the Ancient World*, ed. E. A. Havelock and J. P. Hershbell (New York, 1978), 3–21; *The Greek Concept of Justice: From Its Shadow in Homer to Its Substance in Plato*, (Cambridge, Mass., 1978); *Aux origines de la civilisation écrite en Occident* (1974), French trans. E. Escobar Moreno (Paris, 1981).

2. M. Parry, *The Making of Homeric Verse*, ed. A. Perry, (Oxford, 1971); G. S. Kirk, *Homer and the Oral Tradition* (Cambridge, 1976); J. Svenbro, *La parole et le marbre: Aux origines de la poétique grecque* (Lund, 1976), 11–45; *Oral Literature and the Formula*, ed. B. A. Stolz and R. S. Shannon III (Ann Arbor, 1976), with contributions by: Joseph A. Russo, "Is 'Oral' Or 'Aural' Composition the Cause of Homer's Formulaïc Style?" (31–54); Gregory Nagy, "Formula and Meter" (239–260); Ruth Finnegan, "What Is Oral Literature Anyway? Comments in the Light of Some African and Other Comparative Material" (127–166). Cf. L. E. Rossi, "I poemi omerici come testimonianza di poesia orale," in *Storia e civiltà dei Greci*, vol. 1, no. 1 (Milan, 1978), 73–147.

3. Cf. J.-P. Vernant, "Image et apparence dans la théorie platonicienne de la 'mimésis,' " *Journal de psychologie 2 (1975), 133–160 (in particular, 146–152)*, taken up again in *Religions, histoires, raisons* (Paris, 1979), 105–137.

4. The expression of Joseph A. Russo, in *Oral Literature and the Formula*, ed. B. A. Stolz and R. S. Shannon III ("From Oral to Aural"), 41–42.

5. Cf. Chapter 5, below.

6. *Laws* 3.680d3.

7. *Republic* 3.411a6–8.

8. Cf. pp. 63–68, below.

9. M. Detienne, *Les maîtres de vérité dans la Grèce archaïque* (1967), 3d ed. (Paris, 1979), 9–27; Zs. Ritoók, "Die Homeriden," *Acta antiqua Academiae Scientiarum hungaricae* 18, nos. 1–2 (1970), 1–29; W. Burkert, "Die Leistung eines Kreophylos: Kreophyleer, Homeriden und die archaische Heraklesepik," *Museum Helveticum* (1972), 74–85.

10. That which some call, without reason, "mythic thought." For instance, J. Bollack, P. Judet de la Combe, H. Wismann, *La réplique de Jocaste (Cahiers de philologie* 2) (Lille, 1977), 92. Cf. Chapter 6, below.

11. On the "Homer tradition," its play of innuendo and use of inner references, its systems of repeats from one song to another, cf. Gr. Nagy, *The Best of the Achaeans: Studies of the Hero as Reflected in the Archaic Forms of Greek Poetry* (Baltimore, 1979); and on a precise point of "intertextuality" between the *Odyssey* and the *Iliad*, P. Pucci, "The Song of the Sirens," *Arethusa* 12, no. 2 (1979), 121–132.

12. *Iliad*, 1:268; 1:403; 1:423; 1:590–594.

13. Cf. for the period between the eighth and the fifth centuries, G. L. Huxley, *Greek Epic Poetry from Eumelos to Panyassis* (London, 1969).

14. In social conditions of which new studies have been made by Gr. Nagy, *The Best of the Achaeans.*

15. M. I. Finley, *The World of Odysseus* (New York, 1954), which we quote in the French version (new, revised, and expanded) by Claude Vernant-Blanc and Monique Alexandre: *Le monde d'Ulysse* (Paris, 1978).

16. *Le monde d'Ulysse*, 23–24.

17. Ibid., 27–28.

18. Ibid., 58.

19. Ibid. (appendix I: "Ulysses's Return to the World"), 178: "I am an historian: my professional interest in the *Iliad* and in the *Odyssey* concerns their usefulness as tools, as documents for study of the Bronze Age, centuries unknown and the history of archaic Greece." Soldier of history, only doing his duty.

20. Ibid., 221: "Homer's Trojan War, we suggest, should be severed from Greek *history* of the Bronze Age." Finley underlined the word in the final sentence of "Ulysses's Return to the World."

21. *Le monde d'Ulysse*, 58.

22. The latter are more tenacious: ibid., 192–198.

23. Regarding the "Mycenaean" thesis, cf. lastly R. Hope Simpson and J. F. Lazenby, *The Catalogue of the Ships in Homer's Iliad* (Oxford, 1970), 154–155. Whereas the other thesis is defended by A. Giovannini, *Étude historique sur les origines du Catalogue des vaisseaux* (Berne, 1969), 58; and, with some reservations, by G. Nachtergael, "Le catalogue des vaisseaux et la liste des theorodoques," *Mélanges Cl. Préaux* (Brussels, 1975), 45–55.

24. *Le monde d'Ulysse*, 58: "a world of history and not a world of fiction."

25. Cf. ibid., 105.

26. Ibid., 27.

27. Ibid., 57, 192 ("the decisive point is rather that the pattern should

be consistent, thus eliminating the common assertion that what we find in the poems is either fiction . . . , or a mixture borrowed from different eras").

28. Ibid., 34.

29. For example, P. Vidal-Naquet, "The Iliad undisguised," in a preface to the P. Mazon translation of the *Illiad* (Paris, 1975) ("Folio" Collection), 21. The preface outstrips Finley's interpretation based on history (14–17).

30. Cf. *Le monde d'Ulysse*, 120.

31. Cf. the canto by canto analysis made by Paul Mazon in *Introduction à l'Iliade* (with the collaboration of P. Chantraine, P. Collart, and R. Langumier) (Paris, 1948), 137–230.

32. Documentary comparison is not possible for the *Iliad* and the *Odyssey*, although it is with regard to *La Chanson de Roland* (cf. *Le monde d'Ulysse*, 56): it is possible to read a discussion of this by M. Rouche, "Roland à Ronceveaux," *L'histoire* 3 (July–August 1978), 73–75. The means for verification are lacking. Finley admits it. But the urge to make history is all the more uncontrollable, it seems.

33. "Verification" is an argument whose weakness Finley does not fail to recognize but which he utilizes to reconcile fidelity to a social pattern with the presence of archaisms and anachronisms. But what can it mean for an auditor to demand verisimilitude, probability? What does verisimilitude mean? Surely something other than what Aristotle meant.

34. H. M. Chadwick, *The Heroic Age* (Cambridge, 1912), 432, 458.

35. *Le monde d'Ulysse*, 54.

36. Cf. J. Svenbro, 27. If Svenbro rightly emphasizes the performance of each recitation, he sociologizes radically the "social control" to the point of envisaging the Muse as a collective representation, a religious one, to be sure, but one that allows the poet to understand "his function in the group, his ability to see the future, his sensitivity to the most subtle nuances— precisely the proficiency of which he could not boast" (34). The Muse, daughter of Memory, would be the social control internalized by the singing poet in his poetic work.

37. *Le monde d'Ulysse*, 120.

38. "It is more than probable that the *Iliad* and the *Odyssey*, in their present form, were composed in writing and not orally" (*Le monde d'Ulysse*, 35). In the first French version (1969) he wrote: "It is even possible" (28).

39. Cf. A. Lalande, *Vocabulaire technique et critique de la philosophie*, 8th ed. (Paris, 1960), s.v. "consistency."

40. Cf. Tz. Todorov, *Théories du symbole* (Paris, 1977), 211–219.

41. Even before Socrates Homer divined that man is "that being capable of giving a rational answer to a rational question" (Cassirer, quoted by Finley, *Le monde d'Ulysse*, 27).

42. E. A. Havelock, *Preface to Plato* (Oxford, 1963), 118.

43. Ibid., 61 ff.

44. E. A. Havelock, "Prologue to Greek Literacy," 2:1–59.

45. E. A. Havelock, *Preface to Plato* (chap. 4: "The Homeric Encyclopedia").

46. Plato, *Republic* 10.598e1; 599c6–d1.

47. E. A. Havelock, *Preface to Plato*, 119.

48. Ibid., 141–142.

49. W. F. Otto, *Die Götter Griechenlands: Das Bild des göttlichen im Spiegel des griechischen Geistes* [1941], 6th ed. (Frankfurt-on-Main, 1970), 279. Same praise for Homer but this time on the scale of universal mankind, in W. Jaeger, *Paideia: La formation de l'homme grec*, 2d ed. (Cambridge, 1945), French transl. A. and S. Devyver (Paris, 1964), 1:64–68.

50. M. Lejeune, "La diffusion de l'aphabet," *Comptes rendus de l'Académie des Inscriptions et Belles-Lettres* (1966), 505–511 (506 in particular).

51. V. Segalen, *Les immémoriaux* [1907] (Paris, 1956).

52. That history has been written by the missionary-printer of those islands, W. Ellis, *Polynesian Researches, during a Residence of nearly eight Years in the Society and Sandwich Islands*, vols. 1 and 2 (London, 1829). Cf. G. Duverdier, "La pénétration du livre dans une société de culture orale: le cas de Tahiti," *Revue française d'histoire du livre* (1971): 27–49.

53. Moerenhout, *Voyages aux îles du grand Océan* (Paris, 1837), 1:393.

54. Cf. on problems of alphabetization and the spread of writing, *Literacy in Traditional Societies*, ed. J. Goody (Cambridge, 1968); Fr. Furet and J. Ozouf, "Trois siècles de métissage culturel: En France, XVIIᵉ–XIXᵉs," *Annales E.S.C.* (1977), 488–502; and *Lire et écrire: L'alphabétisation des Français de Calvin à Jules Ferry* (Paris, 1977); R. Chartier, "L'entrée de l'écrit," *Critique*, no. 377 (1978), 973–983; and "L'ancien régime typographique," *Annales E.S.C.* (1981), 191–209. *Libri, editori e pubblico nell'Europa moderna: Guida storica e critica*, ed. A. Petrucci (Bari, 1977).

55. W. Ellis, 1:452: "Pour civiliser un peuple, il faut d'abord qu'il soit christianisé."

56. G. Duverdier, 42.

57. Ibid., art. cit., 40.

58. Ibid., art. cit., 39.

59. Ibid., art. cit., 41.

60. Cf. J.-P. Vernant, *Les origines de la pensée grecque* (Paris, 1962), 40–45.

61. Cl. Préaux, "Du 'linéaire B' créto-mycénien aux ostraca grecs d'É-gypte," *Chronique d'Égypte* 34 (1959), 79–85.

62. Not professional scribes according to J.-P. Olivier, *Les Scribes de Cnossos* (Rome, 1967).

63. Of which the definitive list was drawn up by J. Labarbe, "Les premières démocraties de la Grèce antique," *Bulletin de l'Académie royale de Belgique: Cl. des Lettres, Sciences morales et politiques* (1972), 223–254.

64. Cf. Ed. Will, "La Grèce archaïque," in *Trade and Politics in the Ancient World* (Second International Conference on the History of Economics) (Paris, 1965), 1:85–86.

65. Frag. 24.18–20 Diehl. "The shepherds, in the mountains, survivors of the deluge, are not acquainted with 'lawmakers' for in those earliest times writing did not yet exist" (Plato, *The Laws* 3.680a5).

66. M. Lejeune, 510.

67. M. Lejeune, art. cit., 510. Cf. 507.

68. *Sylloge Inscriptionum Greecarum*, 4th ed. (Leipzig, 1915), 1:1–15.

69. Cf. Fr. A. G. Beck, *Greek Education: 450–350 B.C.* (London, 1964), 72–146; F. D. Harvey, "Literacy in the Athenian Democracy," *Revue des études grecques* 79 (1966), 629–633.

70. Whereas the theater is city business, the school is in the private sector, not in the public, that is, the political one: D. Lanza, *Lingua e discorso nell'Atene delle professioni* (Naples, 1979), 65.

71. E. Posner, *Archives in the Ancient World* (Cambridge, Mass.: 1972), 91–118. Cf. G. Busolt and H. Swoboda, *Griechische Staatskunde*, 3d ed. (Munich, 1926), 2:1037–1041.

72. Aristotle *Politics* 6.7.1321b34–40; 7.11.1331b7–12.

73. E. Posner.

74. Plato, *Phaedrus* 257d5–8.

75. Euripides, *Suppliantes*, 438–439. Cf. M. Detienne in "Espece et temps dans la cité, la littérature et les mythes grecs," *Revue de synthèse* 57–58 (1970), 70–72.

76. Cf. D. Lanza, 53; and N. Loraux, *L'invention d'Athènes* (1981), 180–182.

77. Aeschylus, *Suppliantes*, 434–435.

78. Ibid., 946–949.

79. Tablets to write the minutes and the roll of papyrus that would become the document for the archives. Cf. E. G. Turner, "I libri nell'Atene del V e IV secolo a.c." (revised and augmented version of *Athenian Books in the Fifth and Fourth Centuries* [London, 1952]), in *Libri editori e pubblico nel mondo antico: Guida storica e critica*, ed. G. Cavallo (Bari, 1975), 10. On the processes of "public" writing—drawing, engraving, painting in order to make letters *readable*—cf. the remarks of J. and L. Robert, epigraphic Bulletin (*Revue des études grecques*) (1974): 26, 27; (1978), 13.

80. Cf. for example R. Weil, "Les documents dans l'oeuvre de Thucydide," *L'information littéraire* 26 (1974), 31.

81. Cf. M. I. Finley, *Les premiers temps de la Grèce: L'âge du bronze et l'époque archaïque* [1970], trans. Fr. Hartog (Paris, 1973), 108.

82. M. Lejeune, 510.

83. R. Bogaert, *Banques et banquiers dans les cités grecques* (Leyde, 1968), 376–384.

84. Cf. L. Gernet, *Droit et société dans la Grèce ancienne* (Paris, 1955), 191–193. Acknowledgment of debts, engraved on lead at Korkyra, around 500 B.C., with names of creditors, debtors, witnesses, and the sums involved perhaps relate to maritime loans: P. Calligas, "An Inscribed Lead Plaque from Korkyra," *Annual of the British School at Athens* 66 (1971), 79–93 (cf. J. and L. Robert, epigraphic Bulletin, [*Revue des études grecques*] [1973], 230); B. Bravo, "Une lettre sur plomb de Bezegan: Colonisation et modes de contact dans le Pont," *Dialogues d'histoire ancienne* 1 (1974), 111–187.

85. M. I. Finley, "Censura nell'antichità classica," *Belfagor* (1977), 613.

86. Xenophon, *The Anabasis* 7.5.13–14 (*pollai de bibloi gegrammenai*). Further evidence from H. Alline, *Histoire du texte de Platon* (Paris, 1915), 12, and n. 1 to B. Gentili, *Lo spettacolo nel mondo antico* (Bari, 1977), 6, n. 16; and in

the interim, P. Mazon, *Introduction à l'Iliade* (Paris, 1948), 277, n. 1;
T. Kleberg, *Bokhandel och bokförlag i antiken* (Stockholm, 1962) (Italian transl.
E. Livrea in *Libri, editori e pubblico nel mondo antico: Guida storica e critica*, ed.
G. Cavallo [Bari, 1975], 30); A. Dain, "L'écriture grecque du VIIIe siècle
avant notre ère à la fin de la civilisation byzantine," in *L'écriture et la
psychologie des peuples (Centre international de synthèse)* (Paris, 1963), 174–175.
    87. Cf. D. Lanza, 52–87.
    88. Cf. pp. 72–76, below.
    89. E. G. Turner, "I libri nell'Atene del V e IV secolo a.c.," in *Libri,
editori e pubblico nel mondo antico: Guida storica e critica*, ed. G. Carvallo (Bari,
1975), 18; Plato, *Apologie* 26d10-e1. On literary forms of philosophic discussion, cf. H. Cherniss, *Selected Papers*, ed. L. Tarán (Leyde, 1977), 14–35.
    90. In "Censura nell'antichità classica" (*Belfagor*, 1977), 612, Finley, in
comparing the circulation of writings in Antiquity to a sort of *samizdat* (607),
refers to the example of Euripides, the most well-read of the tragedians but
whose works were promulgated from mouth to mouth, learned and recited
by heart; a number of Athenians, prisoners of the Syracusians in 413, owed
their freedom to the tirades of Euripides which they were able to make their
masters enjoy (Plutarch, *Nicias* 29.2–5).
    91. Cf. L. Canfora, "Storici e societá ateniense," in *Erodote, Tucidide,
Senofonte: Letture critiche*, ed. L. Canfora (Milan, 1975), 24–26; "Dalla logo-
grafia ionica alla storiografia attica," in *Storia e civiltà dei Greci*, vol. 2, no. 3
(Milan, 1979), 355–364; A. Momigliano, "The Historians of the Classical
World and Their Audiences: Some Suggestions," *Annali della Scuola Nor-
male Superiore di Pisa, Lettere e Filosofia* (1978), 59–75; B. Gentili and G. Cerri,
Le teorie del discorso storico nel pensiero greco e la storiografia romana arcaica
(Rome, 1975), 19–45; D. Lanza, 67–74.
    92. The rare exception is silent reading: B. M. W. Knox, "Silent Read-
ing in Antiquity," *Greek Roman and Byzantine Studies* (1968), 421–435. Cf.
P. Chantraine, "Les verbes signifiant 'lire,' " *Mélanges H. Gregoire* (Brussels,
1950), 2:115–126; R. Weil, "Lire dans Thucydide," *Mélanges Cl. Préaux*
(Brussels, 1975), 162–168.
    93. Peculiarity of the intellectual with book in hand and, moreover,
reading to himself: Aristophanes *Grenouilles* 52–53, 1114 (cf. L. Woodbury,
"Aristophanes' Frogs and Athenian Literacy: Ran. 53–53, 1114," *Transactions of the American Philological Association* 106 [1976], 349–357).
    94. Cf. B. Gentili, "Introduction," in E. A. Havelock, *Cultura orale e
civiltà della scrittura: Da Omero Platone*, (Bari, 1973; Italian transl.), v–xi.
    95. A. Leroi-Gourhan, *Le geste et la parole*, vol. 2, *La mémoire et les
rythmes* (Paris, 1965), 22–34; *La mémoire sémantique*, ed. St. Ehrlich and
E. Tulving (*Bulletin de psychologie de l'université de Paris*) (Paris, 1976);
M. Piatelli-Palmarini, "L'entrepôt biologique et le démon comparateur," in
Nouvelle revue de psychanalyse 15 (*Mémoires*) (1977), 105–123.
    96. E. Bernheim, *Einleitung in die Geschichtswissenschaft* (Leipzig, 1889);
J. Vansina, *De la tradition orale: Essai de méthode historique* (Tervuren, 1961).
    97. "La tradition, chaîne de témoignages": J. Vansina, 22–45.
    98. "Le témoignage, mirage de la réalité": ibid., 69–96.

99. Ibid., 8. Cf. 98–100: "how to detect false rumors."
100. I. Meyerson, "Le temps, la mémoire et l'histoire," *Journal de psychologie* (1956), 333–354.
101. Other propositions in J. Vansina, "Once Upon a Time: Oral Traditions as History in Africa," *Daedalus* 2 (1971); C. H. Perrot and E. Terray, "Tradition orale et chronologie," *Annals E.S.C.* (1977), 326–331.
102. Fr. C. Bartlett, "Psychology in Relation to the Popular Story," *Folklore* (1920), 264–293; *Psychology and Primitive Culture* (Cambridge, 1923); *Remembering* (Cambridge, 1932); "Some Experiments on the Reproduction of Folk-Stories," reprinted in A. Dundes, *The Study of Folklore* (New York, 1965).
103. J. Goody and I. Watt, "The Consequences of Literacy," *Comparative Studies in Society and History* (1963), 304–345, reprinted in *Literacy in Traditional Societies*, ed. J. Goody (Cambridge, 1968), 27–68; "Mémoire et apprentissage dans les sociétés avec et sans écriture: La transmission du Bagre," *L'homme* 17 (1977), 1, 29–52; *The Domestication of the Savage Mind* (Cambridge, 1977) (French trans. I. Bazin and A. Bensa, under the title *La raison graphique: La domestication de la pensée sauvage* [Paris, 1979]).
104. M. Mauss, *Œuvres* (Paris, 1969), 3:328–338 (= *Fragment d'un plan de sociologie générale descriptive*, 1934).
105. Ibid., 336. Regarding the Indo-European world, G. Dumézil has always emphasized the important role of powerful priestly groups engaged in maintaining tradition and trained to transmit the ideal corpus of myths, rituals, and sacred terms. Those he calls "the administrators of the collective memory and thought" (*Heur et malheur de guerrier* [Paris, 1969], 48–50).
106. M. Mauss, *Œuvres*, 3:144; 311.
107. Ibid., 2:269–272 (= *Introduction aux mythes*, 1903); 2:209–211 (= *L'art et le mythe d'après*, M. Wundt, 1908).
108. M. Halbwachs, *Les cadres sociaux de la mémoire* (Paris, 1925); *La Mémoire collective* (Paris, 1950), in particular, 78. Cf. comments by I. Meyerson, 336.
109. Cf. P. Mercier, "Histoire et légende: La bataille d'Ilorin," *Notes africaines* 47 (1950), 92–95.
110. J. Goody and I. Watt, 307 (= *Literacy in Traditional Societies*, ed. J. Goody, 30–31).
111. L. Bohannan, "A Genealogical Charter," *Africa* 23 (1952), 301–315. Cf. J. Goody and I. Watt, 309–311 (= *Literacy in Traditional Societies*, ed. J. Goody, 32–34).
112. M. Mauss, *Manuel d'ethnographie* (Paris, 1947), 98.
113. Ibid., 97; R. Finnegan, *Oral Poetry: Its Nature, Significance and Social Context* (Cambridge, 1977), 102–109; J. Dournes, *Le parler des Joraï et le style oral de leur expression* (*Publications de la Société des Orientalistes de France*) (Paris, 1977), 176.
114. J. Goody, *La raison graphique* (Paris, 1979), 204–209.
115. J. Goody, "Mémoire et apprentissage dans les sociétés avec et sans écriture: La transmission du Bagré," *L'homme* (1977), 29–52. Notwithstand-

ing a heavy semiotic apparatus, one may find an attempt at an analysis of "open" truth in R. Mayer, *Les transformations de la tradition narrative à l'île Wallis (Uvea)* (Publications de la société des Océanistes, no. 38) (Paris, 1976).

116. As Cl. Lévi-Strauss says without more ado in *Anthropologie structurale deux* (Paris, 1973), 78.

117. This "plot" Aristotle will be the first to call *muthos* in the *Poetics*. Cf. J. Bompaire, "Le mythe selon la *Poétique* d'Aristote," in *Formation et survie des mythes* (Paris, 1977), 31–36.

118. L. Renou, *Sanscrit et culture* (Paris, 1950), 34–39. Cf. the comments of P. Kiparsky, "Oral Poetry: Some Linguistic and Typological Considerations," in *Oral Literature and the Formula*, ed. B. A. Stolz and R. S. Shannon III (Ann Arbor, 1976), 100–103.

119. Cf. J. Filiozat, "Les écritures indiennes: Le monde indien et son système graphique," in *L'écriture et la psychologie des peuples* (Centre international de synthèse) (Paris, 1963), 147–166.

120. R. Jakobson and P. Bogatyrev, *Le folklore, forme spécifique de la création* [1929], reprinted in R. Jakobson, *Questions de poétique*, trans. under the direction of Tz. Todorov (Paris, 1973), 59–72.

121. Cf. H. R. Jauss, *Pour une esthétique de la réception*, French transl. Cl. Maillard (Paris, 1978).

122. Cl. Lévi-Strauss, *Mythologiques IV: L'homme nu* (Paris, 1971), 560. And development by D. Sperber, (*Le structuralisme en anthropologie* [1968], 2d ed. (Paris, 1973), 114–116; *Le symbolisme en général* (Paris, 1974), 90–94.

Chapter Three

1. S. Moravia, *La scienzia dell'uomo nel settecento* (1970), 2d ed. (Bari, 1978); J. Copans and J. Jamin, *Aux origines de l'anthropologie française: Les memoires de la Société des Observateurs de l'Homme en l'an VIII* (Paris, 1978), 127–169: "Considérations sur les diverses méthodes à suivre dans l'observation des peuples sauvages," par Joseph-Marie de Gérando.

2. J. Copans and J. Jamin, 151.

3. Ibid., 166.

4. Ibid., 165–166.

5. Ibid., 166.

6. Ibid., 169.

7. This is Jan Vansina's reasoning, in 1960 (cf. pp. 33–34, above).

8. Cf. Chapter 1, above.

9. So discreet in the literature of the Société des Observateurs de l'Homme.

10. A. Lang, *Mythes, cultes et religions* [1889], French trans. L Marillier and A. Dirr (Paris, 1896), 13. Cf. A. Lang, *La mythologie*, trans. L. Parmentier (Paris, 1886), 8–9.

11. A. Lang, *Mythes, cultes et religions*, 5.

12. "The Greeks themselves were scandalized by the myths that are a great shock to religious feeling as well as to logical thought, by attributing to

the gods ridiculous and obscene acts and even a nature in contradiction with what mankind longs for in divinity": M.-J. Lagrange, *Études sur les religions sémitiques*, 2d ed. (Paris, 1905), 30.

13. Cf. p. 63 ff., below.

14. Reference marks in E. Hoffmann, *Que ratione epos, mythos, ainos, logos et vocabula ab eisdem stirpibus derivata in antiquo Graecorum sermone (usque ad annum fere 400) adhibita sint* (diss., Göttingen, 1922); H. Fournier, *Les verbes "dire" en grec ancien* (Paris, 1946); L. Müller, *Wort und Begriff Mythos im klassichen Griechisch* (diss., Hamburg, 1953) (typescript which Br. Snell kindly gave me permission to read); K. Kerényi, "Qu'est-ce que la mythologie?" in K. Kerényi, *La religion antique: Ses lignes fondamentales*, trans. Y. Le Lay (Geneva, 1957), 17–42.

15. *Poetae melici graeci*, ed. D. L. Page (1962), 353 (= F. 21 B. Gentili, 1958). The best commentary in G. Perrotta and B. Gentili, *Polinnia: Poesia greca arcaica*, 2d ed. (Messina-Florence, 1965), 230–231. On the forms of tyranny at Samos and the chronology of "Polycrates": J. P. Barron, "The Sixth-Century Tyranny at Samos," *Classical Quarterly* 14 (1964), 210–224.

16. *Fragmente der griechischen Historiker* (= *FGrHist*), 544F1 Jacoby.

17. In which the poet of Samos differs from the historian S. Mazzarino.

18. Herodotus 3.44–45.

19. Suggested by P. Chantraine, *Dictionnaire étymologique de la langue grecque* (Paris, 1968), 3:719.

20. On *stásis*, cf. N. Loraux, "L'oubli dans la cité," in *Le temps de la réflexion* (Paris, 1980), 1:222–242.

21. Hesychius, s.v. "*mutharchoi*." (Trans. note: *pecheurs*—transgressors, sinners—is followed in next paragraph by a pun using the word in its meaning of *fishermen*.)

22. *Iliade* 9.443.

23. Cf. É. Benveniste, *Noms d'agent et noms d'action en indo-européen* (Paris, 1948), 52–54.

24. Xenophanes, frag. 1.13–14 Diels-Kranz. Cf. M. Marcovitch, "Xenophanes on Drinking-Parties and Olympic Games," *Illinois Classical Studies* 3 (1978), 1–16. But there is no reason, as M. Marcovitch (9) suggests, to distinguish, in the "hymn" to the god, between the *muthos* which would be the content, and the *logos*, the verbal expression.

25. Xenophanes frag. 1.21–22.

26. Parmenides frag. 8.1–2; 50–51 Diels-Kranz.

27. Empedocles frag. 17.14 Diels-Kranz.

28. Empedocles frag. 23.9–11. On the difficulty of making a clear-cut division between *muthos* and *logos* in the works of Empedocles, cf. M. Simondon, "La muse d'Empédocle: Patronage mythique des formes de savoir," in *Formation et survie des mythes* (Paris, 1977), 21–29.

29. Aeschylus frag. 231 Mette.

30. Herodotus 2.135 and 143.

31. Hesiod, *Les travaux et les jours*, 106. Here, on the very subtle distinction between *logos* and myth, there has been, for over three quarters of a

century, a difference of opinion between modern interpreters on the subject of the logic of mythic thought or the relationships between philosophic and rational thought and the opposite pertaining to a primordial mythology.

32. *Alathēs logos*: Pindar, *Olympiques* 1.45. Pindar explicitly defines his song and his panegyric to the victor by the word *logos* (*Olympiques* 1.45; 7.38; 9.54; *Pythiques* 2.123; *Nemeennes* 1.51–52; 3.49; 4.51, 116) whose function is sometimes eulogistic, sometimes censorious, on the plane of Memory and Forgetting. Cf. M. Detienne, *Les maîtres de vérite* [1967], 2d ed. (Paris, 1973), 21–24.

33. Pindar, *Nemeennes* 7.39–58.

34. Ibid., 8.55. Cf. M. Detienne, 67–68.

35. Pindar, *Nemeennes* 7.29–44.

36. Ibid., 7.33–34.

37. Pindar, *Olympiques* 1.44–81.

38. Ibid., 1.75–81.

39. Ibid., 1.43–45.

40. Ibid., 1.46–47; *dedaidalmenoi pseudesi poikilois / expatonti muthoi.*

41. Ibid., 1.54.

42. Cf. Fr. Hartog, *Le miroir d'Hérodote: Essai sur la représentation de l'autre* (Paris, 1980), 271–302.

43. Cf. Herodotus 2.48, 51, 62, 81. Egypt seems to preempt those "sacred tales" as though the Greeks had none. The latter relate "myths" about those very Egyptians.

44. J. Rudhardt says in "Cohérence et incohérence de la structure mythique: Sa fonction symbolique," *Diogène* 72 (1972), 46; "In fact, the Greek calls the mythic tale a *hieros logos*, a sacred logos." Immediate advantage: the myth would be a form of rational thought which the Greeks, in their wisdom, must have recognized as being by nature irreducible to conceptual analysis.

45. Herodotus 2.37.

46. Ibid., 2.38.

47. Ibid., 2.39–41.

48. Ibid., 2.43–44.

49. Ibid., 2.45.

50. *FGrHist* 3F17 Jacoby.

51. *Panyassis of Halikarnassos: Text and Commentary*, by Victor J. Matthews (Leyde, 1974), 21–26, 126–128.

52. Herodotus 2.45.

53. Ibid., 2.45: *euēthēs de autōn kai hode ho muthos esti ton peri tou Hērakleos leguosi* . . .

54. Ibid., 2.45.

55. Cf. I. Meyerson and M. Dambuyant, "Un type de raisonnement da justification," *Journal de psychologie* (1946), 386–404.

56. Herodotus 2.45.

57. Ibid., 2.19.

58. Ibid., 2.20.

59. Ibid., 2.20: *sēmēnai* contrasted with *mnēsthēnai*.
60. Ibid., 2.21.
61. Ibid., 2.21: *thōmasiōterē*.
62. Ibid., 2.22.
63. Ibid., 2.23: *es aphanes ton muthon* . . .
64. Ibid., 2.23.
65. Ibid., 2.52–53.
66. Who, in his *Periegesis*, posited the circularity of the river Ocean whence the Argonauts proceeded to the Nile (*FGrHist* 1F302c Jacoby).
67. Aristotle, *De la generation des animaux* 3.5.756b5–10.
68. Thucydides 1.21.1; 1.22.4.
69. Cf. Chapter 4, pp. 63–81, below.
70. Cf. R. Drews, *The Greek Accounts of Eastern History* (Washington, 1973).
71. Thucydides 1.1.1–2.
72. J. de Romilly, *Histoire et raison chez Thucydide* (Paris, 1956); L. Gernet, "Thucydide et l'histoire," *Annales E.S.C.* (1965), 570–575.
73. Thucydides 2.41.1–2.
74. J. de Romilly, 261–266; "Thucydide et l'idée de progrès," *Annali della Scuola Normale Superiore di Pisa, Lettere e Filsofia* (1966), 143–191.
75. Plutarch, *Life of Theseus* 1.5. To make history by removing the part played by the "mythic" is a procedure, a historian's way of writing which awaits its historian. A long story, from Dicéarque (frag. 49 F. Wehrli) to M. I. Finley (*Le monde d'Ulysse*, 105).
76. Cf. R. Weil, "Les documents dans l'oeuvre de Thucydide," *L'information litteraire* (1974), 24–32.
77. Cf. P. Huart, *Le vocabulaire de l'analyse psychologique dans l'œuvre de Thucydide* (Paris, 1968), 222; D. Kurz, *Akribeia: Das Ideal der Exaktheit bei den Griechen bis Aristoteles* (diss., Göttingen, 1970), 40–61.
78. Thucydides 1.22.1. E. Martineau, "A Philological 'Undecidable' (Thucydides 1.22.1)," *Les études philosophiques* (1977), 347–367, has given this text a reading that takes it at face value but which requires M. Heidegger, reinforced by Aristotle, at last to do justice to the first inventor of "historicity as such" (357–358).
79. Thucydides 1.22.3.
80. Ibid., 1.20.1.
81. Ibid., 1.20.2.
82. Ibid., 1.20.3.
83. Ibid., 1.20.3: *ta hetoima*.
84. Ibid., 2.54.1.
85. Ibid., 2.54.2–3. Old men still are at work (*presbuteroi*). It is true that "myths" follow them like their shadow (cf. pp. 96–98, below), and that they seriously threaten both "historicity" and the *République*.
86. Thucydides 2.54.3.
87. Ibid., 1.73.2.
88. Ibid., 1.20.3.
89. Ibid., 1.20.1.

90. Despite the "attenuating circumstances" sought by H. Verdin, "Notes on the Attitude of the Greek Historians with Respect to Local Tradition," *Ancient Society* 1 (1970), 191–194. No doubt there is, in 1.9.2, apropos of Pelops, an allegation of accounts given by those on the Peloponnesus who collected the most accepted tradition from previous generations (*ta saphestata . . . mnēmēi para tōn proteron*). But *archaeology* cannot dispense with them in an effort to construct an intelligible model for discussion of the present of Athens anymore than with evidence given by Homer invoked to confirm what Thucydides already knows through the efficacy of his model (H. Verdin, "Les remarques critiques d'Hérodote et de Thucydide sur la poésie en tant que source historique," *Mélanges W. Peremans* [Leyde, 1977], 70). The censure expressed in 1.20.1 retains all its pith on the threshold of the new history when it calls itself *ktēma . . . es aiei* in 1.22.4.

91. Thucydides 1.21.1.

92. Ibid., 1.21.1.

93. Ibid., 1.22.4. Cf. B. Gentili and G. Cerri, *Le teorie del discorso storico nel pensiero greco e la storiografia romana arcaica* (Rome, 1975), 25, and n. 23.

94. *FGrHist* 552F2 Jacoby.

95. Thucydides 1.22.4.

96. F. Jacoby, *Atthis: The Local Chronicles of Ancient Athens* (Oxford, 1949), 216.

97. Cf. pp. 88–89, below.

98. Herodotus 1, Proème.

99. Herodotus 8.144, for example. Cf. G. Nenci, "Significato etico-polifico ed economico-sociale delle guerre persiane" in *Storia e civiltà dei Greci*, vol. 3, *La Grecia nell'età di Pericle: Storia, letteratura, filosofia*, ed. R. Bianchi Bandinelli (Milan, 1979), 3:12–16.

100. Herodotus 4.166; in the event, mnēmosunon heōutou.

101. Ibid., 2.135.

102. Ibid., 7.24.

103. Ibid., 2.148.

104. Ibid., 2.110.

105. Ibid., 7.226.

106. Ibid., 6.109.

107. Ibid., 2.155.

108. Ibid., 2.20: *sēmēnai* as opposed to *mnēsthēnai*.

109. Cf. pp. 50–52 above.

110. Remarkable resume by O. Longo, "Scrivere in Tucidide: Communicazione e ideologia," *Mélanges A. Ardizzoni* (Rome, 1978), 519–544.

111. Thucydides, 7.8.2–3.

112. Ibid., 7.8.1.

113. Ibid., 7.8.2.

114. Ibid., 7.10.

115. Ibid., 7.8.2.

116. Cf. J. Latacz, *Zum Wortfeld, "Freude" in der Sprache Homers* (Heidelberg, 1966), 174–219.

117. Thucydides 2.65.8 (*hēdonē*).

118. J. de Romilly, "La condamnation du plaisir dans l'œuvre de Thucydide," *Wiener Studien* 79 (1966), 142–148.

119. Thucydides 7.14.4.

120. Ibid., 2.87.4.

121. P. Huart, *Le vocabulaire de l'analyse psychologique dans l'œuvre de Thucydide* (Paris, 1968), 229–230, 304–310. On the art of memory and opportunity, cf. M. de Certeau, *L'invention du quotidien*, vol. 1, *Arts de faire* (Paris, 1980), 156–167.

122. Thucydides 2.41.3–4. With regard to all the questions evoked by the funeral oration and a beautiful death we must now refer to N. Loraux, *L'invention d'Athènes* (Paris, 1981).

123. Thucydides 2.41.2.

124. Ibid., 2.41.4.

125. Ibid., 2.43.2.

126. Ibid., 2.43.3; *agraphos mnēmē.*

127. Ibid., 2.43.2: "Their glory will last forever in memory at every juncture when speech and action come into play."

128. Ibid., 7.69.2.

129. Cf. pp. 88–89, below.

130. Cf. pp. 3–7, above.

131. P. Huart, 167, n. 1: instead of *historia* and of *historein.*

132. Thucydides 8.67.1. Cf. G. Busolt-H. Swoboda, *Griechische Staatskunde*, 3d ed. (Munich, 1920), 1:70–78; 2:460–462.

133. L. Gernet, "Introduction to Plato," *Les lois*, 2 vols. (Paris, 1951), clxxxv–clxxxvi: the *sungraphē*, a promise in writing, in *Les lois*, foreshadows *praxin pasan.*

134. Theophrastus frag. 91 Wimmer.

Chapter Four

1. Xenophon, *L'art de la chasse*, ed. E. Delebecque, 5.5–6.

2. Ibid., 5.20.

3. Cf. n. 1.

4. Xenophanes frag. 11 Diels-Kranz.

5. Xenophanes frag. 19–24 Diels-Kranz. With a few modifications I adopt the version of J. Svenbro, *La parole et le marbre: Aux origines de la poétique grecque* (Lund, 1976), 103 and n. 137.

6. Cf. J. Defradas, "Le banquet de Xénophane," *Revue des études grecques* (1962), 344–365. Critiques in M. Marcovich, "Xenophanes on Drinking-Parties and Olympic Games," *Illinois Classical Studies* 3 (1978), 1–16.

7. Xenophanes frag. 1.1–12 Diels-Kranz.

8. Xenophanes frag. 2.11–12 Diels-Kranz.

9. Xenophanes frag. 2.20–22 Diels-Kranz.

10. Xenophanes frag. 6.15 Diels-Kranz.

11. Even if the Giants are defeated, as well as the Titans, by the

Olympians who bring about world order because of the immoderation of their opponents: F. Vian, *La guerre des geants: Le mythe avant l'époque hellénistique* (Paris, 1952), 286–287.

12. Cf. J. Svenbro, 104, n. 138.

13. Xenophanes frag. 10 Diels-Kranz.

14. Cf. M. Foucault, "Qu'est-ce qu'un auteur?" *Bulletin de la Société française de philosophie* (1969), 73–104.

15. Cf. J. Svenbro, 81–82.

16. Cf. Xenophanes 21A32 Diels-Kranz.

17. Xenophanes frag. 15 Diels-Kranz.

18. Cf. pp. 44–45, above.

19. Hieronymus of Rhodes frag. 42 Wehrli. Cf. M. Detienne, *Homère, Hésiode et Pythagore* (Brussels, 1962), 26.

20. J. Svenbro, 107–138, shows the relation between Theagenes and Xenophanes and supplies useful references.

21. Heraclitus frag. 104 Diels-Kranz.

22. Cf. J. Svenbro, 110–111.

23. Cf. B. Gentili and G. Cerri, "L'idea di biografia nel pensiero greco," *Quaderni Urbinati* (1978), 14–15.

24. Cf. F. Lasserre, "L'historiographie grecque à l'époque archaïque," *Quaderni di Storia* (1976), 127–130.

25. Cf. P. Ricoeur, *De l'interprétation: Essai sur Freud* (Paris, 1965), 30–31.

26. Like H. P. Grice, "Logique et conversation" [1975] in *Communications* 30 (1979), 57–72, followed by Tz. Todorov, *Symbolisme et interprétation* (Paris, 1978), 25–27.

27. In particular, D. Sperber, *Le symbolisme en général* (Paris, 1974), 29–62.

28. Cf. pp. 35–41, below.

29. Cl. Lévi-Strauss, *Mythologiques* (Paris, 1971), 4:585.

30. Another, still more scriptural, is in the Old Testament, for linguistic reasons of a consonantal text whose tradition, through scribes, determines the vocality as well as the meaning. Cf. J. Koenig, "L'activité herméneutique des scribes dans la transmission du texte de l'Ancien Testament," *Revue de l'histoire des religions* (1962), 2:141–174; "Le texte de la Bible," in *Vérité et poésie de la Bible* (collected work) (Paris, 1969), 275–289; "L'existence et l'influence d'une herméneutique sur la transmission du texte hébreu de la Bible," *Bulletin de la Société E. Renan* (= *Revue de l'histoire des religions* [1974], 122–125), 8–11.

31. Thucydides 1.21.1.

32. Herodotus 2.134, 2.143, 5.36, 5.125.

33. Hecataeus of Miletus, *FGrHist* 1F1a Jacoby.

34. Herodotus 5.30.

35. Ibid., 5.36.

36. This is what M. Vegetti discerned, "Nascita del scienziato," *Belgafor* 28 (1973), 647.

37. Herodotus 5.49.
38. Hecataeus of Miletus, *FGrHist* 1F36–359 Jacoby.
39. Hecataeus of Miletus, *FGrHist* 1F1–35 Jacoby.
40. Hecataeus of Miletus, *FGrHist* 1F1*a* Jacoby.
41. Cf. G. Nenci, "Il sigillo di Teognide," *Rivista di Filologia e di Instruzione Classica* 41 (1963): 30–37.
42. Cf. J. Svenbro, 186–209. But nothing indicates that those accounts are for sale like a piece of pottery nor that this disucssion about the "He" and the "I" stems from mental derangement. The social status of the Milesian "maker of accounts" escapes us completely.
43. Thus the Egyptian priests enumerate the names of 330 other kings but, under the circumstances, according to a book (*bublos*): Herodotus 2.100. Herodotus's Egyptians are, simultaneously, they who, more than any other men, exercise their memory the most (2.77) and are the only ones to make a count of years in writing (2.145).
44. Cf. Charles H. Kahn, *Anaximander and the Origins of Greek Cosmology* (New York, 1960), 81–84. In Hecataeus of Miletus, *FGrHist* 1T12*a* Jacoby, the same sentence can be translated in terms of the double meaning of *graphein*: Anaximander dared to describe the inhabited world on a tablet or else had the audacity to draw a map of it.
45. Hecataeus of Miletus, *FGrHist* 1F1*a* Jacoby.
46. This phenomen of the plurality of narratives emphasized by G. Nenci, "Ecateo de Mileto e la questione del suo razionalismo," *Rendiconti dell'Accademia Nazionale dei Lincei, Cl. Scienze Moral. Stor. Filos.*, series 8, vol. 6, nos. 1–2 (1951), 51–58, does not necessarily imply that Hecataeus seeks "myth with one version only."
47. *Histoire des animaux* 9.23 (= Hecataeus of Miletus, *FGrHist* 1T8 Jacoby).
48. Hecataeus of Miletus, *FGrHist*1F26 Jacoby. The second version is adopted by Hesiod, *Theogony*, 287–294.
49. Cf. Herodotus 4.8.
50. Hecataeus of Miletus, *FGrHist* 1F26 Jacoby.
51. Hecataeus of Miletus, *FGrHist* 1F27 Jacoby (= Pausanias 3.25.4–5).
52. *Pap. Caire* 65741 = *Scholies à Antimaque*, ed. Wyss, col. 2, 26 ff., p. 83. Expanded by Jacoby in *FGrHist*, suppl. vol. 1, 2d ed. (1957) (1. Addenda), 1F27*b*.
53. A. Rivier, "Remarques sur les fragments 34 et 35 of Xenophanes," *Revue de philologie* 30 (1956), 37–61 (taken up again in *Études de littérature grecque*, ed. F. Lasserre and J. Sulliger [Geneva, 1975], 337–367).
54. *Iliad*, 20.203–204.
55. *Iliad*, 6.245–211. For a genealogical note on so-called feudal societies: G. Duby, "Remarques sur la littérature généalogique en France aux XIe et XIIe siècles," in *Hommes et structures du Moyen Âge* (Paris, 1973), 287–298; "Mémoires sans historien," *Nouvelle revue de psychanalyse* 15 (1977), 213–220.
56. Cf. J. Schwartz, *Psuedo-Hesiodeia: Recherches sur la composition, la*

diffusion et la disparition ancienne d'œuvres attribuées à Hésiode (Leyde, 1960), 265–548, 629.

57. Cf. D. W. Prakken, *Studies in Greek Genealogical Chronology* (diss., Columbia, 1943).

58. Herodotus 2.143.

59. Ibid.

60. Ibid., 2.144.

61. Ibid., 2.77, 2.145.

62. Ibid., 3.122. Cf. P. Vidal-Naquet, *Le chasseur noir* (Paris, 1981), 81–82.

63. Cf. Cl. Préaux, "L'élargissement de l'espace et du temps dans la pensée grecque," *Bulletin de l'Académie royale de Belgique, Classe des Lettres, Sciences morales et politiques* 54, series 5 (1968), 208–267.

64. Cf. S. Mazzarino, *Il pensiero storico classico* (Bari, 1966), 1:211–212. Only very slowly do the Greek cities adopt a chronological system based on magistrates or annual priesthoods: the eponymous archontate is only obligatory at the top of a decree beginning with the fourth century B.C. Cf. D. Van Berchem, "L'éponymie d'Idalion," in *Chypre: des origines au Moyen Âge* (Geneva: University of Geneva, Séminaire interdisciplinaire, 1975 [ronéoté]), 69.

65. Hecataeus of Miletus, *FGrHist* 1F119 Jacoby.

66. Ibid., *FGrHist* 1F15 Jacoby.

67. Dionysius of Halicarnassas, *Essay on Thucydides*, chap. 8, ed. comment. G. Pavano, (Palermo, 1958), 20–22. We have underlined the nodal sentences. A lecture confident of those beginnings of history by S. Gozzoli, "Una teoria antica sull'origine della storiografia greca," *Studi classici e orientali* 19–20, (1970–1971), 158–211. Cf. also the notes on chap. 5, edited by the historian W. Kendrick Pritchett, *Dionysius of Halicarnassus. On Thucydides* (Berkeley, 1975), 50–55.

68. In as exemplary a way as revealed to Solon in Egypt according to Plato, *Timaeus* 23a1–5.

69. Dionysius of Halicarnassus, chap. 7.

70. Grammatically, *graphai* is placed with *mnēmai*. And Dionysius does not separate spoken from written tradition, contrary to what H. Verdin suggests in "Notes sur l'attitude des historiens grecs à l'égard de la tradition locale," *Ancient Society* 1 (1970), 199–200. In *The Laws* 5.741c6–7, in order to keep intact the initial division of city lands, Plato recommends placing in sanctuaries "memoranda" (*mnēmai*) of cypress, written (*katagragegrammenai*) for times to come. Even slipping from traditional memory to written memory, here and there. In the same sense Callimachus frag. 75.54–55 Pfeiffer evokes the "mythological memorial" (*mnēmē . . . muthologos*) in which Xenomedes of Ceos, one of the historians on Dionysius's list, tells the love story of Akontios and Kudippe. A story probably written in a "foundation" or an "archaeology" of his city (F. Jacoby, *Fragmente der griechischen Historiker* 3.*b*1955, Kommentar zu 442.288–290).

71. Cf. A. Momigliano, "Tradition and the Classical Historian" (1972),

in *Quinto contributo alla storia degli studi classici e del mondo antico* 1 (Rome, 1975), 23–25; and F. Lasserre, "L'historiographie grecque à l'époque archaïque," *Quaderni di Storia* 2 (1976), 118–119.

72. S. Gozzoli looks to the Orient and its influnce on the earliest historiography of the Greeks for substantiation of Dionysius's theory ("Una teoria antica sull'origine della storiografia greca," *Studi classici e orientali* 19–20, (1970–71), 179–189.

73. Chr. Blinkenberg, *Lindos: Fouilles de l'Acropole* (1902–1904), vol. 2, *Inscriptions* (Berlin and Copenhagen, 1941), n. 2.

74. Cf. F. Jacoby, *Atthis: The Local Chronicles of Ancient Athens* (Oxford, 1949), 180–181.

75. The "forgeries of myths" (*muthica . . . plasmata*), Dionysius of Halicarnassus explains (*Essai sur Thucydide*, chap. 7), are the natural productions of memory in all societies in which tales are transmitted which are inseparable from cities and other places.

76. Cf. 88–89, below.

77. Admirable first historians who assign to themselves the mission of preserving native traditions faithfully! *Sic*, H. Verdin, 1:200. Bearing witness, himself, to another historiography in which the Greeks are "the gods of our history" (M. de Certeau).

78. For example, the Delians's decree in honor of the poet Demoteles, son of Aischylos of Andros: he wrote "local myths" (IG, 11.544.7-8 = Dittenberger, *Sylloge*, 3d ed., 382.7-8).

79. Inversely, in another passage, Tylor is to ask historians, experts in "facts," to unravel myths from the chronicle, in order to delete from true history the excrescence, mythology (pp. 12–13, above).

80. Cf. H. Van Effenterre, "Le contrat de travail du scribe Spensithios," *Bulletin de correspondance hellénique* (1973), 31–46. In "Phoenician" letters or in "red" letters? Cf. the discussions of P. Chantraine, "À propos du nom des Phéniciens et des noms de la pourpre," *Studii Clasice* (1972), 7–15; and of G. Patrick Edwards–Ruth B. Edwards, "Red Letters and Phoenician Writing," *Kadmos* (1974–1975), 48–57.

81. A. Momigliano, "Tradition and the Classical Historian" (1972), in *Quinto contributo alla storia degli studi classici e del mondo antico* 1 (Rome, 1975), 30–31. True, Momigliano indicates distance, at the same time: the historian, who is not a public functionary, would only account for events of his choosing. A more subtle judgment than that of the following note.

82. A Momigliano, "Storiografia su tradijione scritta e storiografia su tradijione orale" (1961–1962), in *Terzo contributo alla storia degli studi classici e del mondo antico* 1 (Rome, 1966), 14–15 (praise of Herodotus).

83. As R. Drews says, "The Greek Accounts of Eastern History" (Washington, 1973), 133.

84. K. von Fritz, *Die griechiesche Geschichtsscheibung*, vol. 1, *Von den Anfängen bis Thukydides* (Berlin, 1967), 48–76.

85. F. Lasserre, "L'historiographie grecque à l'époque archaïque," *Quaderni di storia* (1976), 118–119.

86. Herodotus 4.36.

87. Ibid., 2.20–23.
88. Theophrastus, *Characters* 8.

Chapter Five

1. The survey would have been awkward to do without the material supplied by the exhaustive index of L. Brandwood, *A Word Index to Plato* (Leeds, 1976). We have also benefited by the studies of Luc Brisson on *muthos* and his compendium of the corpus of Plato's work.

2. *Philebus* 14*a*3–5. Mythology is filled with contradictory tales: *Republic* 2.380*c*3.

3. *Politics* 304*c*10–*d*3.

4. *Greater Hippias* 286*a*1–2.

5. *Sophist* 234*c*4–7.

6. *Phaedrus* 229*c*4–5.

7. Ibid., 230*a*2.

8. *Laws* 10.887*c*8–*e*1.

9. Pluche, *Le spectacle de la nature*, new ed. 1750, vol. 8, pt. 2, 348 (according to B. Groethuysen, *Origines de l'esprit bourgeois en France* [1927] [Paris, 1977], 6).

10. *Laws* 10.887*d*4.

11. Ibid., 10.887*d*5–*e*1.

12. Cf. J. Pouillon, *Fétiches sans fétichisme* (Paris, 1975), 155–160.

13. *Phaedrus* 274*c*1–3.

14. *Odyssey* 8.550 ff.

15. Ibid., 11.368.

16. Ibid., 7.240–297.

17. Ibid., 12.450–453.

18. Ibid., 1.351–352.

19. *Politics* 268*e*4–10.

20. *Republic* 2.377*a*4–5.

21. *Laws* 7.808*d*5–8.

22. *Republic* 2.378*d*–*e*.

23. Ibid., 377*d*6.

24. *Laws* 3.680*d*3.

25. *Republic* 3.387*b*8–*c*3.

26. Ibid., 3.394*b*–*c*. Cf. Thucydides 1.21.1.

27. Ibid., 3.392*a*3–8. Cf. V. Goldschmidt, *Questions platoniciennes* (Paris, 1970), 141–159.

28. Two versions: *Timaeus* 21*a*5–25*e*1; *Critias* 108*c*8–110*b*4.

29. Herodotus 2.178.

30. Cf. K. Kerényi, *La religion antique: Ses lignes fondamentales*, trans. Y. Le Lay (Geneva, 1957), 98–117.

31. *Timaeus* 22*a*1–6.

32. *Aux origines de l'anthropologie française: Les mémoires de la Société des Observateurs de l'Homme en l'an VIII.* Tests published and presented by J. Copans and J. Jamin (Paris, 1978).

33. *Timaeus* 22b3–9.

34. Ibid., b1–2: *muthologein* associated with *genealogein* and paraphrasing *ta archaiotata legein*, that is, the *archaiologia* in which the sophist Hippias excels (*Hippias Majeur* 285d–e).

35. Ibid., 22d7–23a5.

36. Ibid., 23a9–b1.

37. *Critias* 109d6–e1.

38. Ibid., 109e3–110a3.

39. Ibid., 110a6–7.

40. *Timaeus* 23c3.

41. *Critias* 110a2–3.

42. Ibid., 110a3–6.

43. *Timaeus* 22b4–5.

44. Ibid., 22a6–b3.

45. In ibid., 26e5–6, Socrates recognizes a *logos* of truth, not a fictional *muthos* which has been molded (*plastheis*). Critias's discourse establishes the authenticity of the tale in *The Republic*, told, at least in part, as a *muthos* of leisure (2.376d11–12; cf. *Timaeus* 26c9).

46. *Greater Hippias* 285d–e; Philostratus, *Vie des Sophistes* 1.11.3 = T2 in *Sofisti*, ed. Untersteiner (Florence, 1953), 3:40.

47. Cf. pp. 74–75, above.

48. *Greater Hippias* 286a1–2.

49. Semonides T97 West = *FGrHist* 543T1 Jacoby. Cf. F. Lasserre, "L'historiographie grecque à l'époque archaïque," *Quaderni di Storia* 2 (1976), 113–142. According to E. Norden (*Agnostos Theos* [Berlin, 1913], 370–374), the Sophists of the fifth century created a genre centered on cultural history.

50. Phanodemus is the author of a work called *Attikē Archaiologia.* Cf. F. Jacoby, *Atthis: The Local Chronicles of Ancient Athens* (Oxford, 1949), 83–84. Ancient stories must be differentiated from invented myths (*muthoi . . . peplasmenoi*): Diodorus 2.44.3; 2.46.6. Cf. Also A. E. Wardman, "Myth in Greek Historiography," *Historia* 9 (1960), 408.

51. *Greater Hippias* 286a1–2.

52. *Laws* 11:913a3–c 3. "Myth" appears here in the plural, *hoi . . . legomenoi muthoi*, and in the words "De tels gains ne profitent pas aux descendants."

53. *Laws* 9.872c7–e4.

54. Ibid, 9.865d3–866a1.

55. Ibid., 4.719c1.

56. *Republic* 2.381e1–5.

57. *Schol. Aristophanes, Paix, 758; Comm. anon. in Aristot. graeca* (Berlin, 1892), 20:427, 1.38–40. Cf. Aristophanes, *Guêpes*, 1179.

58. Cf. *Republic* 3.392a9 (*peri anthrōpōn . . .*); a6 (*muthologein*).

59. Cf. *Timaeus* 22a7–b1.

60. Aristophanes, *Lysistrata*, 781–794. Cf. P. Vidal-Naquet, *Le chasseur noir* (Paris, 1981), 151–174.

61. *Lysistrata*, 806–820.

62. *Laws* 4.719c1.
63. *Republic* 3.401b2.
64. Ibid., 3.401b8–d2.
65. *Laws*, 1.638c5–8.
66. *Republic*, 3.386c4.
67. Hesiod, *Works and Days*, 764.
68. Pausanias 1.17.1. Cf. Voigt, s.v. "Pheme, *Real-Encylopädie der classischen Altertumswissenschaft*" (1938), col. 1954–1955.
69. Hesiod, *Works and Days*, 763–764.
70. In thirty-seven instances in the body of Plato's work, twenty-two in *Laws*.
71. *Laws* 2.672b3.
72. Ibid., 4.713c2.
73. *Cratylus* 395e5.
74. *Laws* 2.672b3; *huporrein*.
75. Ibid., 10.906c1.
76. *Apology* 18c1.
77. *Laws* 7.822c4.
78. Or evil tongues which are the tongues of women, *gunaikeioi phēmai* (*Laws* 11.934e7–935a2), when shrews insult each other without a real debate taking place.
79. To permit to escape, to scatter, *kataskedannunai*: the same verb in Plato, *Apology* 18c1, and in Hesiod, *Works and Days*, 95.
80. *Timaeus* 72b3. Cf. the *manteias phēmē*: *Laws* 7.792d3.
81. *Philebus* 16c8.
82. *Laws* 12.966c5. And the *phēmai* who represent the basic maxims sing *humnein* to children: *Republic* 5.463d6–7. In the *Laws* 7.799e10–12, Plato plays on the double meaning of *nomos*: the ancients gave the name of *nome* to the tunes played on the zither, songs sung at public gatherings (F. Lasserre, *Plutarque: De la musique*, ed. trans. comm., [Lausanne, 1954], 22–27).
83. *Laws*, 1.625a–b.
84. Ibid., 1.624b2.
85. Ibid., 8.836b1.
86. Ibid., 8.838a4–839d2.
87. Ibid., 8.839c4.
88. Ibid., 8.839b3–6.
89. Ibid., 8.839b7–c2.
90. Ibid., 8.839d4–6.
91. Ibid., 8.840b10–c2.
92. *Republic* 5.463d6–7.
93. Cf. J. Jouanna, "Le médecin, modèle du législateur dans *Les lois* de Platon," *Ktema* 3 (1978), 77–92.
94. "Il faut placer et tête de chaque loi un prélude approprié" (*Laws* 6.772e2–3). And by this preamble, often called *paramuthion* (*Laws* 6.773e5; 9.880a7; 10.885b3; 11.923c2), Plato means "the myth which prefaces the law" (*ho pro tou nomou muthos*: *Laws* 11.927c8–9).
95. Ancient myths of the Sauromatians for the education of women

(*Laws* 7.804*e*4–5); tales about the spirit of revenge in victims of manslaughter (*Laws* 9.865*d*5–6); myth on the suffering in store for the murderer of his parents (*Laws* 9.872*d*8–*e*1); proverb invoked for the protection of treasure (*Laws* 11.913*c*1–3); the story of Patroclus concerning the surrender of weapons (*Laws* 12.944*a*1).

96. *Laws* 6.773*b*4–6; *e*5.

97. Cf. P. Boyancé, *Le culte des muses chez les philosophes grecs* (Paris, 1936) (reedited with supplement, 1972), 149–165.

98. *Republic* 2.382*c*. In this instance the story of the sown teeth and of the armored foot soldiers born of them: the Thebes of Cadmus.

99. Ibid., 3.414*c*1–415*d*2.

100. Ibid., 9.592*b*3–4.

101. Ibid.

102. Ibid., 2.663*c*1–2.

103. Ibid., 2.663*e*1–2.

104. Ibid., 2.663*e*5–6.

105. *Republic* 2.377*c*3.

106. Ibid., 2.378*d*1.

107. Cf. *Theaetetus* 176*b*7.

108. Cf. *Sophist* 234*c*4–7.

109. *Republic* 3.395*c*8–*d*3.

110. Ibid., 2.380*c*7–8.

111. Ibid., 2.377*a*12–*b* 3. Cf. *Theaetetus* 191*d*2–9.

112. Cf. *Greater Hippias* 286*a*1–2.

113. G. Roux, "Le sens de ΤΥΠΟΣ," *Revue des études anciennes* (1961), 5–13.

114. *Republic* 2.378*e*7–379*a*4; 380*c*8.

115. Ibid., 2.378*e*1.

116. Ibid., 2.378*d*1–3.

117. *Timaeus* 26*b*; *c*3–4.

118. Ibid., 26*e*5–6.

119. *Republic* 2.377*b*9–*c*1.

120. Ibid., 2.377*c*8–*d*1.

121. Ibid., 3.386*b*7–8.

122. Ibid., 3.386*c*4; 387*b*2.

123. Ibid., 3.387*b*8.

124. P. 96, n. 101, above.

125. *Timaeus* 23*a*2–3.

126. Ibid., 24*d*7.

127. Ibid., 23*e*7–24*a*1.

128. Ibid., 23*a*2–3.

129. Ibid., 21*a*7.

130. Ibid., 21*b*4–5.

131. *Laws* 2.663*e*8–664*a*6.

132. Ibid., 2.664*b*4–*c*1.

133. Ibid., 2.664*c*4–*d*2.

134. Ibid., 2.664*d*2–4.
135. No discrimination between old men and old women in *The Republic* (2.378*d*1). Whereas, in *The Laws*, despite Socratic method, there is no dialectical nurse.
136. Aristotle, *Rhetoric* 2.21.1395*a*.
137. Aristotle, *Politics* 3.1.5.1275*a*14–19.
138. Plato, *Laws* 2.659*d*1–4.
139. *Laws* 2.659*e*3.
140. Ibid., 2.659*e*1–5.
141. Ibid., 7.793*a*10–*b*1.
142. Ibid., 7.793*b*7.
143. Ibid., 7.793*c*1–2.
144. Ibid., 6.769*a*1–2.
145. Ibid., 3.685*a*7–8.
146. Ibid., 4.712*b*2.
147. Ibid., 6.752*a*2.
148. *Republic* 9.591*e*1–2.

Chapter Six

1. M. Mauss, *Manuel d'ethnographie* (Paris, 1949), 9.
2. Ibid., 5.
3. Ibid., 10.
4. Ibid., 200.
5. Ibid., 202.
6. Ibid., 203.
7. Cf. J. Starobinski, "Le mythe au XVIIIᵉ siècle," *Critique*, no. 366 (1977), 979.
8. M. Mauss, *Œuvres* (Paris, 1969), 2.161.
9. E. Cassirer, *La philosophie des formes symboliques*, vol. 2; *La pensée mythique* [1924], French transl. J. Lacoste (Paris, 1972).
10. Ibid., 27.
11. Ibid., 39.
12. Ibid., 29.
13. E. Cassirer, *Langage et mythe: À propos des noms des dieux* [1924], French transl. O. Hansen-Love (Paris, 1973), 110–111.
14. E. Cassirer, *La philosophie des formes symboliques*, vol. 2, *La pensée mythique*, 8–9.
15. Ibid., 20–21.
16. *L'année sociologique* 2 (1899), preface, iv–v.
17. É. Durkheim, *Les formes élémentaires de la pensée religieuse* (Paris, 1910), 612–623.
18. Ibid., 612.
19. Ibid., 613.
20. Ibid., 622–623.
21. Ibid., 624.

22. Ibid., 623.

23. E. Cassirer, *La philosophie des formes symboliques*, vol. 2, *La pensée mythique*, 16–17.

24. Ibid., 8.

25. Ibid., 11.

26. Ibid., 12.

27. Ibid., 15.

28. Ibid., 20.

29. Cf. p. 19, above.

30. Cf. G. Van Riet, "Mythe et vérité," *Revue philosophique de Louvain* 58 (1960), 15–87.

31. Proofs and analyses collected in *Revue philosophique* 4 (1957): "Centenaire de Lucien Lévy-Bruhl."

32. Unpublished letter of M. Leenhardt, 6 February 1944, published by R. Dousset-Leenhardt, *L'homme* 17 (1977), 113.

33. Lucien Lévy-Bruhl, *La mythologie primitive* (1935), v–vi.

34. Fontenelle, *De l'origine des fables* [1724], critical edition J. R. Carré (1932), 30–31.

35. Dr. Fortune, *Sorcerers of Dobu*, 30–31, quoted by L. Lévy-Bruhl in *La mythologie primitive*, xi.

36. Lévy-Bruhl, xi.

37. Ibid., 176–178.

38. Ibid., 180–186.

39. Ibid., 217–222.

40. A. Lang, *Mythes, cultes et religions* [1889], French trans. (Paris, 1896), 307.

41. M.-J. Lagrange, *Etudes sur les religions sémitiques*, 2d ed. (Paris, 1905), 7.

42. L. Lévy-Bruhl, *Mythologie primitive*, 218–221.

43. Ibid., vi.

44. L. Lévy-Bruhl, *Les fonctions mentales dans les sociétés inférieures*, 9th ed. (1951), 434–435.

45. Ibid., 436.

46. Ibid., 435.

47. Ibid., 449.

48. Louis Bréhier, "Originalité de Lévy-Bruhl," *Revue philosophique* (1949), 385–388.

49. This is the interpretation that is to be chosen by G. Van Der Leeuw, *L'homme primitif et la religion: Étude anthropologique* (Paris, 1940); and by M. Leenhardt, *Do Kamo: La personne et le mythe dans le monde mélanésien* (Paris, 1947).

50. L. Lévy-Bruhl, *Mythologie primitive*, 222.

51. Ibid., 290.

52. Ibid., 302.

53. Ibid., 314–315.

54. Ibid., 317.

55. Ibid., 317–318.

56. Ibid., 319, and the project mentioned on p. vii.

57. L. Bréhier, 385–388.

58. L. Lévy-Bruhl, *Fonctions mentales dans les sociétés inférieures*, 438. It is the main artery for comparisons between primitives, children, and the insane outlined by G. Van Der Leeuw, 145–156.

59. "For instance, after a generation an idiot will only be remembered as a *Dema*, "L. Lévy-Bruhl, *Mythologie primitive*, xxviii.

60. "Logique de l'ambigu, de l'équivoque, de la polarité," by J.-P. Vernant, *Mythe et société en Grèce ancienne* (Paris, 1974), 250.

61. M. Mauss [1903], in *Œuvres*, ed. V. Karady (Paris, 1969), 2:269.

62. Ibid. [1903], 2:269–272; ibid. [1908], 206–211.

63. Ibid. [1939], 2:165.

64. "Mentalité primitive et participation" in ibid. [1923], 2:125–131.

65. Cl. Lévi-Strauss, *Anthropologie structurale* (Paris, 1958), 232.

66. Cf. N. Ruwet, "Linguistique et sciences de l'homme," *Esprit* (November 1963), 565.

67. A. J. Greimas, "La mythologie comparée" [1963], taken up again in *Du sens* (Paris, 1970), 117–134.

68. Cf. the preface written by A. J. Greimas, "Les acquis et les projets," in J. Courtès, *Introduction à la sémiotique narrative et discursive* (Paris, 1976), 5–25.

69. It is in reply to G. Dumézil who states in 1970 that he has never understood the difference between myth and story, that A. J. Greimas suggests this solution (*Sémiotique et sciences sociales* [Paris, 1976], 210–213).

70. A. J. Greimas, "La mythologie comparée" [1963] taken up again in *Du sens* (Paris, 1970), 117–118.

71. Cl. Lévi-Strauss, *Miel aux Cendres* (Paris, 1966), 407–408.

72. C. R. of M. Detienne, *Les jardins d'Adonis: La mythologie des aromates en Grèce* (Paris, 1972), in *L'homme* 12, no. 4 (1972), 97–102.

73. Cl. Lévi-Strauss, in *L'homme* 12, no. 4 (1972), 97.

74. Cl. Lévi-Strauss, Interview (with R. Bellour, summer 1972), in *Claude Lévi-Strauss: Textes de et sur Cl. Lévi-Strauss*, collected by R. Bellour and C. Clément (Paris, 1979), 175–176.

75. Fontenelle, 31–32.

76. Cf. É. Benveniste, *Le vocabulaire des institutions indo-européennes* (Paris, 1969), 1:9.

77. M. Granet, *Danses et légendes de la Chine ancienne* (Paris, 1926), 1:36–37, 41.

78. Ibid., 1:1, 51.

79. L. Gernet, *Anthropologie de la Grèce ancienne* (Paris, 1968), 21–61, 93–137.

80. Ibid., 185.

81. Ibid., 185, n. 23: "Au niveau où nous prenons la pensée mythique, nous admettons sans autre forme de procès qu'elle a un rapport direct avec la donnée sociale."

82. Ibid., 100.

83. Ibid., 131.

84. Cf. the comments of J.-P. Vernant, *Bulletin de la société française de philosophie* 56 (1963), 17: "Le langage, dans le cadre duquel le mythe se constitue et se formule, déborde le domaine de l'activité mythique; il exprime la totalité de l'expérience sociale; il est tout à la fois l'instrument, le véhicule, la manifestation d'une culture globale." Does this mean that a place must be reserved for myth to come in mythic thought, this total language?

85. John Burnet, *Early Greek Philosophy* [1892], trans. A. Reymond (Paris, 1919) (reedited 1952).

86. Ibid., 6.

87. Ibid., 7.

88. Ibid., 2.

89. Ibid., 4.

90. Ibid., 7–8.

91. Ibid., 10–11. Another fate of a work: Hesiod, congratulated by W. Jaeger for having made the most useful contribution toward disengaging philosophic content from myth and giving to mythology its religious scope (*Die Theologie der frühen griechischen Denker* [1947] [Stuttgart, 1953], 23). Regarding Jaeger's Christian humanism, the Greeks give evidence of a natural theology: the religion of philosophers "which will last as long as there are men on earth."

92. F. M. Cornford, *From Religion to Philosophy* (London, 1912); "A Ritual Basis for Hesiod's Theogony" [1941], in *The Unwritten Philosophy and Other Essays*, ed. W. K. C. Guthrie (Cambridge, 1950; paperback, 1967), 95–116; *Principium Sapientiae: The Origins of Greek Philosophical Thought* (Cambridge, 1952).

93. J.-P. Vernant, "La formation de la pensée positive dans la Grèce archaïque" [1957], in *Mythe et pensée chez les Grecs* (Paris, 1965), 290. Cf. *Les origines de la pensée grecque* (Paris, 1962), 96–114.

94. Cf. M. Griaule, "Connaissance de l'homme noir," in *La connaissance de l'homme au XXᵉ siecle* (*Rencontres internationales de Genève*) (Neuchâtel, 1952), 11–24; "Réflexions sur les symboles soudanais," *Cahiers internationaux de sociologie* (1952), 8–26.

95. "Une fois initié l'ethnologue, bien qu'il ait rapporté une très riche moisson, n'a finalement rien de plus à dire sur la société dogon que ce qu'en disent les Dogon eux-mêmes." (P. Smith, "La nature des mythes," *Diogène*, no. 82 [1973], 96).

96. Synthesis of existential lectures on mythology in G. Gusdorf, *Mythe et métaphysique: Introduction à la philosophie* (Paris, 1953); cf. M. Dufrenne, "La mentalité primitive et Heidegger," *Les études philosophiques* 9 (1954), 284–306; P. Ricoeur, "Le symbole donne à penser," *Esprit* 27 (1959), 60–76.

97. That of the ancient manuals such as the *Library* of the pseudo-Apollodorus or else the systematic narration of the *muthos* of Protagoras when the great realities of the spiritual world abandoned him: K. Kerényi, *La religion antique: Ses lignes fondamentales*, trans. Y. Le Lay (Geneva, 1957), 20, 42.

98. J. Rudhardt, "Une approche de la pensée mythique: Le mythe considéré comme un langage," *Studia philosophica* (1966), 208–237; "Images et structures dans le langage mythique," *Cahiers internationaux de symbolisma* (1969), 87–109; "Cohérence et incohérence de la structure mythique: Sa fonction symbolique," *Diogène 77* (1972), 19–47; "La fonction du mythe dans la pensée religieuse de la Grèce," in *Il mito greco*, ed. B. Gentili and G. Paioni (Rome, 1977), 307–320.

99. Maurice Leenhardt has reservations when mythology rediscovered its primary meaning in New Caledonia a century after the beginnings of evangelism and commerce sanctified by the Book. Behold the myth in all its pristine "freshness" in a primitive world and "everything in it still vibrates with the adventure or the emotion which gave birth to it." Leenhardt laments it: the ethnologists are not prepared to observe the forms of myth they encounter (9). The great classic myth obscures "speech in the sense of the Word," the "internal reality" that the spirit experiences in actual mythology. But the question remains of integrating a "mythic mentality" with the reasoning faculty of the human species. And the Protestant minister worries about teaching us where religion begins and where mythology ends. Moses' relation to his God is religious: in itself the Burning Bush is not; it is mythic. The transition, this time, occurs in Israel, peninsula of monotheism where thought frees itself from mythology by creating the "internal myth" (unedited letter of M. Leenhardt, 6 February 1944, published by R. Dousset-Leenhardt, *L'homme* 17 (1977), 1, 113–114.

Chapter Seven

1. Natalis Comes, *Mythologiae* (Venice, 1551) (cf. J. Seznec, *La survivance des dieux antiques*, 2d ed. [Paris, 1980], 199–228). But Fontenelle read it at the Jesuits in the French version published in Rouen in 1611: Noël Le Comte, *Mythologie, c'est-à-dire explication des fables, contenant les généalogies des dieux, les cérémonies de leurs sacrifices, leurs gestes, aventures, amours et presque tous les préceptes de la philosophie naturelle et morale.* Cf. Fontenelle, *De l'origine des fables* [1724], ed. J. R. Carré (Paris, 1932), 41–42.

2. Cf. J. Starobinski, "Le mythe au XVIIIᵉ siècle." *Critique*, no. 366 (November 1977), 996. "Il ne nous est pas permis d'avoir avec les Grecs quelque chose d'*identique*": Hölderlin, plunged into mourning, giddy over the ruination of the imitable. Acerbic point made by Ph. Lacoue-Labarthe, "Hölderlin et les Grecs," *Poetics* 40 (1979), 465–474.

3. For instance, this is the position of M. I. Finley, *Les anciens grecs*, trans. M. Alexandre (Paris, 1971), 47.

4. Cf. pp. 8–10, above.

5. *Prolegomene zu einer wissenschaftlichen Mythologie* (Göttingen, 1825). On K. O. Müller, cf. H. Pinard de la Boullaye, *L'étude comparée des religions*, 2d ed. (Paris, 1925), 1:268–276; and B. Bravo, *Philologie, histoire, philosophie de l'histoire: Études sur J. G. Droysen, historien de l'Antiquité* (Warsaw, 1968).

6. Fr. Vian, *La guerre des géants: Le mythe avant l'époque hellénistique* (Paris, 1952).

7. Fr. Vian, *Les origines de Thèbes: Cadmos et les Spartes* (Paris, 1963), 5.

8. Ibid., 6-7. A matter of correcting the main defect of a mythology, "several from its cultist connections" tending to deteriorate into a collection of "fables" at the mercy of the "imagination of the narrator." Even though, elsewhere, the writer does not preclude that a kind of "creativeness born of free phantasy" could develop according to "pre-existing schemata" (ibid., 12).

9. Pp. 12–13, above.

10. Lucien Lévy-Bruhl, *Fonctions mentales dans les sociétés inférieures* (Paris, 1910), 434–435.

11. Cl. Lévi-Strauss, *Tristes Tropiques* (Paris, 1955), 318. Some repercussions: L. de Heusch, *Pourquoi l'épouser?* (Paris, 1971), 141–146; J. Derrida, *De la grammatologie* (Paris, 1967), 145–202.

12. Cl. Lévi-Strauss, *Anthropologie structurale* (Paris, 1958), 232. We underline the word "reader."

13. In *Anthropologie structurale deux* (Paris, 1973), 78, Cl. Lévi-Strauss recalls that the title of his chair at the École pratique des hautes études, created in 1888, "Religions des peuples, non civilisés," was changed at his request in 1954: "Religions comparées des peuples sans écriture." Still primitive but less shocking to an audience from overseas.

14. Cl. Lévi-Strauss, *Anthropologie structurale deux*, 78.

15. As Jack Goody does in a new way in *Une récitation du Bagré* (Paris, 1980).

16. Ed. Leach, *Les systèmes politiques des hautes terres de Birmanie*, 2d ed. [1964], French transl. (Paris, 1972), 304–318.

17. Lévi-Strauss's propositions developed by P. Smith, "La nature des mythes," *Diogène* 82 (1973), 91–108; *Le récit populaire au Rwanda* (Paris, 1975), 114–115.

18. Hypothesis of R. Barthes, "Introduction à l'analyse structurale des récits" [1966], taken up again by R. Barthes, W. Kayser, W. C. Booth, Ph. Hamon, *Poétique du récit* (Paris, 1977), 7–57; A. J. Greimas, *Du sens* (Paris, 1970), 185–230; H. Weinrich, "Structures narratives du mythe," *Poétique* 1 (1970), 25–34. Etc.

19. For instance, J.-Fr. Lyotard, *Discours, figure* (Paris, 1971), 149–151.

20. Plotinus, *Ennéades* 3.5.9, 3.7.6, with comments by J. Pépin, "Espace et temps en Grèce," *Revue de synthèse*, nos. 57–58 (1970), 97–102.

21. E. Cassirer, *La philosophie des formes symboliques*, vol. 2, *La pensée mythique*, French transl. J. Lacoste (Paris, 1972), 17.

22. E. Bréhier, "Philosophie et mythe," *Revue de métaphysique et de morale* 22 (1914), 361–381.

23. As has been shown by J. Bompaire in "Le mythe selon la *Poétique* d'Aristotle," in *Fonction et survie des mythes* (Paris, 1977), 31–36.

24. R. Dupont-Roc and J. Lallot, *Aristote: La poétique. Texte, traduction, notes* (Paris, 1980), 149.

25. *Sustasis*: Aristotle, *Poétique* 1450a15; 32; *sunthesis*: 1452b31; 1459a22.

26. Ibid., 1451a36–38.

27. Ibid., 1451a1–2 (*eumnēnoneuton*).

28. Ibid., 1453b3–6. An "intellectualized" point of view R. Dupont-Roc and J. Lallot, 13, observe: "The poet writing his story *must bring things to the attention*" (Aristotle, *Poétique* 1453b23).

29. The slogan is: invent (*heuriskein*), Aristotle, *Poetics* 1453b25.

30. Ibid., 1453a17–22. Cf. R. Dupont-Roc and J. Lallot, 247–249.

31. For there are other meanings of *muthos*: hearsay, the incredible, the false (*Histoire des animaux* 6.30.579b2–4; 35.580a16–21; 8.12.597a7); the stories, the gossip of those who waste their time talking about anything at all; the *philomuthos*, the chatterbox (*Nichomachean Ethics* 3.13.117b34); the "myth" composed of miraculous tales, astonishing, with philosophic merit (*Metaphysics* 1.2.982b15–20); in short, the "mythic" form borrowed from an "ancient tradition about divinity" (that the stars are gods), a form chosen with the view of convincing the masses and serve common laws and interests (*Metaphysics* 11.8.1074a38–b14). Cf. J. Bollack, "Mythische Deutung und Deutung des Mythos," in *Poetik und Hermaneutik* (Munich, 1971), 4:67–119 (in particular, 76–78, 96-99).

32. Pp. 111–12, above.

33. Sextus Empiricus, *Adversus mathematicos* 1.252–253, 91–96, with comments by B. Bravo, "Remarks on scholarship in Ancient times," *Eirene* (1968), 325–335.

34. J. Starobinski, 976–977.

35. Based on his research in Rwanda (*Le récit populaire au Rwanda* [Paris, 1975], 114–115), Pierre Smith concludes that, in his bailiwick at least, myths do not exist as a type of tale, definable by a certain interesting phenomenon to be communicated or by producing a certain effect. There remain "mythic themes": the origin of death, the advent of inequality, how women became dominated by men. An equivocal position, set forth by Luc de Heusch, "Mythologie et littérature," *L'homme* 17, nos. 2–3 (1977), 101–109, which attempts to save Rwanda myth by the indirect means of mythology and mythic thought (106), that is, "the sum total of ancient deeds and titles, guarantees—royal, cosmogonic and devine—which are expressed at various levels of literary, popular or scholarly creation" (108).

36. Knowledge of categories or knowledge of the world? was asked in unison by P. Smith and D. Sperber, "Mythologiques de Georges Dumézil," *Annales E.S.C.* (1971), 583–585.

37. The most "general" suggests P. Smith, *Le récit populaire au Rwanda*, 115. More recently, in a new journal, *Le temps de la réflexion* (1980), 61–81, the same writer, in a subtle and respectful lecture on the *Mythologiques*, recalls that, concerning anthropology, "the myth is a concept similar to post-operative shock" (84), not the myth tale but the "mental myth," a concept that does not seem to relieve all anxiety about the health of "mythic thought."

38. Cf. D. Sperber, "La pensée symbolique est-elle pré-rationnelle?" in *La fonction symbolique: Essais d'anthropologie*, ed. M. Izard and P. Smith (Paris, 1979), 17–42.

39. Remarks by Antiphanes, writer of comedies in the first half of the fourth century B.C. (quoted by Athenaeus, *Les Diepnosophistes* 6.222b1–7), who finds that tragic poets have a remarkably easy task.

40. Cf. The example propounded by Ed. Leach and expounded on by D. Sperber, *Le symbolisme en général* (Paris, 1974), 91.

41. Lists, pictures, turns of phrase: J. Goody, *The Domestication of the Savage Mind* (Cambridge, 1977); "Mémoire et apprentissage dans les sociétés avec et sans écriture," *L'homme* 17 (1977), 1, 29–52.

42. Silenos de Caléacte, in *FGrHist* 175F4 Jacoby. Cf. M. P. Loicq-Berger, *Syracuse: Histoire culturelle d'une cité grecque* (Brussels, 1967), 138, n. 5; Cl. Vatin, "Jardins et vergers grecs," *Mélanges G. Daux* (Paris, 1974), 345.

Index of Classical References

General Index

Greeks, xi, 3–5, 6, 8, 11, 13–15, 21,
  43, 44, 49, 50, 80, 87, 88, 99,
  107–113, 115–18, 121–23, 127,
  129
Greimas, A. J., 115, 163 n.67,
  n.68, n.70, 166 n.18
Griaule, M., 120, 121, 164 n.94
Grice, H. P., 153 n.26
Groethuysen, B., 157 n.9
Gusdorf, G., 164 n.96

Hades, 73, 87, 93, 98
Halbwachs, M., 35, 146 n.108
halieis, 45
Hartog, F., 149 n.42
Harvey, F. D., 144 n.69
Havelock, E. A., 22, 26, 27, 28,
  140 n.1, 142 n.42–n.45, n.47, 143
  n.48, 145 n.94
hearsay, 55, 58, 60, 62, 89, 91, 93,
  99
Hecataeus of Miletus, 46, 51, 63,
  70–77, 79–81, 99, 150 n.66, 153
  n.33, 154 n.38–n.40, n.44, n.45,
  n.47, n.48, n.50, n.51, 155 n.65,
  n.66
Hegel, 8, 137 n.42
Hephaestus, 88
Hera, 67
Heracles, 49–51, 72–74, 80
Heraclitus, 67, 153 n.21
hermeneutics, 69–70
Herodotus, 32, 46–52, 56–58, 70,
  76, 79–80, 83, 125, 148 n.18,
  n.30, 149 n.43, n.45–n.49, n.52–
  n.54, n.56–n.58, 150 n.59–n.65,
  151 n.90, n.98–n.108, 153 n.32,
  n.34, n.35, 154 n.37, n.43, n.49,
  155 n.58–n.62, 156 n.86, 157
  n.87, 157 n.29
heroes, 74, 87, 89, 91, 102, 131
Hesiod, 51, 64–66, 73, 75, 87, 92,
  119, 148 n.31, 159 n.67, n.69,
  n.79, 164 n.91, n.92
Hesychius, 148 n.21
Heusch, Luc de, 166 n.11, 167
  n.35

Hieron, 133
Hieronymus of Rhodes, 153 n.19
Hippias the Sophist, 89, 158 n.34,
  n.46, n.48, n.51
historiography, 77
history, 24–25, 26, 32, 33, 34, 43,
  52–53, 78–81
Hoffmann, E., 148 n.14
Hölderlin, F., 124, 165 n.2
Homer, 22–28, 51, 64–67, 69, 75,
  82, 87, 102, 119, 140 n.1, n.2,
  141, 142, 148 n.22, 154 n.54,
  n.55. See also epic
Huart, P., 150 n.77, 152 n.121,
  n.131
hubris, 65
hupomnēmata, 31
Husserl, Edmund, 8
Huxley, G. L., 141 n.13

illusions, 10, 14, 18, 42–62, 74, 78,
  97, 102, 108, 109, 113–14, 125,
  128–29, 130, 131
imitation, 95, 97
incantation, 95, 100, 101–2
inconsistency, 111, 121–22, 125
interpretation, 8, 23, 26, 63–81, 84,
  113, 114, 115, 116
intuition, 105
irrational, 8, 11, 17, 18, 20

Jacoby, F., 151 n.96, 155 n.70, 156
  n.74, 158 n.50
Jaeger, W., 143 n.49, 164 n.91
Jakobson, Roman, 39–40, 147
  n.120
Jamin, J., 147 n.1–n.6, 157 n.32
Janicaud, D., 137 n.42
Jauss, H. R., 147 n.121
Jensen, Adolphe E., 17, 139 n.86
Jouanna, J., 159 n.93
Julia, D., 137 n.36

Kahn, Charles H., 154 n.44
katalegein, 70, 86
Kerényi, K., 148 n.14, 157 n.30,
  164 n.97

Panyassis of Halicarnassus, 50,
149 n. 51
paramuthion, 95, 101
Parmenides, 107, 148 n.26
parphasis, 47
Parry, M., 22, 140 n.2
participation, 110, 111, 112
Pascal, 13–14
past, 34, 42, 52, 53, 55, 65, 79, 88, 89,
102
Pausanias, 159 n.68
pedagogues, 27, 65
Pelasgos, 31
Peleus, 45
Pelops, 3, 48
Peoples of Nature, 3–4, 12, 13, 18,
20, 109–12, 127, 129
Pépin, J., 166 n.20
Pericles, 31, 53, 59, 60
Periegesis, 70–72
Perrot, C. H., 146 n.101
Perrotta, G., 148 n.15
persuasion, 95–96
Phaedrus, 83, 157 n.6, n.7
Phanodemus, 158 n.50
phēmē, 92, 93, 100. *See also* rumor
Phemius, 86
phenomenology, 120
Pherecydes of Athens, 49
philosophy, 32, 43, 44, 46, 63, 65, 67,
68, 69, 80, 98, 102, 108–9, 115–17,
199–22, 126, 128, 129, 130
Phoenix, 45
Phoroneus, 88, 90
Piatelli-Palmarini, M., 145 n.95
Pinard de la Boullaye, H., 135 n.2,
138 n.46, 139 n.74, 165 n.5
Pindar, 47–48, 83, 149 n.32–n.41
Plato, xi, 22, 27, 30, 44, 82–102, 107–
8, 109, 125, 130, 140 n.6, n.7, 142
n.46, 143 n.65, 144 n.74, 155 n.70,
157–61
pleasure, 5–6, 58–59, 89, 95, 97, 101,
113
plot, 131
Plotinus, 130, 166 n.20
Pluche, 157 n.9

Plutarch, 150 n.75
poetry, 22, 55, 61, 78, 95, 97, 98, 106,
126
poets and chanters, 23, 25, 65, 85,
86, 89, 126. *See also* singing poet
poliētai, 45
politics, 120
Polycrates, 44–45
polytheism, ix, 17, 104
Pomare, kings, 28–29
Poseidon, 48, 67, 73
Posner, E., 144 n.71, n.73
Pouillon, J., 157 n.12
power and writing, 30, 31
praise, 47, 48, 96
Prakken, D. W., 155 n.57
Préaux, C., 143 n.61, 155 n.63
prelogical, 110, 111, 112–13, 121, 127
present, 37, 52, 53, 65, 85
priests, 49, 50, 88, 99, 154 n.43
Primitives. *See* Peoples of Nature
Pritchett, W. Kendrick, 155 n.67
probability, 73, 74, 76, 81, 84, 131
Propp, V., 115
proverb, 23, 34, 40, 86, 89, 95, 102
Pucci, P., 141 n.11
Pyrrha, 89
Pythagoras, 66

Ranke, 34
rationalism, 5, 6, 8, 15, 16, 18, 24, 26,
32, 46, 76, 79, 82, 107, 109, 110,
111–12, 113, 114, 119, 120, 121,
123, 125, 129
reading, 28, 29, 30, 38, 59, 65
reason. *See* rationalism
recollection, 37, 38
recitation, public, 32, 39, 56, 67, 99
relics, 13
religious idea, 4, 5, 14–16, 17, 18, 20,
43, 64, 103, 105–7, 111, 112, 129
Renou, L., 147 n.118
repetition, 37, 38, 39, 41, 86, 91, 130
Revel, J., 137 n.36
rhapsodists, 49, 66, 67, 69, 99
rhetoric, 83
Richardson, Robert D., 135 n.2